# BROKEN HEART

# A TRUE HISTORY
# BROKEN
## OF THE VOICE
# HEART
## REFERENDUM

### SHIREEN MORRIS

LA TROBE
UNIVERSITY PRESS

IN CONJUNCTION WITH BLACK INC.

Published by La Trobe University Press,
in conjunction with Black Inc.
Wurundjeri Country
22–24 Northumberland Street
Collingwood VIC 3066, Australia
enquiries@blackincbooks.com
www.blackincbooks.com
www.latrobeuniversitypress.com.au

La Trobe University plays an integral role in Australia's public intellectual life, and is recognised globally for its research excellence and commitment to ideas and debate. La Trobe University Press publishes books of high intellectual quality, aimed at general readers. Titles range across the humanities and sciences, and are written by distinguished and innovative scholars. La Trobe University Press books are produced in conjunction with Black Inc., an independent Australian publishing house. The members of the LTUP Editorial Board are Vice-Chancellor's Fellows Emeritus Professor Robert Manne and Dr Elizabeth Finkel, and Morry Schwartz and Chris Feik of Black Inc.

Copyright © Shireen Morris 2024
Shireen Morris asserts her right to be known as the author of this work.

ALL RIGHTS RESERVED.
No part of this publication may be reproduced, stored in a retrieval system, or transmitted in any form by any means electronic, mechanical, photocopying, recording or otherwise without the prior consent of the publishers.

9781760645205 (paperback)
9781743823712 (ebook)

 A catalogue record for this book is available from the National Library of Australia

Book design and typesetting by Beau Lowenstern
The lyrics of Paul Kelly's 1992 song 'Special Treatment' on pp. 209–10
are reproduced by kind permission of the artist and Sony Music.

*For Ashaan and baby brother,*
*with love and hope for a fairer Australia*

# CONTENTS

*Timeline* — ix

*Introduction* — 1

1. Counterfactual — 15
2. A Failed 'Radical Centre' Referendum — 25
3. Repudiating the Radical Centre — 36
4. The Illusion of Bipartisanship — 47
5. Grab Them by the Lapels — 63
6. On Constitutional Compromises — 73
7. Flip-Floppers — 89
8. Albanese's Voice — 106
9. Where Is the Detail? — 121
10. Topsy-Turvy World — 128
11. Black Robe Returns — 137
12. A Radical Splinter — 145

| | |
|---|---|
| 13. A Final Compromise | 155 |
| 14. A Noble Politician | 163 |
| 15. Tipping Points | 179 |
| 16. Broken Heart | 196 |
| *Acknowledgements* | 223 |
| *Notes* | 225 |
| *Index* | 245 |

# TIMELINE

**2012** — The Expert Panel on Constitutional Recognition of Indigenous Australians recommends Indigenous constitutional recognition with a racial non-discrimination guarantee. The proposal gets blasted by conservatives as a 'one-clause Bill of Rights'.

**2014** — Cape York Institute (Noel Pearson and Shireen Morris) collaborates with constitutional conservatives (Julian Leeser, Greg Craven, Damien Freeman and Anne Twomey) to co-devise a compromise: a constitutionally guaranteed Indigenous advisory body to provide 'advice to the Parliament and the Executive Government on matters relating to' Indigenous peoples.

**2015**

*May* — Frank Brennan opposes a constitutional advisory body, claiming it cannot be achieved in a legally sound way.

Anne Twomey publishes the draft amendment, as co-developed by Cape York Institute and constitutional conservatives, to demonstrate how it can be done.

*June* — Malcolm Turnbull privately tells Noel Pearson and Shireen Morris he supports the idea of a constitutionally guaranteed Indigenous advisory body. (Tony Abbott, Christian Porter, the attorney-general's office, and other Coalition politicians also indicate support at various times.)

*July* — Indigenous leaders issue the Kirribilli Statement, rejecting constitutional symbolism and calling for a process to facilitate consensus on constitutional recognition.

*September* — Turnbull overthrows Tony Abbott to become prime minister.

*7 December* — Turnbull and Opposition leader Bill Shorten appoint the Referendum Council to consult and make recommendations on Indigenous constitutional recognition. Its Indigenous members organise First Nations regional dialogues to assess all options.

| 2016 | July | Julian Leeser, Liberal politician and conservative co-creator of a constitutional Voice, enters Parliament. |
| --- | --- | --- |
| | November | Turnbull attempts to push the Referendum Council towards symbolism. Says the Voice proposal has a 'snowflake's chance in hell'. |
| 2017 | 19 May | Warren Mundine publicly declares support for a constitutional amendment to empower Indigenous voices. Liberal MP Tim Wilson is also publicly encouraging. |
| | 26 May | The Indigenous regional dialogues issue the Uluru Statement from the Heart, which calls for a constitutionally guaranteed First Nations Voice and rejects mere symbolism. |
| | 30 June | The Referendum Council makes its recommendation for a constitutional Voice, acknowledging that it addresses conservative objections to a racial non-discrimination guarantee. |
| | 26 October | Turnbull rejects the Voice and misrepresents it as a 'third chamber of Parliament' that Australians will reject. But polls show most Australians support it (frequently 56–60 per cent) until mid-2023. |
| 2018 | August | After a leadership spill, new prime minister Scott Morrison repeats the 'third chamber' misrepresentation. |
| | November | Indigenous leaders Noel Pearson, Megan Davis and Pat Anderson propose further compromises in Voice constitutional drafting submitted to the Joint Select Committee on Constitutional Recognition, chaired by Julian Leeser and Patrick Dodson, to address the 'third chamber' objections. |
| | 29 November | The Leeser–Dodson Committee recommends processes to determine legislative, executive and constitutional options for the establishment of a Voice. |
| 2019 | 18 May | The Morrison government is re-elected with a commitment to implement the Leeser–Dodson recommendations to co-design a Voice, and a funding commitment to hold a referendum. Liberal Voice supporters Andrew Bragg and Bridget Archer enter Parliament. |
| | 18 July | Former chief justice Murray Gleeson delivers speech endorsing the original Voice constitutional drafting, as co-devised by Cape York Institute and constitutional conservatives, and published by Twomey. He says the amendment demonstrates how the Voice can be achieved without 'derogation from parliamentary supremacy'. |

|      |              |   |
|------|--------------|---|
|      | *30 October* | The Morrison government announces the Indigenous Voice Co-Design Process under Minister for Indigenous Affairs Ken Wyatt, to be overseen by a senior advisory group chaired by Marcia Langton and Tom Calma. |
| **2021** |          | Danny Gilbert and Pearson start advocating further refinements to the constitutional drafting, developed with former High Court judges, making it more legally modest. |
|      | *December*   | The final report of the Indigenous Voice Co-Design Process is released, showing how a national Voice can be anchored in local and regional voices. |
| **2022** | *21 May*  | Labor wins the federal election. Albanese promises a Voice referendum in his first term. Peter Dutton becomes the new Opposition leader, and Jacinta Nampijinpa Price enters Parliament. |
|      | *5 June*     | Julian Leeser, co-creator of the Voice, becomes shadow attorney-general and shadow minister for Indigenous Australians. |
|      | *27 July*    | Price's maiden speech to Parliament stridently opposes a constitutional Voice. |
|      | *30 July*    | Albanese releases the Gilbert, French and Gleeson Voice drafting for further consultation at Garma. The media starts calling it 'Albanese's Voice'. |
|      | *August*     | Frank Brennan, long-time opponent of a constitutional Voice, begins to publicly criticise the government's constitutional drafting, especially the Voice's ability to advise the executive government. Greg Craven, a conservative co-creator of the original 2014 constitutional drafting, later joins these public attacks. |
|      | *September*  | The government appoints the Referendum Working Group to advise on the referendum. |
|      | *29 September* | The Referendum Working Group releases its Voice Design Principles. |
|      | *27 November* | The Nationals oppose the Voice referendum. Andrew Gee resigns from the party because he supports a constitutional Voice. |
|      | *December*   | Pearson meets with Dutton, who says he is open to a constitutional Voice and does not believe it will divide the country by race. |

| | | |
|---|---|---|
| **Summer break** 2022–2023 | | Advance's 'No' campaign starts proliferating 'this will divide us by race' messages. Questions about the details of the Voice are repeatedly issued by the Liberals. |
| 2023 | February | Objections to the Voice constitutional drafting have been proliferating from the right. Albanese issues a letter inviting Dutton to suggest changes to the drafting. Dutton never responds. |
| | 13 March | Attorney-General Mark Dreyfus proposes a further compromise in the constitutional drafting to appease conservatives' concerns. |
| | 22 March | Indigenous leaders negotiate an alternative compromise with the government, expanding Parliament's power over the Voice's operations, to address conservative objections. |
| | 23 March | The revised drafting is announced by the government. The original Voice compromise now has several additional concessions built in. But Craven claims the Indigenous radicals have got their way and blasts their failure to compromise. |
| | 27 March | Leeser pressures Labor with legal questions in Parliament. Albanese challenges Leeser to show courage and stand up for the proposal he has long supported. |
| | 30 March | The Joint Select Committee on the Aboriginal and Torres Strait Islander Voice is established to inquire into and report on the Constitutional Alteration Bill containing the proposed constitutional drafting. |
| | 1 April | The Liberals lose the Aston by-election to Labor (the first time since 1920 that a government has won a seat from the Opposition at a by-election). |
| | 3 April | Leeser delivers a Press Club speech suggesting the Voice's constitutional function of advising both Parliament and the executive government be removed. |
| | 4 April | Somehow, a Newspoll survey still shows majority public support for a constitutional Voice, which has been consistent since 2017. |
| | 5 April | Dutton announces the Liberals will oppose the referendum. He will not allow a conscience vote. Bipartisanship is now off the table. |
| | 11 April | Leeser resigns from the shadow ministry to advocate a constitutional Voice. Jacinta Nampijinpa Price subsequently takes his spot as shadow minister for Indigenous Australians. |

| | |
|---|---|
| *19 April* | The solicitor-general's legal advice endorses the Voice constitutional amendment as an 'enhancement' of Australia's parliamentary democracy. |
| *12 May* | The Joint Committee on the Aboriginal and Torres Strait Islander Voice endorses the Constitution Alteration Bill without further changes. |
| *22 May* | Dutton delivers a speech saying the Voice would 're-racialise' the nation. |
| *12 June* | Polls show the 'Yes' vote has dropped below 50 per cent. The 'No' vote is now ahead. |
| *19 June* | The Constitution Alteration Bill is passed by both houses. The focus turns to the community campaign. |
| *August* | Polls show the 'Yes' vote at around 44–46 per cent and dropping. The 'No' vote is increasing. |
| *September* | Polls now show the 'Yes' vote falling below 40 per cent. |
| *14 October* | On referendum day, around 40 per cent of electors vote 'Yes' to a constitutional Voice, while approximately 60 per cent vote 'No'. |

# INTRODUCTION

This book is the sequel to *Radical Heart*, which tells the story of my initial seven years of work with Noel Pearson on Indigenous constitutional recognition, from 2011 to 2018. It explains how Indigenous leaders collaborated with constitutional conservatives in 2014 to develop the idea of a constitutionally guaranteed Indigenous advisory body – a concept adopted via an unprecedented consensus of Indigenous peoples in the Uluru Statement from the Heart in 2017. *Radical Heart* closes after then prime minister Malcolm Turnbull rejected the Voice proposal in October 2017, seriously damaging future chances of bipartisanship.

*Broken Heart* is the next instalment. It zooms out from the present moment to capture the whole trajectory of the Voice, reanalysing the early years with the benefit of new hindsight, before zooming in on the final years to unpack the history of the failed referendum. I felt compelled to write this book because from the moment the voting results started coming in on 14 October 2023 – and throughout the referendum campaign – politicians, advocates and commentators have been trying to rewrite history.

Pundits called it a 'no compromise' referendum. Its failure was the fault of Indigenous leaders and a Labor government that stubbornly refused to negotiate or compromise. According to *The Australian*, Prime Minister Anthony Albanese had to take responsibility for his government's mistakes in managing the referendum, while Indigenous leaders needed to 'accept their own part in insisting Mr Albanese take the toughest possible stand on the referendum question'.[1] The whole referendum approach was 'crash or crash through', said constitutional lawyer and Jesuit priest Frank Brennan.[2] It was a phrase repeated ad nauseam during and after the campaign. The Labor government and 'Yes' proponents were 'pig-headed',[3] was the story, and this led to referendum defeat.

That narrative is false, and inverts reality. It points the finger solely at Labor and Indigenous leaders for failing to find common ground with the right. Yet it exonerates the Coalition for its obstruction of any form of substantive constitutional recognition (notwithstanding individual outliers and private indications to the contrary), its refusal to negotiate with Indigenous leaders who wanted more than empty symbolism and, ultimately, its politically motivated choice to oppose and kill the Voice referendum.

As this book will describe, Indigenous leaders repeatedly compromised to try to win Coalition support that was never forthcoming – though their compromises were sometimes imperfectly timed and executed, poorly publicised and not widely understood. The Coalition never compromised. The right's failure to meet Indigenous people in the middle cruelled the referendum and, with it, all hopes of achieving Indigenous constitutional recognition. Peter Dutton and the Coalition must wear that legacy.

The 'crash or crash through' narrative was true only in one tangential and metaphorical respect. As the referendum campaign proceeded, its momentum became unstoppable. It became a freight train, hurtling forward with the force of its own velocity. In earlier years, I had always thought the government in charge would pull the plug if polls showed certain defeat. Yet in the heat of battle, with election promises made, advocates committed, donations received, the date set and hearts on the line, pulling the pin seemed impossible. Indigenous leaders might not have agreed, for a start. After decades of advocacy for rightful recognition, after a hundred or more years of asking for a fairer voice in their affairs, and after more than fifteen years of formal processes, the question they posed to non-Indigenous Australians needed an answer. The compromise Voice proposal, devised with bipartisanship in mind, needed to either float or sink. Australia needed to see itself. And now we will.

I'm writing this book to interrogate and articulate the real reasons for the referendum's defeat for the historical record. It is a complicated story, but it needs to be told.

⚘ ⚘ ⚘

Let me first address the perspective from which I write. I occupy a strange position in Indigenous and Australian politics. I am neither Indigenous nor white. My ancestors hail from India, via Fiji, where the British took indentured servants to work on sugar cane plantations. My parents migrated to Australia in the 1970s, towards the end of the White Australia policy. Though I was born here, my migrant ancestry is one perspective I brought to the referendum debate.

I am also a constitutional lawyer and reform advocate whose primary focus for over twelve years, under the mentorship of Aboriginal leader Noel Pearson, was Indigenous constitutional recognition. I facilitated the collaboration between Indigenous leaders and constitutional conservatives that in 2014 devised the 'radical centre' concept of a constitutionally guaranteed Voice, building on decades of Indigenous advocacy. A constitutional Voice was the topic of my PhD thesis, and I advocated the reform for nine years up until the referendum. I learned much during this time. The privilege of working with Noel and other leaders for more than a decade has afforded me a distinct insight on this chapter in Australia's history.

Some will say a non-Indigenous person shouldn't write this book. They will say I shouldn't have been involved in Indigenous constitutional recognition at all. Matters of identity increasingly require more than explanation; they require justification. Especially when you are a brown-skinned but non-Indigenous advocate for reconciliation and justice. The contemporary trend is to critique who gets to speak, rather than engaging with the speaker's argument. We are told to 'stay in our lane'. An Indian Australian can talk about multiculturalism, but not Indigenous recognition. Perhaps that's why I ended up working on multicultural engagement in the final years before the referendum, as director of the Radical Centre Reform Lab at Macquarie University Law School. Multifaith and multicultural engagement were not my expertise, but there seemed no other space for me in the formal 'Yes' campaigns. I worked on the issue from around the edges. An insider, yet an outsider at the same time.

As a non-Indigenous advocate for the Voice, I always felt a tension between being urged, and feeling a responsibility, to speak up in support of the reform Indigenous people requested through the Uluru Statement – the proposal I helped devise – and feeling pressure to stay passive and silent. These contradictory forces informed and frustrated my twelve years of work, notwithstanding the many Indigenous leaders consistently calling for non-Indigenous solidarity with Indigenous causes.

Indigenous actor and playwright Nakkiah Lui urged all Australians to be active and vocal during the Black Lives Matter debate in 2020. 'We can all help by advocating for people of colour and ensuring we are actively taking part in the conversation to dismantle systemic racism,' she told *The Project*.[4] Summer May Finlay reiterated that message after pop star Ed Sheeran wore a T-shirt featuring the Aboriginal flag while performing in Australia. 'We need good allies,' Finlay wrote. 'We are only 3 per cent of the Australian population. We can't raise the profile of issues affecting us without our allies.'[5] At the same time, she correctly insisted that Indigenous voices must lead debates about Indigenous rights.

I, too, took the view that it need not be either/or: we can and did have both. Principles of self-determination mean reform solutions in Indigenous affairs must be Indigenous-owned and must empower Indigenous voices. This is part of what Noel calls Indigenous people's 'right to take responsibility' over their own lives. It was the fundamental logic behind the Uluru Statement's call for a constitutional First Nations Voice, which arose from an unprecedented process of Indigenous self-determination, culminating in the first-ever national Indigenous consensus on how they want to be constitutionally recognised. The Uluru Statement, achieved under the leadership of Megan Davis, Pat Anderson and Noel, deserved widespread non-Indigenous support.

It was a political reality that the Indigenous 3 per cent minority would need supporters and advocates from the 97 per cent to achieve their desired reforms. The Uluru Statement invited non-Indigenous Australians to 'walk with' Indigenous people because the country cannot be healed, and the Constitution cannot be changed, by the 3 per cent alone. As Palawa elder Rodney Dillon observed in 2018, 'We've been flat out campaigning for the last 200 years. We've done well in some places but not well in other places. We need supporters like you campaigning on these things, talking to pollies ... I think that non-Indigenous peoples' support and influence can be really, really important to make change.'[6] According to Wiradjuri and Wailwan lawyer Teela Reid, those with special expertise had an extra responsibility to share their knowledge. In the referendum debate, lawyers in particular had 'an obligation to step up and ... ensure the community gets the right information and can make informed decisions about where they stand on the issue'.[7]

I took that responsibility seriously, but identity was a hindrance. The observation that 'Shireen is not blak' was sometimes posted or noted in response to my advocacy – sometimes by the same people calling for non-Indigenous solidarity with Indigenous causes. The chastisement was not generally applied to the many white constitutional lawyers and advisers involved, perhaps because their non-blakness was more self-evident. White experts and lawyers seemed revered and respected, part of the accepted terrain in Indigenous affairs, whereas non-Indigenous, non-white involvement required special justification.

It is notable (if my survey is correct) that in the various official and expert committees put together by Australian governments to progress Indigenous recognition over the last fifteen years, there has never been a sitting participant of a non-European migrant background. All the relevant bodies, including the Expert Panel on Constitutional Recognition of Indigenous Australians (the Expert Panel) in 2011, the various parliamentary committees, the Referendum Council in 2016–2017 and the co-design groups of 2021, were made up of Indigenous and white Australians. And in 2023, the Labor government set up an exclusively Indigenous Referendum Working Group, supported by a small committee of Indigenous and white constitutional experts. There was never a Chinese, Japanese, Indian or Vietnamese Australian expert or advocate in sight – almost as if this was a conversation exclusively between the Indigenous peoples and the white colonisers, with non-white migrants playing no allowable role. This was also true of the campaign bodies: Australians for Indigenous Constitutional Recognition (which oversaw Yes23) was headed only by Indigenous and white Australian leaders. Ditto the Uluru Dialogue under Megan Davis. Ditto Uphold & Recognise, the conservative outfit co-founded by Julian Leeser and Damien Freeman.

I floated around the edges, in-between and often unseen. I advised Noel, co-wrote submissions and joined meetings with him, and continued to advocate and persuade, but in later years I was not a key player, strategically speaking. Still, invisibility allows a different perspective and perhaps some objectivity. I can write this book with the benefit of some distance from key decisions in the lead-up to the referendum, which I hope enables a clearer critique.

So here is my justification for butting in where I am not wanted, one last time. To those who have told me to shut up because 'Shireen is not blak': tough luck. I am brown and I spell it with all the letters. More importantly, I'm Australian. Non-white migrants and their descendants have a role to play in reckoning with our country's history and achieving just reform. You might not always see us, but this is our country too. The Australian Constitution belongs to all Australians and has to be changed by all Australians. We all bore responsibility to advocate and achieve this constitutional reform. This was our shared cause: to work together to achieve the Uluru Statement. We failed. This is my take on why.

∾ ∾ ∾

Noel and I always believed that if we worked with conservatives and created broad coalitions for change, then with hard work and perseverance, a double majority of Australians could be persuaded to vote 'Yes' to a constitutional Voice for Indigenous peoples. We had no illusions about the difficulty of this challenge. Politically, changing Australia's Constitution is one of the hardest things to do. It requires both a national majority and a majority of voters in four out of six states to say 'Yes'. Only eight of forty-five referendums have succeeded since 1901, and the Constitution was last changed in 1977 – over forty-seven years ago. Since then, the nine referendums held have all been defeated. The Voice referendum did not win a majority in any jurisdiction except the ACT. The failure was comprehensive.

The key killer was lack of bipartisanship, long considered a prerequisite for referendum success. But in an era of sharpening political polarisation, social fragmentation and tribalism – exacerbated by social media's amplification of disinformation, hate and dumbed-down debate – sensible cross-party policy discussion conducive to bipartisan reform ultimately proved elusive. Though the Voice germinated in collaboration across divides, the referendum became a partisan war zone, with politicians opting for political point-scoring rather than cooperation for the national good. The reasons behind the failure of bipartisanship are examined in the following chapters.

Why did Indigenous leaders and the Labor government persevere with the referendum absent bipartisan support? This book grapples with that question too. But to put it in perspective, Indigenous people had been waiting 122 years for a government willing to put worthwhile constitutional recognition to the people. And, as I will suggest, genuine bipartisanship may never have been forthcoming for any substantive form of constitutional recognition, given the Coalition's longstanding resistance to anything other than constitutional symbolism, and its opportunistic tactics, which sought to exploit every avenue for electoral and political advantage – even avenues that damaged the country. Given this reality, lack of bipartisanship notwithstanding, this was still viewed as the best chance of finally recognising Indigenous people in the Constitution in the way they wanted to be recognised, and in a way that would deliver tangible improvements to Indigenous communities. As prolific Voice campaigner Thomas Mayo reflected after the referendum defeat: 'I don't have regrets … it was a rare opportunity where there was a government and a prime minister that listened to that request from a majority of Indigenous people. It was something Indigenous people wanted … We had to try because this is an urgent matter.'[8] They had to try.

The failure of the October referendum concluded my twelve years of work towards Indigenous constitutional recognition. I watched the pragmatic proposal developed in collaboration with constitutional conservatives win unprecedented Indigenous consensus through the Uluru Statement in 2017. I watched it gain political traction through dogged persuasion by Indigenous leaders. Then I watched it become a political football. I saw firsthand how our radical centre coalition with constitutional conservatives faltered and then fractured under political pressure. The nasty tribalism of our politics ultimately could not be overcome.

*Introduction*

In the final few months leading up to the referendum, I was flying around the country to speak at events, sometimes more than ten a week. I visited several Indigenous communities and was reminded how much this meant to them: the urgency of the need for change was palpable. There were communities up north where kids were known to break into houses, not to take laptops or mobiles, but to take food from the fridge. It made me think of my own son: I couldn't fathom him facing such deprivation. 'They have nothing,' I told my husband on the phone, conveying the passion of the adults of one particular community, who spoke with such hope about peace, inclusion and friendship. Those remote Indigenous communities voted 'Yes' in the highest numbers. Their need was greatest. After weathering the cruelties of history, they desperately wanted reform and reconciliation, and were reaching out to their fellow Australians for love and acceptance. But they were not the focus of the debate.

Increasingly, I witnessed a debate mired in polarisation, disinformation, confusion and racism. I heard claims that voting 'Yes' would allow Indigenous people to take away our backyards. That voting 'Yes' would force businesses to give stuff away to Indigenous people. That voting 'Yes' would mean we would all have to pay rent for living on Indigenous land. None of this was true. Yet these claims went viral on social media and were whispered to voters at the polls.

The referendum was an opportunity for a national settlement of historical wrongs. Viewed in this context, the profound modesty of Indigenous Australians' invitation to non-Indigenous Australians to advance reconciliation via an advisory constitutional Voice – a proposal forged in compromise – should have been clear. The problem was many Australians probably did not see this as a settlement of our nation's troubled history. If they focused on the issue at all (and polling research suggests some didn't), the historical context was likely missing. The political context – the collaboration and compromise across political divides that gave rise to the Voice proposal – was also absent. Many Australians voted 'No' in a context vacuum.

Identifying and unpacking mistakes is crucial if reformers are to learn from the referendum's failure. In addition to critiquing the choices, lies and hypocrisies of Voice opponents, this book analyses what I assess to be the errors made by Voice advocates and the government.

I want to be clear, however, that acknowledging strategic missteps does not exonerate the Coalition. Ultimately, the political right chose not to play ball. They chose to oppose a modest proposal for Indigenous constitutional recognition instead of owning and refining it. The Coalition should have made the Voice its own while in government, especially given the concept was co-created with conservatives, including one who became a Liberal Party parliamentarian. The Coalition should have continued that collaboration with Indigenous people and led a 'Nixon goes to China' referendum. Instead, it shirked that historic opportunity for leadership, and when Labor finally took the reins in 2022 it chose to sow division for political gain. The Coalition wanted to derail the referendum to hurt Albo. Indigenous people were cannon fodder in the ensuing partisan war.

Nor does acknowledging failures on both sides of politics completely exonerate the Australian people for the choice we collectively made. At the end of the day, we decided. A significant majority of Australians voted 'No' based on the information we had before us. We had the 'Yes' and 'No' booklets, although legally they did not need to be truthful. We heard the basics of what was proposed. Whether we chose to seek out the facts or rely on lies was our choice. We exercised our democratic rights. Australians, too, must wear that legacy.

I don't accept the truism, repeated by politicians in the wake of this defeat, that 'the Australian people always get it right'. The quip intends to reject Trumpian mistrust in democracy and democratic outcomes, to bolster faith in the system and respect for the electorate, but it incorrectly insinuates that anyone who respects democracy must endorse all outcomes of democratic processes. It reveals political cowardice: 'I'm too scared to acknowledge that Australians made a poor decision in rejecting the Voice, in case they reject me too, so I'll pretend they got it right.' This lets us off too lightly. It evades political responsibility for mistakes and choices that led to the devastating outcome. It avoids grappling with the polarised and petty state of our politics, which rendered this modest reform conceived with conservatives ultimately impossible to achieve.

I take a contrary view. The Australian people, acting through our democratic procedures, do not always get it right. We did not get it right when our policies and laws enabled Indigenous Australians to be paid unequal or non-existent wages during the protection era, nor when our democratically endorsed decisions sanctioned the forcible removal of Indigenous children from their families, the banning of Indigenous languages and the denial of Indigenous property rights. We did not get it right when we enacted legislation that denied Indigenous Australians the vote in some jurisdictions right up until the 1960s. And we did not get it totally right in the 1967 referendum, when a massive majority of citizens approved the conferral of constitutional power to the Commonwealth, allowing it to make special laws and policies about Indigenous people – under a power it has only ever used to make laws about Indigenous people – without also requiring that Parliament and government hear advice from Indigenous communities when making decisions impacting their lives.

The Australian people got it wrong in the Voice referendum. We chose fear over love. Though voting 'Yes' would have cost us little, we fell for nitpicking and division over a chance at reconciliation. That was our right: our collective decision was of course democratically legitimate. But we made a mean and miserly choice. The ask, after all, was small. After everything Indigenous people have been through in this country – the discrimination, the dispossession and the bloodshed of the past – all they were asking for was a guaranteed advisory Voice in their affairs. Theirs was a hand of friendship extended, asking only for the ability to have a say in decisions affecting them, and we slapped it away. We couldn't find it in ourselves to give them even that.

We can reflect that Australians were misinformed or confused or distracted, that the 'Yes' campaigns were ineffective and the 'No' campaigns too effective, that social media favours lies and hate, and that lack of bipartisanship killed it – and that may all be true. But these are also excuses. Whatever the myriad reasons for failure – and we must learn from them – Australians said 'No' to our nation's best opportunity to settle our fraught founding history. The chance to achieve Indigenous constitutional recognition has been lost, likely forever. I know many Indigenous people will be experiencing pain for a long time.

∾ ∾ ∾

The referendum result has changed the way I see Australia and my fellow Australians. I worry we have lost the ability to empathise and cooperate across divides to achieve reform in the interests of our most disadvantaged, and in the interests of the country. Division and base politics trump genuine policy discussion, creating reform timidity and inertia. Australia's rigid Constitution now seems basically unamendable – and what does that say about our democracy? Our ineptitude at constitutional change ultimately threatens our democratic stability and constitutional longevity, for a structure that cannot bend is prone to break. As conservative philosopher Edmund Burke observed, 'A state without the means of some change is without the means of its conservation.' Lacking the ability to forge the consensus needed to change our Constitution via referendum, we lack a crucial element of democratic self-governance. Learning lessons from the referendum defeat is therefore important.

I hope this book challenges Australia's next generation to come up with new solutions where previous generations have failed. To develop better ideas and strategies to make our country fairer and heal history's wounds. There are serious issues gripping our society, and too few bright minds building the consensus needed to implement compelling solutions. We face growing inequality, climate change, declining educational competitiveness. We face a housing crisis that renders the dream of home ownership increasingly unattainable for anyone without wealthy parents. We face year after year of failed efforts to close the gap on Indigenous disadvantage, growing racism and worsening social cohesion. Current leaders seem to view these problems as intractable, but the next generation must break through the division and inertia – if you don't, who will?

Though this book tells a story of defeat, I urge readers not to be disheartened: be energised. The lesson should be to try harder, work smarter, learn from the mistakes unpacked here and persevere with better strategies. Don't be scared to try to change things, even though change is hard. Don't be scared to fail, even though failure hurts. Try your best to do something great. That's what advocates for the Voice referendum did: we tried to do something good for Indigenous people, and for the country. We failed despite our earnest efforts. Maybe future generations will succeed where we did not.

# 1

# COUNTERFACTUAL

In his 2022 Boyer Lectures, Noel Pearson asked Australians to consider the following thought experiment:

> Easter Saturday 1891: the leading lights of the six colonies have come together to draw up the Constitution on the paddle steamer *Lucinda*, anchored on the western foreshores of Pittwater in Sydney's north. They are to spend 'a mammoth 13-hour session' drafting the Constitution of the proposed Commonwealth of Australia. The Constitutional Committee is hosted by Sir Samuel Griffith, Premier of Queensland and later first Chief Justice of the High Court. Edmund Barton, later the nation's first Prime Minister, is there, as is Charles Kingston, future Premier of South Australia. Sir John Downer is there for some time with other Founding Fathers of the new nation, once described by Professor Marcia Langton – with great affection of course – as a collection of beards, moustaches and whiskers protruding from venerable ears, noses and eyebrows. The core of the Australian Constitution is drafted here. The work done over that Easter weekend is decisive in the constitutional history of the nation.
>
> Imagine the Committee on board the *Lucinda* is made aware of a gathering of ambassadors representing tribes from all compass points of Ancient Australia: North, South, East and West. At the

invitation of the Eora peoples they have come to make representations to those drafting the constitution of the new Commonwealth. Their people have suffered great depredations in the past hundred years of frontier conflict and dispossession – their numbers are now much diminished and many tribes are near driven off the face of the earth.

If these representations included the constitutional recognition of Aboriginal and Torres Strait Islander peoples through a Voice to the Parliament and executive government in order to create a dialogue between the old and new Australians in respect of the country's heritage and its future – what would those on board the *Lucinda* respond with the benefit of our hindsight today? I ask each of us: what would our response be if we were on board the *Lucinda*?[1]

Let us explore this counterfactual more deeply, to better comprehend the magnitude of Australia's decision on 14 October 2023.

Imagine a Gadigal man watched the *Lucinda* chug down the river, his son by his side. The white man on the deck smoked a pipe and gazed at the water. Its smoke curled and conjoined with the ship's steam, which puffed up into the low-hanging clouds. The water reflected the smoke and sky; it was grey, like the white man's beard. For a moment, the black man and the white man locked eyes in fleeting recognition across the water. The white man's eyes glinted and squinted through his smoke. The black man stared, gripping his spear, watching for guns. He made hand gestures, comprehensible in any language: *You, me, talk,* his hands said. *Your people. My people. Let's talk together.* The white man raised his eyebrows, nodded, then retreated below deck.

That Easter weekend in 1891, the *Lucinda* was a drafting retreat. Samuel Griffith, from Queensland, Charles Kingston, from South Australia, and Edmund Barton, from New South Wales, were all on board as it cruised the Hawkesbury River. Inglis Clark was away with a bad cold, but his draft Constitution was refined by the subcommittee aboard the boat. The decisions made that weekend provided the constitutional framework that today governs Australia.

Let's imagine something changed after those two men saw themselves reflected in each other's eyes: perhaps the idea dawned on Samuel Griffith, the white man, that they might talk across divides.

Back in the dining room, Griffith might have sat in one of the leather armchairs where his colleagues drank tea and conversed as they anchored at Pittwater. His mind was troubled by the encounter on deck, which made him think of happenstance and history. Had their boat not sailed into Broken Bay and up the Hawkesbury to avoid the rough swell and vomit that forced John Downer to disembark, would he have seen that man with fierce eyes and a wiry frame, or his boy, whose wondering gaze reminded him of his own son? Would he have felt this whispering in his heart, or the disquiet in the most pragmatic parts of his lawyer's brain? It got him thinking how unexpected detours can alter one's perspective, and perhaps a nation's history.

Imagine Griffith told his colleagues about the man on the shore and asked them to turn the ship around to pursue a conversation with the man and his people. Barton might have resisted. 'We are already behind schedule,' he said. 'And how do you propose we converse, even if we could find the naked rascal in the scrub?' But Griffith could have insisted they invite the man on board to talk. They could find him some clothes if that was Barton's concern. And they could organise an interpreter – he knew of learned men studying the languages of the blacks. The others acquiesced to their Queensland colleague, who they assumed was harried by violence he'd witnessed on the northern frontiers and was therefore seeking a more peaceful resolution.

As the boat turned back, they might have discussed the fact that New Zealand representatives had been invited to participate in discussions pertaining to Australia's federation (they later decided not to join the new nation), but the Indigenous peoples of their own continent had not been extended the same courtesy. The Constitution that would unify the colonies risked failing, in a fundamental sense, to unify its peoples.

Griffith recalled how New Zealand's colonial secretary, Captain Russell, had told the Australasian Federation Conference of his reservations about conjoining with Australia. New Zealand's settlers had to struggle against 'a proud, indomitable, and courageous race of aborigines', Russell explained, and the Kiwi settlers had treated the natives 'in a manner so considerate that the condition of no other native and savage race on the face of the globe can be compared to it'. This might have been due to their 'missionary zeal' or the fact that New Zealand's settlers were more 'pure in spirit' than colonisers elsewhere. More pragmatically, Russell revealed, they knew 'the natives could defend their own interests and look down the sights of a rifle better than any other savage people'. The Māori outnumbered the white settlers, which perhaps also explained why their 'hearts and policy were softened'. They appreciated 'the necessity for keeping the natives at peace' while still 'obtaining enough of their lands to further colonization'. The New Zealanders were thus reluctant to transfer their native management to a Parliament of 'mostly Australians' that by comparison 'cares nothing and knows nothing about native administration', and which had 'dealt with native races in a much more summary manner than we have ventured to deal with ours in New Zealand'.[2]

Would Australia's new Constitution deal with Indigenous peoples in a 'summary manner' too? Remembering Russell's speech might have got Griffith thinking of the 1864 Battle of Mitchell River, up at Cape York in Queensland, where Olkolo warriors had attacked drovers and been run into the water and shot. Blood spilled on both sides, and though the Australian tribes were significantly depleted and less fearsome than they had once been, they could still uprise. Even by 1885, those working on the pearling boats would occasionally rebel, kill the Europeans and steal the boat. The Native Police counteracted their resistance, but frontier conflict continued.

'In New Zealand, we have the Treaty,' John Hall, the other Kiwi delegate, might have explained privately. Hall had become the premier of New Zealand in 1879 and was in power for the violent conflict at Parihaka in 1881, which was fresh in his mind, as the Queensland conflicts were in Griffith's. 'We give the Māori representation in the Parliament. Since 1867, they have had special seats,' Hall noted. The seats were initially a tool for control and the limitation of Māori political power. 'You need to think about how to minimise bloodshed,' and how to access land 'without unnecessary resistance'. Some kind of agreement might help, Hall might have suggested. 'Perhaps give them some representation, a political voice. Invite them to participate within proper rules and processes.'

As the *Lucinda* chugged back to shore, maybe the Australian men debated the merits of including the natives in their constitutional discussions. 'The idea is preposterous,' Barton might have insisted. 'The Aborigines are a dying race. There is no need to entreat with them, for they will be gone in a few decades. They are not fearsome warriors like the Māori. Look at what has been happening in Tasmania.' Yet while the natives had been weakened, formal inclusion could still facilitate a more productive peace. They might have shared nagging worries, perhaps anchored in conscience, especially when they imagined the boy of no more than ten staring in wonder at the boat. What would become of him, and his children and grandchildren, in a new nation that excluded them?

Charles Kingston might have made the moral case, passionate liberal that he was. South Australia under his leadership had included women in the electoral franchise in 1894, making it one of the first places in the world to do so. 'We should strive to be true to the Royal Instructions that were conveyed to the first explorers and settlers of this land,' he could have urged. 'We should do that which till now has not successfully been done: obtain the consent of the natives for the establishment of this new Commonwealth on this soil. We should do unto these others as we would have them do unto us, were the situations reversed.'

Let's imagine the crew found the Aboriginal man and his boy. The man was persuaded to leave his spear on shore, on the assurance that the white men's guns were also put away. After coaxing, he came on board. Imagine history was rewritten because two men locked eyes after a ship changed course to avoid rough seas.

Indigenous people across the continent might have been invited to send representatives to a final Constitutional Convention. They might have called it a 'constitutional corroboree'. Word was first sent to the Yolngu Dilak in Arnhem Land. For them, the time was ripe to talk peace: Makarrata. Message sticks travelled to the Noongar in Western Australia, to the Yorta Yorta down south, to the tribes of central Australia and to Tasmania, where Truganini's descendants fought to retain the vestiges of their peoplehood.

The tribes would have convened and strategised. They knew the precariousness of their position. If they asked for too much, their claims might not be taken seriously. They could be dismissed altogether, and uncaring arbitrators would decide what form of recognition (if any) the constitutional compact would grant them. Conversely, nothing about their pitiful circumstances would change if they asked for too little. They would forever be at the whim of the white man's harsh policies – powerless and unheard. The colonisers had the guns; they increasingly had the numbers. The Indigenous tribes were on the back foot. Strategy was everything. They would have to appeal to conscience and common humanity. They would need persuasive wit. Crucially, despite their internal disagreements, they would need to stand united. If they were divided in their claims, any splits would be exploited. With a unanimous voice, however, they might create some leverage.

Imagine they formed a constitutional Dilak with Indigenous representatives from around the continent – an Indigenous negotiating party. The Dilak was highly pragmatic, having been advised in this vein by Griffith and other supportive colonialists. They didn't ask for reserved parliamentary seats. They didn't, at that time, ask for a Treaty. Those negotiations could be saved for later. They asked for constitutional recognition of their Dilak – a national body that could advocate and negotiate into the future on behalf of the native peoples of the land. They asked that the existence of their Dilak be guaranteed by the Constitution, and enacted flexibly to enable its evolution, allowing Indigenous people to provide advice to the new Commonwealth Parliament and government on the laws and policies that would impact them. With the assistance of interpreters, and in collaboration with Griffith and others, they drafted a constitutional provision to guarantee their voice would be a permanent part of the new Commonwealth.

Imagine the black man who had locked eyes with Griffith spoke to the proposal at the final Convention, with a translator conveying his words in English:

> Our people have lost so much. We have seen our ancestors and family members gunned down and poisoned. Once proud warriors have been felled. Our songlines, cultures and languages are already disappearing, our peoples wiped out by diseases and war. We are losing much of our land, so we cannot hunt and fish like as we once did. Now in many places we are beggars on the fringes of your society, struggling to survive. We rely on handouts, and our children are taken from us. We do not agree with such treatment, which denies our humanity.
>
> Should you establish a new nation on our land as you propose, we ask to be formally included and recognised within it. We do not wish to be annihilated, nor assimilated. We do not want to disappear. We want to be recognised as the unique peoples we are. We want a rightful place in the new nation, and a rightful say in our own affairs.
>
> So we implore you, newcomers: we will share our land, our home, with you. Despite all that has befallen us, we will welcome

you to our country so this will be your country too. All we ask in return is that you always include us in the decisions you make about us, by guaranteeing us an advisory voice. We will respect the overarching authority of the new Parliament and government. You will remain the ultimate decision-makers.

But, please, recognise us in a real way by promising to always hear our voices. Recognise our national Dilak. In return for sharing our country with you, this is all we ask.

The white men might have conferred and debated. Maybe there was consternation and grumbling, as their differences fomented division. Maybe Griffith and the few other supporters spoke in favour of the proposal to their colleagues. 'Put yourself in their shoes,' Griffith might have urged, thinking of blood already spilled. 'They are offering us a very good deal. They have had their country taken from them. They are no longer the rulers of their own land. Their people have been killed, their livelihoods usurped and their languages often banned. And they are not asking for reserved seats, as the Māori have in New Zealand. They are not asking for sovereign territory upon which their own laws shall prevail, as some Indian tribes have in America. They are not asking for a separate state in the new Commonwealth. They are not even asking for monetary compensation for their losses. They are asking only for a permanent ability to advise Parliament and government on decisions impacting their affairs. I ask you: if we were in their place, if we had lost our land and had our people killed and our children taken, is this all *we* would ask for? I am certain that if it were me, if it were my people who had possessed this whole continent since God's beginnings, I would be asking for much more.'

The men might have considered Samuel's pleading with respect. However, there was an overwhelming view that the blacks should be given no special privileges. Most felt they should be assimilated. They should not exist in any kind of separate sense. And, strategically, there was no real need to give them anything in the name of peace and reconciliation anyway – they had already been defeated.

To overcome division on the issue, and to forestall an uprising from the blacks who would be present for a potential 'No' vote, the white delegates might have decided an Indigenous Voice should not be included in the Constitution of 1901. For the time being, they decided, the Constitution would explicitly exclude Indigenous people,[3] as had been previously planned. Instead, a referendum on a constitutional Voice would be held some years later. That way, they argued, the Australian people could have their say on that issue separately and directly.

Imagine that by the time that vote came there was insufficient appetite for the change. The government initiated the referendum at the urging of persistent Indigenous advocates, who had kept their promise to quell retaliatory violence. But, by now, the proposal's few white champions faced different political circumstances. Their backing for the Indigenous Voice idea diminished as they protected new positions of power and fought new political enemies. Less willing now to share any power, some began to publicly critique the proposal they once shaped and supported. The Indigenous advocates did not know how to answer their criticisms: they had been counting on their support.

Imagine Australian sympathies declined further as the vote approached. Many felt the blacks had only themselves to blame for their wretched situation, and an advisory body would not fix anything anyway. The proposed change did not seem legally safe, given some of its original proponents were now equivocating and others were raising concerns. Nor did they see the proposed reform as a necessary settlement of the fact of Indigenous dispossession, for that dispossession was not a wrong that required settling. It was just what happened: the superior people prevailed.

Some saw the proposal as unfair: why should the blacks get a special advisory body when the white settlers had no equivalent? If they want a political Voice, they should get elected to Parliament like everyone else. Granted, Indigenous people in some jurisdictions had not yet secured the right to vote. And although they still complained about their exclusion from the Constitution, their unequal wages, their children and land being taken, and Protectors controlling various aspects of their lives, such inequities (past or continuing) were no excuse for favourable special treatment – for that would turn the whites into second-class citizens, which would be intolerable.

Imagine the Indigenous advocates could not convince voters otherwise. Having been treated as inferior and unequal by the whites, under a Constitution that specifically excluded the 'Aboriginal race', Indigenous people could not answer the objection that giving them a Voice would somehow divide the country on racial grounds.

Imagine the new Australians voted 'No' to constitutionally recognising the original peoples through an advisory Voice in their affairs.

# 2
# A FAILED 'RADICAL CENTRE' REFERENDUM

We always understood the centrality of bipartisan support. From the moment we began working together in 2011, Noel would say that 'Nixon needed to go to China' to achieve constitutional reform in Australia. The metaphor referred to President Nixon's 1972 visit to the People's Republic. It emphasised the importance of conservatives championing reforms that would otherwise be viewed as progressive and automatically opposed by the right. Constitutional recognition needed a sympathetic conservative leader to bring the right on board.

Constitutional change is not a typical electoral or reform battle. Securing the left – those naturally most amenable to reform – is not enough. A consensus across some three-quarters of the political spectrum is needed to fulfil the four-out-of-six-states approval threshold, plus the requirement of a national majority. Noel would use an image of a clock face to illustrate the importance of building this support. It showed the Greens at seven, Labor occupying most of the left-hand side, the Liberals spanning the right, and the Nationals and One Nation at four and five o'clock respectively. Noel challenged us to plant a 'stake in the ground' at four o'clock. If we secured the support of good-hearted and rational conservatives, then everyone to the left of that should be easier to persuade. The aim was to foster conservative co-ownership of the reform in the hope that, with conservative champions, bipartisan support could be achieved.

Our strategy was informed by Noel's pursuit of the 'radical centre', defined as 'the intense resolution of the tensions between opposing principles ... that produces the synthesis of optimum policy'.[1] Finding the radical centre requires engagement across divides, in contrast to the entrenched ideological positions and point-scoring of ordinary partisan politics. It is not simply about splitting the difference between two opposing principles to reach a lowest-common denominator. Rather, it is about harnessing the 'dialectical tension' in enduring disagreements to uncover a creative and ambitious reform solution.

Radical centrism draws on Hegelian dialectical argument. It seeks to resolve apparent contradictions to innovate new ideas. A thesis is proposed, which attracts a counterargument, the antithesis. The radical centre endeavours to synthesise these contradictory insights into a richer truth or a more correct and consensus-building position. Such an approach encourages balance, because a good society – and the best policy – is usually an amalgam of insights from conservatism, liberalism and socialism.[2] The radical centre thus eschews simplistic categories like left and right. Finding it is an empathetic endeavour, requiring us to see the humanity and intelligence in our opponents, and the kernels of truth in their opinions. This demands both humility and creativity. As Noel explained in 2016:

> If politics is the art of the possible, then the radical centre is about *maximum* possibility [my emphasis]. If politics is necessarily about tension and struggle, then the radical centre is the highest compromise. The radical centre is the policy and political source of innovation.
>
> If you want innovation, then keep innovatively exploring the tensions between left and right; keep hunting the radical centre. Creativity and imagination are the means to creating the radical centre.[3]

We sought a radical centre synthesis of the core disagreement in Indigenous constitutional recognition.

Indigenous advocates always insisted that constitutional recognition must entail substantive, empowering reform – if it wouldn't make a genuine difference to Indigenous communities and outcomes, what was the point? The opportunity of constitutional change could not be squandered: it must reform the power relationship between Indigenous peoples and the Australian state, to make it fairer than in the past, so that better practical outcomes could be achieved. This required more than a static, symbolic constitutional statement of no operational effect. As the late activist Galarrwuy Yunupingu put it, Indigenous people sought 'serious constitutional reform'[4] to ensure past wrongs were not repeated.

Many political leaders, by contrast, thought Indigenous recognition was just about symbolism. Reluctant to share power with the powerless peoples of the country, they preferred cosmetic tinkering with the Constitution's race clauses and the insertion of a new symbolic preamble – but no real reform to any power relationships.

The distance between these starting points presented a roadblock to consensus. Indigenous people wanted substantive constitutional reform. Political elites kept rejecting or ignoring such calls. The two groups were having parallel conversations. They just couldn't connect.

In 2013, working with Noel out of Cape York Institute (CYI), we had reached an impasse in our efforts towards constitutional reform. ACU professor Greg Craven and other right-wingers had lambasted the Expert Panel's 2012 recommendation for a racial non-discrimination clause to be included in the Constitution – a substantive proposal CYI had championed – as a 'one-clause Bill of Rights'.[5] Noel realised bipartisanship could not be achieved with this proposal, but he also knew Indigenous people could not settle for symbolism. We needed to rethink the whole thing by 'stepping to the right and up':[6] this meant taking on board conservative concerns while nonetheless achieving something empowering and substantive that Indigenous people could champion. I had no idea what the solution might be.

I went on exploratory missions to Samuel Griffith Society conferences to try to understand where our conservative opponents were coming from.[7] There I identified a group of constitutional conservatives – Craven; the convenor of the Samuel Griffith Society (and later federal Liberal MP) Julian Leeser; philosopher Damien Freeman; and leading constitutional law expert Anne Twomey – with whom we endeavoured to find common ground. We built relationships and held several meetings and workshops over many months to discern an alternative path forward.

As I recounted in *Radical Heart*, this engagement was initially difficult. The constitutional conservatives (dubbed the 'con cons') didn't understand why Indigenous leaders were pushing for a racial non-discrimination guarantee. We didn't understand why they didn't understand, given the history of discrimination Indigenous people had suffered under the Constitution. Eventually, after vigorous discussion, the parties began to grasp each other's perspective.

The constitutional conservatives acknowledged Indigenous concerns were justified, given the history. The Constitution should ensure Indigenous people are treated more fairly – just not through a constitutional amendment that would empower the High Court to strike down Parliament's laws, thus undermining parliamentary supremacy and creating legal uncertainty. In turn, we came to understand the importance to conservatives of upholding the Constitution, respecting parliamentary supremacy and minimising legal uncertainty.

Our intense conversations uncovered a sweet spot. We discovered it was possible to uphold the Constitution *and* recognise Indigenous interests in a meaningful, substantive way. Instead of empowering the High Court to invalidate laws and policies found by judges to be discriminatory, the Constitution could empower Indigenous peoples *themselves* to have a fairer say in laws and policies affecting them. The idea of a constitutionally guaranteed Indigenous advisory body was a political and procedural solution, rather than a litigious solution, to the competing concerns. The proposed constitutional change would create no veto, but would give Indigenous peoples a non-binding, advisory voice in political decisions relating to them.

Contrary to the 'crash or crash through' narrative propagated by Frank Brennan[8] and others, this is how the Voice began in 2014. It was forged in collaboration across divides, to reconcile Indigenous aspirations for substantive and empowering constitutional change with the conservative desire to uphold the Constitution.

Ironically, the advisory body solution was also far more in keeping with Indigenous calls for greater self-determination and political agency than a racial non-discrimination guarantee ever was. It fused conservative priorities with one-hundred-plus years of Indigenous activism asking for a fairer political voice.

In the following months, Indigenous leaders Megan Davis and Marcia Langton joined the discussions. In later years, human rights commissioner (and later Liberal MP) Tim Wilson and Indigenous advocate Warren Mundine[9] made contributions showing how a constitutional Voice could address liberal as well as conservative concerns (back then, both were supporters of constitutional change to empower Indigenous voices).[10]

Our engagement with constitutional conservatives had a profound effect on me as a fledgling constitutional lawyer and advocate. Mine was not the only perspective altered. In a speech to the Sydney Institute two weeks before the October 2023 referendum, Leeser explained how our 2014 collaboration helped shape his thinking:

> I too found myself challenged. I found myself being drawn more deeply into reflecting on the genuine aspirations of Aboriginal and

Torres Strait Islander Australians to be recognised in their Constitution and for this to result in some sort of practical change in outcomes in their communities and in their lives ...

Out of those discussions came an idea that went with the grain of our existing constitutional arrangements.

The idea was not flowery language, which is inconsistent with the dry, sparse, technical nature of our Constitution, but an advisory body that would sit within our existing arrangements.

The body recognised the supremacy of Parliament in our constitutional arrangements, and could inform the Parliament as well as the ministers and public service about how to implement policies that work with Aboriginal culture and practice ...

Not only a Voice to the Parliament and Government, but one that could also speak through local and regional bodies to public servants, mayors and decision makers.

Then, rightly, the idea was taken back to Aboriginal and Torres Strait Islander Australians.

This process wound across Australia and culminated in the release of the Uluru Statement from the Heart.[11]

Our alliance in 2014 negotiated every word, comma and semicolon of a proposed constitutional amendment requiring Parliament to establish an Indigenous body with the core function of 'providing advice to the Parliament and the Executive Government on matters relating to Aboriginal and Torres Strait Islander peoples'. Anne Twomey published our agreed drafting in *The Conversation* in 2015.[12]

Those original words were an important site of agreement, representing the convergence of our disparate agendas. They were a meticulously negotiated noble compromise. With the formulation of those words, we at CYI abandoned our previous advocacy for a racial non-discrimination guarantee to advocate instead the Indigenous advisory body as co-devised with constitutional conservatives. We proceeded on the basis of their support. Over the next nine years (as explained further in Chapter 6), several iterations of the 2014 drafting simplified and streamlined the amendment and led to the final words put to the Australian people on 14 October 2023. The words Australians voted on were directly descended from, and very similar to, the amendment our alliance originally drafted.

Those constitutional conservatives advocated the Voice for many years. In December 2014, the group met with Tony Abbott, who around that time famously declared he would 'sweat blood' for Indigenous recognition,[13] to pitch our proposed Voice amendment to him. Leeser and Freeman established the conservative organisation Uphold & Recognise (U&R) in 2015, dedicated to championing the proposal in conservative circles.

The conservative case for a constitutional Voice developed from there. As Leeser put it in 2016, the proposed amendment provided the kind of machinery clause that 'Griffith and Barton and their colleagues might have drafted, had they turned their minds to it'.[14] Craven for many years described the proposal he co-created as 'modest yet profound'. In 2015, he called it 'genuinely brilliant'. Combining 'minimal constitutional exposure with maximum moral impact', the advisory body would work 'with the Constitution, not against it... It can advise, but not dictate to government, inform but not instruct Parliament. Our democracy is enhanced not undermined.'[15]

Coming from the most constitutionally conservative figures in the country, this endorsement was important, though we understood that much more work would be required to ultimately achieve bipartisan support. At this early stage, CYI and U&R were lonely advocates of the proposal. There were also early opponents. Brennan publicly argued against the proposal from at least 2015. He favoured constitutional minimalism and repeatedly advised Indigenous people to settle for something symbolic.[16] He claimed it was 'impossible' to design a constitutional provision 'that was technically and legally sound' and ensured 'the untrammelled sovereignty of parliament'. Some Labor representatives were also unhappy with our shift in position in those early days, viewing it as a sellout to conservatives. Back then many preferred the Expert Panel's more ambitious racial non-discrimination guarantee, and viewed the advisory body proposal as too weak.[17]

⁕ ⁕ ⁕

Three years later, that compromise devised with constitutional conservatives won Indigenous consensus. The concept of a First Nations constitutional Voice garnered Indigenous endorsement by clear majority consensus in 2017. This extraordinary achievement was led by Indigenous leaders such as Megan Davis, Pat Anderson and Noel. Through the First Nations regional dialogues, Indigenous people assessed and debated all the options on the table, including symbolic recognition, a racial non-discrimination guarantee and a constitutional advisory body. As Davis explained, the dialogues involved 'a structured deliberative decision-making process' that included 'intensive civics education, an explanation of the legal options' and 'a preference matrix that would enable communities to assess reform proposals and rank them according to the interests of the region'. The Indigenous organisers 'took very seriously the importance of the process being bottom up and driven by the people themselves'.[18]

Through this rigorous process, a national Indigenous consensus was reached and the Uluru Statement from the Heart was issued. The statement asked that Indigenous peoples be recognised through a constitutionally guaranteed Voice. It also asked for a Makarrata Commission, which could be set up in legislation, to oversee agreement-making and truth-telling.

Thomas Mayo has spoken powerfully about the hard work and passion that went into achieving the majority position. 'There were people embracing each other with tears in their eyes, who had debated each other throughout the process. It was an incredible moment,' Mayo recalled.[19] The Uluru Statement was a historic achievement in Indigenous peoples' struggle for constitutional recognition. Most advocacy of the past had emanated from particular regions or individuals; never before had a national consensus been realised.

The majority position was strong, though there were of course dissenters. Dissent is healthy and normal. Of the 250 delegates elected by their Indigenous peers across the regions to convene at that final constitutional convention at Uluru, seven walked out of final talks,[20] citing concerns about giving up their sovereignty – Lidia Thorpe, who later became a federal senator, was among them. But more than 97 per cent of delegates agreed. That consensus deserved the deep respect of non-Indigenous Australia.

Indigenous people achieved such consensus despite north–south rivalries, despite remote, regional and urban divides, despite all the usual personal and political differences, and notwithstanding the immense cultural and linguistic diversity of the First Nations of Australia. I have often wondered: if you got 250 representatives of any other cultural or ethnic group together and asked them to forge a consensus on a complex matter of constitutional reform, could they achieve that level of agreement? The Indian Australian community wouldn't reach a 97 per cent consensus on anything, that's for sure.

There was a strange reciprocity in those numbers. Uluru presented an extraordinary 97 per cent Indigenous consensus behind the Voice, with only 3 per cent dissent among the delegates at the final convention. And Indigenous people were only 3 per cent of the Australian population. They needed to convince the 97 per cent non-Indigenous majority that the constitutional recognition they proposed was sensible and worthwhile, and deserved the nation's support.

Indigenous people needed fair media coverage to get their message across to non-Indigenous Australia. Too often, however, the media picked holes in the Indigenous consensus, because division makes good news and outlets were under pressure to appear 'balanced' – even at the cost of downplaying true levels of Indigenous support. The validity and power of the Uluru consensus was diminished in the media coverage, and successive polls showing majority Indigenous support (often at over 80 per cent)[21] were downplayed. 'Not all Indigenous people agree with the Voice,' reporters and the 'No' campaign would remind us time and again. A minority of high-profile Indigenous opponents were platformed and amplified to convey false balance, creating the skewed impression that advocates such as Jacinta Nampijinpa Price, Warren Mundine and Lidia Thorpe represented the views of 50 per cent or more of the Indigenous population. The prosecution of such false balance would be massively detrimental to the 'Yes' campaign. It was disproved too late by referendum booth results, which showed remote communities with the highest proportions of Indigenous people overwhelmingly voted 'Yes' to recognition through a constitutional Voice in their affairs.[22]

Their consensus was pragmatic. Indigenous people stepped away from minimalist tinkering with the 'race' clauses and insertion of symbolic statements into the Constitution. They also moved away from a racial non-discrimination clause as a means of achieving constitutional empowerment through litigation, the predominant solution recommended by past reports. Through the Uluru Statement, Indigenous people adopted the noble compromise position. The delegates understood the pragmatism of their choice. As Mayo explained, the proposed Voice was 'powerful enough to influence the decisions that affect us', yet 'conservative enough to succeed at a referendum'. It was 'both radical and conservative'.[23] He was right: the Voice was the radical centre. An advisory body with no veto powers, the existence of which was nonetheless constitutionally guaranteed, was balanced.

The Referendum Council – the Indigenous and non-Indigenous expert body convened in 2015 by the Turnbull government and the Opposition to advise on the next steps towards Indigenous constitutional recognition – grasped the compromise. Endorsing the Uluru

Statement's call for a constitutional Voice, its report explained that the proposal 'took account of the objections raised' to a racial non-discrimination clause. The Voice recommendation was therefore 'highly reasonable'[24] because it addressed conservative concerns.

Then the dynamics started to change. The Voice began to be viewed in mainstream politics as a progressive reform, rather than a pragmatic compromise.

# 3
# REPUDIATING THE RADICAL CENTRE

If the 1999 republic referendum got crushed by an 'unholy alliance' between monarchists and direct electionists,[1] the Voice referendum was repudiated by an unprincipled union between the separatist Indigenous left and the reactionary right – though the right's opposition was more electorally impactful. The reactionary right wants assimilation. No special place for Indigenous people can be accommodated – let's even get rid of welcomes to country, some 'No' proponents have argued. At the other extreme, the separatist left seeks Indigenous 'sovereignty'. It rejects any Indigenous inclusion in Australia's 'racist and colonial' Constitution, the authority of which it disputes – although the figurehead of the Blak Sovereign Movement, Lidia Thorpe, is open to 'infiltrating' the Australian political system in other ways, including by being a federal senator.[2] These two groups hated each other. They nonetheless joined forces to defeat the Voice referendum, which proposed a sensible middle way between their extremes.

The Uluru Statement peacefully posited that Indigenous peoples' 'spiritual sovereignty' could 'shine through' Australia's constitutional arrangements in a way that fully respected parliamentary supremacy and the dominant authority of Australian governments. Its aims were integrationist and unifying, not separatist or assimilationist. A constitutional Voice was the inclusive 'third way' solution that reconciled

Indigenous difference with national unity, offering a form of constitutional recognition deeply in keeping with Australian constitutional tradition. The approach enmeshed the best instincts of progressivism and conservatism: it was innovation grounded in tradition.

Its conservatism was underappreciated. In 2022, journalist Paul Kelly asked whether the 'practical conservatism enunciated by Edmund Burke' had been 'consigned to the dustbin' of Australian history.[3] What he as a Voice opponent and too many others failed to understand was that although pragmatic conservatism was being repudiated by the reactionary right, it was nonetheless being kept alive by Indigenous peoples through their middle ground proposal for a Voice, as developed with constitutional conservatives. That this was not understood raises serious questions about Australia's ability to conduct rational debates to sensibly evolve our constitutional institutions. Intransigence entails risks. As Burke recognised, a structure that cannot bend can become brittle.[4]

After the Voice was championed by Indigenous people through the Uluru Statement, it became framed as an Indigenous proposal. Its Indigenous credentials were valid and to be celebrated: Indigenous Australians had been asking for a stronger voice in their affairs for decades, and the Uluru Statement was the culmination of that advocacy. It was Indigenous self-determination in action. But the concept of a constitutional Voice had also benefitted from the input of non-Indigenous constitutional conservatives. This fact could have been more of a selling point for broader Australia. Any resultant loss of progressive brownie points could have been accepted as part of efforts to encourage bipartisanship. However, the Voice's conservative history was undersold as the Indigenous campaign gathered steam – a tendency encouraged by political advisers telling campaigners that the Voice needed to be seen as an Indigenous proposal if it were to succeed.

Parts of the leftist media spun the radical centre origins of the Voice as a narrative of sneaky conservatives manipulating unsuspecting

Indigenous people – a spin CYI rebutted as condescending and untrue. In *The Saturday Paper*, for example, Karen Middleton suggested some would 'see the behind-the-scenes negotiations' with constitutional conservatives in 2014 as 'sinister'.[5] The collaborations were neither 'behind-the-scenes' nor 'sinister' – they were detailed publicly on numerous occasions – but such framing caused concern among progressive elements of the Indigenous leadership, who passionately advocated a constitutional Voice but viewed the involvement of conservatives with suspicion. Given how some of these conservatives behaved in later years, I now concede such suspicion was justified. But this tension led to a denial of conservative involvement by some parts of the Indigenous leadership.

The Indigenous-owned Voice became automatically viewed as progressive, which risked alienating the right. This was a weakness in the framing, but also reflected the relative quietness of its conservative co-creators, who in the face of Coalition resistance did not always loudly celebrate their contributions to the reform, nor the national opportunity the Indigenous–conservative convergence had created – though at times they tried. The fact that prominent conservatives, including Liberal Party parliamentarian Julian Leeser, had helped conceive of the Voice was not widely appreciated. Even by 2023, many Coalition politicians we spoke to did not know of Leeser's involvement. This history was also often lost to the public, which had political ramifications. Conservative Australians might have found the involvement of old fuddy-duddy white conservatives comforting, whereas something that came from Indigenous people alone may have been viewed as scary and automatically radical. The leftist framing was amplified when successive Liberal leaders rejected Indigenous people's call for a Voice. It solidified when Anthony Albanese won the May 2022 election for Labor and made the Voice referendum an election-night commitment. From that moment, the proposal was officially owned by the left, and the radical centre vanished almost entirely from view.

This became Labor's Indigenous-led referendum, which further enhanced its progressive credentials. The government established a Referendum Working Group: 'a broad cross-section of representatives from First Nations communities across Australia' charged with providing advice on 'successfully implementing a referendum within this term of Parliament'. The twenty-one-person group – assisted by a small committee comprising Indigenous and non-Indigenous constitutional experts, including Twomey, Craven and Noel – gave advice on timing, what information to provide to the public and how to refine the constitutional amendment and referendum question. Forming part of a broader sixty-one-member Referendum Engagement Group – again an Indigenous-only committee – tasked with advising the government on building community support for the referendum, it was co-chaired by Linda Burney, the Minister for Indigenous Australians, and Senator Patrick Dodson, Special Envoy for Reconciliation and Implementation of the Uluru Statement from the Heart.

It is unclear how the decision was made to create Indigenous-only working groups, given past Indigenous recognition committees had all consisted of both Indigenous and white leaders. Noel occasionally expressed incredulity that – apart from the small expert committee – only Indigenous advice was formally sought by the government on the best way to win a referendum that the non-Indigenous majority would ultimately decide.

The consequences of underselling non-Indigenous and conservative input into the Voice hit home during the final weeks of the campaign. I was addressing a gathering in a wealthy suburb of Melbourne. The attendees were sceptical Liberal voters, but by the end of our discussion many said they were switching from soft 'No' to 'Yes'. As usual, I had explained how we at CYI had collaborated with constitutional conservatives in 2014 to develop a compromise proposal, which was then endorsed by Indigenous people through the Uluru Statement. One woman said: 'I am now voting "Yes", but I'm confused. You've used several key words: *compromise, collaboration, conservatives, pragmatism, middle ground.* This is all crucial, but why am I just hearing it now? Why is this not part of the mainstream message? No one knows about it.' She was right.

It reflected a perennial problem for the radical centre. Though there were moments of productive collaboration across divides, political partisanship kicked in as the Voice proposal got legs: ultimately, neither side could tolerate the involvement of the other. The participation of conservatives made progressives and some Indigenous people wary. But when Indigenous people took ownership of the Voice through the Uluru Statement, and it was tragically rejected by Turnbull, the proposal became cast as progressive, providing increased fodder for the right's opposition. Eventually, when Labor took charge of the Voice, even some of its conservative co-designers began to attack their own creation, anxious not to be fully associated with what was by then viewed as an overly ambitious and progressive reform.

The far left's behaviour exacerbated the tribal dynamic. While the right-wing 'No' case claimed the Voice was too risky and radical, the leftist anti-compromise crew argued it was too weak. The far left's objections were especially frustrating because they came from a minority of Indigenous activists who ostensibly wanted progress on Indigenous rights yet were proactively helping to defeat the best chance at achieving it. These activists favoured different solutions – 'sovereignty', treaties first and full implementation of the UN Declaration on the Rights of Indigenous Peoples – but had no effective political strategy to realise their objectives.

Weeks after the referendum defeat, Lidia Thorpe urged Parliament to legislate the UN Declaration, which calls for Indigenous consultation and participation in laws and policies impacting them. Her proposal attracted bipartisan opposition.[6] A constitutional Voice would have helped Australia realise those principles: the proposal was adopted by the Indigenous delegates with the UN Declaration in mind,[7] and was backed by UN experts as facilitating Indigenous rights as articulated under international law.[8] Australia is now no closer to implementing the UN Declaration, and Thorpe's advocacy for treaties has been understated since the referendum's defeat.

The 'No' campaign utilised both right-wing (the Voice is too risky and radical) and left-wing (the Voice is too weak) objections to rally opposition. Some right-wing social media 'No' ads even quoted Thorpe and used her image, much to her annoyance.[9] Like the right, however, left-leaning Voice opponents had no viable plans for progressing Indigenous interests once the referendum was defeated. The contributions of both extremes were more about protest and politics than real progress. All this fed the tribalism that derailed the referendum.

⁂

Given these dynamics, it should have been unsurprising that progressive support for the Voice began to grow when Malcolm Turnbull rejected the Uluru Statement in 2017. Labor representatives who had initially been unenthused began to come on board – if the Liberals rejected it, it must be good! Off the back of the inspiring Indigenous consensus, non-Indigenous support also began to grow – highlighting possibilities of consensus across divides.

Polls showed the Voice had majority support for around six years prior to the referendum. A 2017 OmniPoll survey showed 61 per cent would vote 'Yes' to a First Nations voice in the Constitution.[10] A February 2018 Newspoll survey showed the proposal had 57 per cent support. By July 2019, another showed support was at 66 per cent,[11] despite opposition from the Coalition. Some outlier polling even showed support was at 81 per cent.[12] Compare that with the 61 per cent result achieved in the same-sex marriage postal survey – a voluntary vote, which skews the result higher – under a Liberal prime minister advocating for the change. Polling showed support for a constitutional Voice at similar levels, notwithstanding the lack of Coalition leadership and Liberal prime ministers' advocating 'No'. The proposal initially seemed capable of uniting black and white, and left and right.

New conservative advocates started to emerge. In 2015, I engaged with right-leaning commentator Chris Kenny, who arguably became the most effective conservative champion for the Voice, alongside Leeser – only Kenny's support never faltered. Former Labor leader Kevin Rudd and right-wing radio personality Alan Jones were inspired to declare a 'unity ticket' of support on the ABC's *Q&A* in 2017 – an unprecedented moment. The shock jock explained the proposal's simple pragmatism:

> There has been, and there always will be … standing Indigenous advisory bodies. Now, as I understand it, all Pearson and co are saying, which is pretty reasonable sort of stuff, [is that] the Constitution is to mandate the existence of such a body … And they would then be able to advise the government of the day on matters relating to Indigenous affairs. I don't think that's in any way controversial, we already have it …
>
> It's to simply say, 'Well, we'll alter the constitution to mandate the fact that there will be a statutory Indigenous advisory body. It won't be binding on the government but we'll have the capacity to recommend to the government on all matters in relation to Indigenous affairs.' How hard is that?[13]

Jones put it well: the proposed reform was not much to ask. It was reasonable. It was simple. But he later switched to rabid opposition. Once the Voice became a Labor policy, Jones argued it would divide Australia by race and derail government.

There were many other right-wing supporters of the Voice who ended up changing sides. Jeff Kennett was one. In 2016, I asked Kennett to launch *The Forgotten People*, a collection of essays by conservatives making their case for a constitutionally guaranteed advisory body. I edited the book with Damien Freeman, and it featured contributions by Leeser, Craven and Twomey, among others. Kennett agreed and launched it at the Melbourne Town Hall. He then published his unequivocal support for a constitutionally enshrined Indigenous advisory body in the *Herald Sun*, arguing such a council would provide 'invaluable advice' and 'help us to celebrate our first peoples'. His article even quoted the constitutional drafting published by Anne Twomey, calling it 'not a bad starting place in my opinion', so long as the First Peoples 'agree on the form and the wording', which 'should be the sole objective in their forums to be held this year'.[14] Kennett was talking about the First Nations regional dialogues that would soon kick off under the Referendum Council.

In 2019, Kennett was still 'open-minded' about a constitutionally enshrined Voice.[15] Yet by January 2023, with Labor championing the proposal, he argued the Voice should be enacted in legislation but not constitutionalised.[16] As the October referendum drew nearer, he became a staunch opponent. A constitutional Voice seeks to give 'one section of our community ... a special place of influence and representation with the federal government of the day over all other Australians ... [which is] inappropriate, unfair, and discriminates against all other Australians', he declared. 'We should all be treated equally through and by our Constitution.'[17] Quite the turnaround. Kennett also accused the Labor government of 'rolling two questions into one' by proposing an amendment that combined Indigenous recognition with the creation of an advisory body.[18] Yet in 2016, Kennett himself proposed adding symbolic recognition to the introductory sections of the *Constitution Act*, to complement the Voice amendment. He argued that 'recognition should commence with the phrase, "This Constitution recognises Aboriginal and Torres Strait Islanders as the continent's first peoples"'.[19] As it turned out, the beginning of the Voice amendment put to referendum in 2023 used a very similar introductory line: 'In recognition of Aboriginal and Torres Strait Islander peoples as the First Peoples of Australia'. But by then Kennett was an ideological opponent of Labor's referendum.

Chris Merritt, the former legal affairs editor at *The Australian*, is another conservative who supported the Voice in the early years but opposed it when it became a Labor proposal. In 2017, Merritt said a constitutional Voice 'would do nothing more than provide advice to the government on proposed laws affecting the Indigenous community'. He characterised it as a historical settlement. 'Here's the harsh reality,' Merritt wrote. 'Our forebears took this country from the original inhabitants. We are not about to give it back. So the least we can do is oblige ourselves to listen when Indigenous people ask to be heard.'[20] After Labor won the May 2022 election, however, Merritt opted for strident opposition: the Voice was divisive, he said, in column after column. It would upend democracy and divide Australia by race.

❧ ❧ ❧

'No constitutional reform proposal has done more to address the concerns of conservative opponents than the proposal for a constitutionally guaranteed Indigenous voice.' These words were uttered by a prominent senior Liberal who understood the true history of compromise that informed the Voice, at a dinner in 2022. The observation was correct. A constitutional Voice was probably the first proposed constitutional amendment in Australian history to arise from collaboration between ambitious reformers and constitutional conservatives dedicated to preserving the Constitution.

I expected that fact to generate goodwilled engagement between left and right, and Indigenous people and the right, to perfect the execution of the elegant compromise forged. It didn't: my expectation was naive. It assumed some basic level of good faith and flexibility on the part of Coalition parliamentarians. It assumed that honest and principled conversations could be had about how Indigenous people and the Coalition might meet in the middle.

Honest and direct conversations proved mostly impossible because too many politicians would say one thing in private and another in public. Their positions were too slippery; they couldn't be pinned down. Consensus cannot grow in such conditions. In the end, most of the Coalition did not seem to care how much Indigenous people had done to address conservative concerns. They cared about their political fortunes over and above principles. And the radical centre cannot survive without protagonists who care about principles.

Our underpinning belief was that if we gave conservatives shared ownership of a co-designed reform, then, with hard work, Indigenous people could win wider conservative support. As I came to learn, however, this only really worked for the individual conservatives directly involved in conceiving the Voice – and even their support dissipated when the progressives got into power and political battle intensified.

I now also see that the original compromise was forgotten partly because the significance of the disagreement it resolved had faded. Perhaps, in politics, radical centre syntheses are momentary: the dialectical tension that propels them disperses over time.

Prior to 2014, Indigenous people had proposed a thesis: a racial non-discrimination clause should be introduced into the Constitution to guarantee their fairer treatment. This attracted an antithesis from conservatives, who said, 'No, that does not uphold the Constitution and it undermines parliamentary supremacy'. The reconciliation of these positions gave rise to the idea of a constitutionally guaranteed advisory body – a synthesis of the competing concerns.

At first the Voice was an outlier proposal. Then it was adopted by Indigenous people in the Uluru Statement. It later became Labor policy. For five to six years it enjoyed approval levels of around 60 per cent. The Voice became the new thesis: the compromise it represented was eclipsed and it became seen as a progressive-owned orthodoxy, ripe for rebuttal by parties looking for something to oppose.

A new dialectical tension emerged. The new thesis was a constitutional Voice. The new antithesis, propounded by right-wing objectors, was that the Voice was a 'third chamber' – a misrepresentation coined by Barnaby Joyce, then perpetuated by Malcolm Turnbull – and a breach of equality.

Voice proponents later began seeking a new synthesis of the conflict – a refined radical centre – through adjustments to the constitutional drafting (as Chapter 6 explains). But these solutions did not resolve the competing concerns, because the new dialectic was mostly performative: there was no further genuine dialogue or negotiation across divides. Key opponents were not truly open to compromising in aid of bipartisanship. Their opposition was about opposing Albanese's referendum for political gain.

# 4
# THE ILLUSION OF BIPARTISANSHIP

Lack of bipartisanship was the Voice's major killer. Support among Coalition voters plummeted by more than 30 per cent in 2023, with most of the decline ensuing after the Liberal Party's formal opposition was declared in April. According to ANU expert Ian McAllister, who co-led a large study on voter attitudes throughout the campaign, the referendum would likely have succeeded with bipartisan backing because division would have been minimised.[1] It is hardly a revolutionary observation.

History shows that changing Australia's Constitution generally requires bipartisan support. Historically, the 'Labor urge to reform' the Constitution has offset the conservative propensity to protect it.[2] Labor tends to support proposals for change. An 'ironic consequence' is that most amendments have occurred under right-wing governments,[3] underscoring the centrality of strategies to secure conservative support.

Though some commentators argued bipartisanship should be deprioritised,[4] the 2023 referendum's failure reiterates its importance, exposing the naivety of claims that bipartisanship had become less necessary for constitutional reform in the social-media age. On the contrary, bipartisan reassurance is now more crucial to counteract platform algorithms amplifying negativity, tribalism and misinformation. As Twomey observed after the defeat: 'In a hyper-partisan and post-truth world, the prospects of referendum success now depend more than ever on an elusive spirit of bipartisan cooperation.'[5]

The Voice referendum was preceded by fifteen years of ostensible bipartisan commitment to Indigenous constitutional recognition. The Uluru Statement's call for a Voice was not only the culmination of a century of Indigenous advocacy but a response to that longstanding bipartisan pledge to recognise Indigenous peoples in the Australian Constitution.

Prime Minister John Howard first committed to a referendum to recognise Indigenous peoples in the Constitution in 2007.[6] Kevin Rudd, as Opposition leader, matched Howard's commitment. Since then, no Australian prime minister, whether Labor or Liberal, has gone to an election without a promise to recognise Indigenous peoples in the Constitution. (That changed at the 2022 election, when a Coalition commitment to a referendum was notably absent.) Yet, over this period, no prime minister ever put a referendum to the people – until Albanese. As Noel remarked, 'Albanese on election night was the first sign of real leadership since 2007.'[7] No other leader made it a first-order issue, worthy of the expenditure of serious political capital. So how genuine was the bipartisan commitment really?

I now see that bipartisanship on Indigenous constitutional recognition was an illusion. The facade began to crumble in 2017, when Turnbull rejected the Uluru Statement's call for a Voice. It was then obliterated between November 2022 and April 2023, when the Nationals and then the Liberals decided to formally oppose the referendum. But it was a farce from the start. Let me explain why.

꙳ ꙳ ꙳

The professed bipartisan commitment obscured an enduring disagreement: most politicians, especially those on the right, preferred recognition to entail something purely symbolic, whereas Indigenous people have always wanted it to involve substantive and empowering change to address the 'torment of their powerlessness'.[8] The fifteen years that followed Howard's initial commitment were therefore punctuated by clashes about the meaning and purpose of constitutional recognition: was it about making a symbolic statement or was it about effecting structural reform for improved practical outcomes?

While most right-wing politicians never let go of their preference for constitutional symbolism, the consistent resistance of Indigenous leaders made it politically difficult to proceed with a referendum on that basis – especially given the guiding principles of all formal processes since the Expert Panel in 2011 included the requirement that any proposal 'accord with the wishes of Aboriginal and Torres Strait Islander Peoples'.[9] Besides, a symbolic recognition referendum would have no momentum without numerous Indigenous champions: Indigenous opposition would kill its chances of success. This created a tension between Indigenous and political leaders that was prone to periodic eruption. There could be no recognition referendum until that impasse was somehow resolved.

The first clash occurred between Howard and Noel at the time of Howard's 2007 speech. Howard proposed introducing a statement of Indigenous recognition through a new symbolic preamble to the Constitution. You would think his flopped preamble referendum of 1999 might have turned him off the idea of re-running that failure. Several conservatives had been 'highly suspicious' of the 1999 proposal: Dame Leonie Kramer derided it as an 'adolescent "wish list"', while Greg Craven characteristically described it as a 'time bomb' awaiting detonation by a future High Court (he carried a proclivity for violent constitutional metaphors well into old age).[10] Australians rejected it, but eight years later, Howard was unable to learn from his mistake: he planned to put a symbolic preamble to the people again.

In his 2022 Boyer Lectures, Noel reflected on his reaction to Howard's 2007 commitment:

I never supported preambular recognition. It was and is insufficient. The preamble that accompanied the 1999 referendum on the republic was rejected by the Australian people. I believed it would be rejected again not least because Indigenous people reject it and because constitutional conservatives warn it would empower the High Court to re-interpret the entire constitution. It is not a legally safe nor politically viable option.[11]

Though Noel had pushed Howard to move on constitutional recognition prior to 2007, he subsequently told him he could not support a symbolic preamble. According to Noel's speech, Howard promised that 'different options' would be discussed with Indigenous leaders if his government was returned for a fifth term. But Howard lost the election.

Noel's 2022 recounting of this disagreement probably prompted Howard to announce his opposition to the Voice a few days later,[12] but it was nonetheless important for Noel to pitch the Voice to conservative voters and politicians. The example of Howard's early commitment was key. It showed that the Liberal grandfather did not believe recognising Indigenous peoples in the Constitution would divide the country by race – even if he was ultimately only prepared to countenance symbolic recognition.

In the twenty-four years after 1999, Howard's position didn't shift – despite consistent Indigenous rejection of a symbolic approach and despite the 2017 consensus of Indigenous peoples behind a constitutional Voice. It demonstrated the insincerity of the prime minister's private assurance that he was open to considering other options in consultation with Indigenous leaders. In 2023, he still insisted that a symbolic preamble approach was the superior solution: 'More than twenty years ago … what I had in mind was an acknowledgment of their prior occupancy. I mean, nobody can argue with that,' he complained.[13] The media reported his remarks as those of an ancient oracle declaring what constitutional change was allowed and what wasn't. But what about the fact that Indigenous people didn't want it, constitutional conservatives warned against it and the majority of the country rejected his preamble idea in 1999?

With this conflict about the fundamental objective of Indigenous recognition bubbling beneath the surface, successive governments ran laborious public processes to further the Indigenous recognition agenda. Each had to grapple with the same conundrum. Prime Minister Julia Gillard established an expert panel to advise her government on the issue. As noted, the panel's 2012 report recommended a racial non-discrimination guarantee, which constitutional conservatives blasted as a 'one-clause Bill of Rights'. The Labor government did nothing about the recommendations, probably because there was no consensus pathway forward. In response to this impasse, CYI began to engage constitutional conservatives, with Tony Abbott's encouragement, which led to the idea of a constitutionally guaranteed Voice.

After Abbott became prime minister in 2013, he established the 2014 Joint Select Committee on Constitutional Recognition of Aboriginal and Torres Strait Islander Peoples, chaired by Ken Wyatt, to explore options for recognition. CYI's concept of a constitutionally guaranteed Indigenous body was initially unpopular, even with Labor, and the committee's 2015 recommendations stuck with variations on the racial non-discrimination guarantee. However, Wyatt subsequently admitted these would not be accepted by his Coalition colleagues, who saw such a guarantee as 'effectively a bill of rights'[14] – a fact we had tried unsuccessfully to convey to the committee. This left only minimalistic constitutional changes on the table, which Indigenous people did not want.

Indigenous leaders yet again made clear that they wanted more than just symbolism – they wanted real reform. They issued the Kirribilli Statement in July 2015, which declared:

Any reform must involve substantive changes to the Australian Constitution. It must lay the foundation for the fair treatment of Aboriginal and Torres Strait Islander peoples into the future. A minimalist approach that provides preambular recognition, removes section 25 and moderates the races power (section 51(xxvi)) does not go far enough and would not be acceptable to Aboriginal and Torres Strait Islander peoples.

The statement noted the need for further engagement with Indigenous peoples in relation to a constitutionally guaranteed Indigenous advisory body. By this time, some Indigenous leaders were seeing it as a potential 'third way'. The statement called for 'ongoing dialogue' between Indigenous people (via a referendum council, steering committee or other mechanism) and called upon the government to 'negotiate on the content of the question to be put to referendum'.[15]

Abbott subsequently announced the Referendum Council, which was then appointed under Prime Minister Turnbull and Opposition leader Bill Shorten. Its Indigenous members convened First Nations regional dialogues around the country. Turnbull tried to steer the Referendum Council towards a minimalist outcome, saying the Voice proposal had a 'snowflake's chance in hell'.[16] But the Indigenous leadership resisted these attempts at manipulation, and in 2017 issued the Uluru Statement, which endorsed the middle way: a First Nations Voice to be enshrined in the Constitution. The Referendum Council's final report recommended the constitutional enshrinement of a Voice. Turnbull was not pleased. 'This is not what I asked for,' he told the council. 'Take it or leave it,' was co-chair Mark Leibler's reply. Yet again, there was a standoff.

Then, in October 2017, the Turnbull government rejected the proposed Voice, misrepresenting it as a 'third chamber of Parliament'. The illusion of bipartisanship was shattered.

Somehow, hope survived and semblances of cross-party cooperation remained. The Coalition government established the Leeser–Dodson

Joint Select Committee on Constitutional Recognition in 2018, which recommended more work be done on the Voice as the only viable pathway for Indigenous recognition. This kept the Voice alive. On the committee's recommendation, the Morrison government established the Indigenous Voice Co-Design Process, led by Minister Wyatt, which ran public consultations on the potential design of a Voice. Convened by Marcia Langton and Tom Calma, it delivered its final report in 2021, setting out detailed design options. But Morrison made only negative public remarks about the idea of constitutional enshrinement.

The recurring theme is of right-leaning politicians rejecting recommendations from their own official committees that did not adhere to their predetermined preference for constitutional minimalism. That the press gallery, which is supposed to hold politicians to account, shared the same overwhelming preference for symbolism illuminates how power reinforces and protects power. The Canberra bubble reinforced the views of the Canberra bubble. The right never wanted to share power with Indigenous peoples, not even the minuscule levels of empowerment that would be enabled through a constitutionally guaranteed non-binding advisory body. Official recommendations asking for anything more than symbolism were therefore ignored or rejected by successive governments – until Labor won the 2022 election and Albanese committed to holding a referendum on a First Nations Voice in his first term.

The default analysis by commentators is that the referendum failed because Indigenous Australians did not settle for symbolism. *The Australian*'s Peter van Onselen argued the referendum should have 'enshrined constitutional recognition of Indigenous Australians, leaving a body to advise government to be established with legislation', because a symbolic insertion would attract overwhelming public support,[17] whereas a Voice would not. This was also the preferred approach of Frank Brennan,[18] whose analysis the press seemed to regard as gospel.

David Crowe argued in *The Sydney Morning Herald* that 'the Voice is about more than recognition because Indigenous leaders wanted practical change', which he described as 'ultimately about power'. 'The polls suggest many Australians do not want to give Indigenous people more power … Many Australians simply do not want a change of this scale,' Crowe opined. His analysis regurgitated Brennan's characterisation of the Voice referendum as a 'crash or crash through' issue for the prime minister: Labor and 'Yes' campaigners had adopted an 'all or nothing' approach, eschewing symbolic recognition, which was 'the easier path to victory'.[19] The argument was parroted by countless media commentators: Indigenous people were asking for too much. The model was overreach. Had they proposed something just symbolic, Australians would have voted 'Yes' in overwhelming numbers. This framing coloured the whole debate.

The post-referendum ANU survey appeared to back up these views. The results showed 61.7 per cent of respondents who were eligible to vote definitely or probably would have voted 'Yes' to a referendum on recognition, broadly conceived.[20] Commentators, including press-gallery stalwart Michelle Grattan, were quick to say this supported the proposition that symbolic recognition would have succeeded.[21] Yet they consistently ignored contextual considerations that rendered a symbolic approach unviable.

First, what does 61.7 per cent support for a 'broad conception of constitutional recognition' mean, absent a specific proposal? A constitutional Voice also attracted support of around 60 per cent in the six years leading up to the referendum, before an amendment was put forward by government and political division crystallised. The historical trend is that public support drops as the vote nears. The particulars, as they emerge, give opponents ammunition for attack. Why would a symbolic referendum be any different?

Second, Australians overwhelmingly rejected a symbolic constitutional preamble in 1999. Only 39.34 per cent voted 'Yes', a result similar to the Voice referendum.

Third, opposition to mere symbolism from two powerful constituencies would be assured.[22] Constitutional conservatives such as Leeser would have rejected it. They have repeatedly warned that the inclusion of symbolic words in the Constitution would be legally dangerous and ill-fitted to our practical constitutional rulebook, potentially leading to unintended High Court interpretations of the whole Constitution. (Leeser made it clear he would oppose a symbolic insertion into the Constitution, whereas he supported a constitutionally guaranteed Indigenous advisory body.[23]) More importantly, Indigenous Australians have consistently rejected a merely symbolic mention in favour of empowering and practical reform that helps close the gap. They made this clear long before the First Nations regional dialogues that culminated in the Uluru Statement, and they reiterated their firm rejection of mere symbolism during those dialogues.[24] Why would Australians endorse a form of recognition Indigenous Australians say they do not want, and which sensible constitutional conservatives oppose? We wouldn't. Opposition from these two constituencies would create a pincer movement that would kill a symbolic proposal. It would fail, just as it did in 1999.

That most commentators ignored these realities, while rebuking Indigenous people and Albanese for putting anything more than mere symbolism to the Australian people, speaks to the poverty of the media and expert analysis of the referendum.

※ ※ ※

Looking back on this history, it is clear there was only ever bipartisan support for an amorphous but wholly symbolic form of recognition that Indigenous people never wanted and that was politically impossible.

This is why the Coalition did not hold a referendum on symbolic constitutional recognition during its nine years in government, despite its professed commitment to the issue, and it must be partly why Dutton quickly withdrew his tactical promise to hold another symbolic referendum should the Voice fail.[25] Symbolic recognition rejected by Indigenous people is not recognition at all, and it would never be put to a referendum due to Indigenous opposition.

While the political class kept complaining that Indigenous leaders should have compromised (which they did, repeatedly), no amount of compromise – short of a complete capitulation to embrace mere symbolism – was likely to have changed the fact that most of the right wanted nothing but symbolism, if that. This is the great irony of the dominant narrative that Indigenous leaders and Labor derailed the referendum with their 'crash or crash through' failure to compromise. The opposite is far more true: Indigenous people compromised plenty, perhaps more than they should have. They were expected to endlessly concede ground to accommodate right-wing concerns. But the Coalition never reciprocated. Except for a few individual outliers and privately expressed declarations that rarely matched public positions, the Coalition never budged from its 'symbolism or nothing' position.

Some Voice advocates nonetheless overemphasised the history of bipartisan commitment, in the hope of persuading the Coalition to come on board at the right time, but such hope turned out to be in vain. When you understand this, it becomes easier to see why Indigenous leaders and Labor persevered in the face of opposition from Turnbull in 2017 and Dutton and Nationals leader David Littleproud in 2022 and 2023. Substantive constitutional recognition never had Coalition support in the first place.

Once it was clear there was no bipartisanship, Indigenous people had four options. One: accept a wholly symbolic proposal, as Howard, Turnbull, Brennan and others wanted them to do. But this would expend their one chance at constitutional reform on a change that would deliver zero practical benefit to communities. It might expunge some white guilt, but it would do nothing to close the gap and would perpetuate the failing systemic status quo. It is to their credit that Indigenous people rejected this option.

Two: wait for a time when maybe bipartisanship could be achieved. But Labor had waited almost a decade to be in power. What if they didn't get another term? And the Liberal Party's position hadn't really changed in fifteen years. Maybe a future Liberal Party under a Julian Leeser or an Andrew Bragg would be different. But who knew if that would eventuate, or if the politics would allow those individuals to stick to their principles?

Three: abandon any hope of achieving recognition of Indigenous peoples in the Constitution and stop prosecuting this cause.

Or four: attempt to take the Coalition's veto power away by trying to win the Voice referendum absent the bipartisanship that was only ever an illusion anyway.

Indigenous leaders understood the rare opportunity of a prime minister willing to put the Voice to the people. Presumably, they also understood the risks – they were being guided and encouraged by some of the most experienced political advisers in the country. They chose to try.

Reflecting on the campaigns and the government's approach, however, I can see that 'Yes' advocates could have done more to bargain, encourage, coax and cajole support from the highly resistant Coalition. I'm not saying these extra efforts would have succeeded – they probably would have failed, given the Coalition's intransigence and politically driven opposition to Albanese's referendum. Nonetheless, 'Yes' advocates could have made it more difficult for the Coalition to say 'No' to a proposal that had been devised with constitutional conservatives, including a Liberal parliamentarian.

As noted, the government and the 'Yes' campaigns framed the Voice as a wholly Indigenous and therefore progressive proposal, which involved downplaying its credentials as a compromise with conservatives. Perhaps this was inevitable given repeated Coalition rejection of anything substantive, but it was still an error. Though they made important efforts, the Voice's conservative co-creators could also have done more to rebalance the narrative and sell the unprecedented opportunity created by the Uluru Statement to the Coalition and its supporters.

Albanese's choice to champion the cause on election night, to cheers from the Labor faithful, was arguably a mistake too. Though this positively raised the profile of the cause, it also stamped it as a Labor agenda. The prime minister could have announced a bipartisan-backed process a couple of weeks later, standing next to Dutton, though that assumes Dutton would have agreed, which (knowing what we now know) is perhaps unlikely.

There was a sense from some Labor politicians that bipartisanship would not be forthcoming anyway, so what was the point in trying hard to work with the other side? While this perception was probably accurate, there was also a misplaced confidence that a Labor government could win the referendum without Coalition support, because public support for the Voice 'goes very deep'. Yet Labor operatives must have understood that Coalition support was essential, given its centrality in constitutional reform discourse. As Chris Bowen remarked on Q&A in April 2022, 'only eight referendums have passed, none without bipartisan support ... It's unthinkable we would put it to the people and lose.'[26] However, some Indigenous leaders argued that bipartisanship might be less relevant than it once was, given declining trust in politicians, which perhaps comforted the left that support from the right was not essential. This complacency was ill-advised.

Some official reports produced by Voice advocates were also flawed, which gave the Coalition excuses to reject the proposal. Take the 2017 Referendum Council report, which needed to be compelling to readers across the political spectrum. In selling the Indigenous consensus behind the recommendation, it was robust and persuasive. The report meticulously explained that the First Nations regional dialogues had

> engaged 1200 Aboriginal and Torres Strait Islander delegates – an average of 100 delegates from each Dialogue – out of a population of approximately 600,000 people nationally. This is the most proportionately significant consultation process that has ever been undertaken with First Peoples. Indeed, it engaged a greater proportion of the relevant population than the constitutional convention debates of the 1800s, from which First Peoples were excluded.[27]

However, the report was weaker in defending the proposal's legal and conservative credentials. It did not recommend any specific constitutional amendment for a Voice – a major mistake. Apparently, former High Court chief justice Murray Gleeson had advised his fellow Council members to leave the wording to Parliament. Damien Freeman and I had taken Gleeson through Twomey's 2015 draft amendment, which a few years later he endorsed as legally sound.[28] It would have been better if the Council had put forward that drafting as an example of how a constitutional Voice could be achieved. The absence of specific wording gave opponents greater scope for fearmongering. Together with Coalition resistance to substantive constitutional change, it allowed the debate to drift. Not until 2023 did any official government report recommend an amendment for a constitutional Voice. That was six years of missed opportunities for raising awareness, facilitating coherent public and legal discussion, and making drafting refinements in the public eye, with additional compromises in full view.

Given the lack of specific drafting in the report, it was probably unwise for the Referendum Council to tell Turnbull the Voice was 'take it or leave it' when the prime minister pushed back. Take or leave what? The Turnbull government quoted those words in its rejection statement – 'The Referendum Council said the Voice to Parliament was a "take it or leave it" proposal for the Parliament and the Australian people. We do not agree,'[29] it said – and went on about the Council's belligerent approach for years.[30] In the face of Turnbull's resistance, it might have been better to suggest a collaborative process to nut out the specifics of the constitutional drafting and address Coalition concerns.

Turnbull later complained the Referendum Council had presented 'a column of smoke and you couldn't grapple with it ... If you wanted to produce a proposal of this kind, it should have been a detailed bit of drafting.'[31] Yet Turnbull, too, shirked responsibility: he was the prime minister. Upon receiving the Referendum Council's recommendation, he could have convened an expert and/or parliamentary process to flesh out drafting options. Political calculations – and pressure from the right of his party – meant he didn't. Instead, he maligned the proposal as a 'third chamber' and rejected it. This suggests he would not have agreed to a collaborative drafting process had the Council proposed one. Turnbull was more interested in outright opposition than building consensus.

The subsequent 2018 Joint Select Committee chaired by Leeser and Dodson also squibbed the drafting challenge. The committee was required to 'recommend options for constitutional change', and its members privately urged constitutional experts and academics to submit a variety of drafting options to the committee – which many did. However, in the foreword to its final report, the committee complained that 'it is difficult to proceed to referendum today on the Voice when this Committee has received no fewer than eighteen different versions of constitutional amendments which might be put at a referendum'.[32]

It was another excuse. While the omission of specific drafting in the Referendum Council's report was used to justify Coalition inaction, the multiple drafting variations solicited by the Joint Select Committee were unfairly framed as a lack of consensus and used as an excuse for inaction too. Voice advocates could not win. Instead of proposing any specific constitutional drafting, the committee recommended that, 'following a process of co-design, the Australian government consider, in a deliberate and timely manner, legislative, executive and constitutional options to establish The Voice'. This pushed the can down the road.

The absence of drafting in the Referendum Council's report gave rise to other problems down the track. In 2022, it enabled Brennan to claim that the Voice's constitutional ability to advise the executive was recently concocted by Indigenous advocates.[33] It wasn't: it had been part of the proposal since its inception in 2014. It also formed part of the Referendum Council's understanding of the proposal in 2017, as demonstrated by the report's multiple references to the Voice giving advice on both laws and policies.[34]

The omission of specific drafting was a misstep that could easily have been fixed by any well-meaning government that wanted to help Indigenous people achieve something good. But that was the problem: the Coalition was not well-meaning on this issue. Nor was it open-minded. It wanted only minimalism – and its position *was* 'take it or leave it'. There was therefore no room for sloppiness on the part of Voice advocates trying to manoeuvre for something more.

Another misstep was that while the Referendum Council report sensibly recommended a constitutionally guaranteed Indigenous advisory body with no veto powers,[35] it ill-advisedly noted a concern among some Indigenous dialogue participants that the proposed body might have 'insufficient power if its constitutional function was "advisory" only', revealing 'support ... for it to be given stronger powers'.[36] This candid aside risked inflaming right-wing opponents. The Turnbull government cited these comments in its rejection, noting how the council was concerned 'the proposed body would have insufficient power if its constitutional function was advisory only'.[37]

The mistake reflected the fact that the Referendum Council report was written in an open and honest way: it was frank and forthright about the range of Indigenous hopes, views and divergences that were reconciled in forging consensus – and the Turnbull government exploited its honesty. This demonstrated a stark mismatch of intentions. Indigenous advocates were putting their proposal out there with high hopes, immense goodwill and perhaps some naivety. They seemed ill-prepared for the bad-faith political response of the Coalition, which was not interested in working with Indigenous people to understand their arguments, refine their proposal or help sell it to the public. It was only interested in exploiting any weakness to justify its negative response.

What Indigenous advocates achieved through the Uluru Statement was remarkable. But they were only human. The Referendum Council did the best it could, given the circumstances and wisdom at the time, but it could not turn the illusion of bipartisanship into reality. As Turnbull himself said after the referendum defeat: 'There was never any prospect of the Voice amendment receiving formal Coalition endorsement.'[38]

# 5

# GRAB THEM BY THE LAPELS

In our efforts to foster bipartisanship, Noel and I engaged with members of the Coalition over many years. Noel would talk about Lyndon B. Johnson's famous ability to persuade politicians of both sides. Known for tireless doorknocking and hiking up miles of farmers' driveways in Texas to have one-on-one conversations with his constituents, in the halls of power L.B.J. would use every angle possible to persuade his targets, grabbing them by the lapels, debating, pleading, cajoling, until they saw an issue from his point of view. 'L.B.J. did the hard yards of persuasion,' Noel would say. 'We need to take that approach. We have to do everything that needs to be done to win.' With that inspiration, we tried our best to persuade Coalition politicians to support the idea of a constitutionally guaranteed advisory body. But key politicians on the right proved fickle. The changing positions of some are worth recounting.

Turnbull was among several Coalition politicians who privately expressed support for a constitutionally guaranteed Indigenous advisory body before later changing his mind. At a meeting at Parliament House in June 2015, while communications minister, Turnbull told Noel and me that the advisory body proposal seemed 'sensible' and asked how he could help us promote it. He suggested a possible 'politics in the pub' event in his electorate. After the meeting, I emailed Turnbull links to Twomey's constitutional drafting and our committee submissions.[1]

But sometime between 2015 and 2017, Turnbull capitulated. In September 2015, just three months after our meeting, Turnbull overthrew Tony Abbott to seize the prime ministership of Australia. As George Brandis reveals in the ABC *Nemesis* documentary, Turnbull made a 'Faustian bargain' with the right of his party to obtain their support for his leadership. This involved selling out on key principles and committing to do their bidding on certain policy issues. There was even a rumour – promoted by a conservative source – that Turnbull did a deal with Howard to secure his support in the spill. The alleged deal was that Turnbull as prime minister would only support minimalist constitutional change and nothing more. Once in office, Turnbull also had to deal with Abbott spoiling from the back bench. As Liberal MP Andrew Hastie remarked, Abbott was like the 'ghost of Banquo' in Turnbull's government. The prime minister probably had little room to manoeuvre on ambitious policy and must have been under pressure to abandon any support for a constitutionally guaranteed Indigenous advisory body.

Alternatively, Turnbull might have been misleading us in June 2015: perhaps he never supported the proposal to begin with. Here's the thing I learned about politicians over twelve years of engaging with them on Indigenous constitutional recognition: they are prone to tell people what they want to hear and quite often can straight up lie. And even if they are genuine in expressing support in private, they can turn on a dime when political circumstances dictate.

Faced with the likelihood of Turnbull's rejection after the prime minister's negative remarks to the Referendum Council, Noel considered the possibility of legislating the Voice before holding a referendum, to elicit bipartisan cooperation. Although his Indigenous colleagues wanted to persevere with the constitutionalise-first plan, Noel felt a different approach was needed given Coalition resistance. The politicians were not responsive. After unanswered texts and calls, Noel finally spoke with then Indigenous affairs minister Nigel Scullion, but only after *The Courier-Mail* had reported the leaked cabinet decision to reject a constitutional Voice on 25 October 2017.

The story revealed that Scullion and the attorney-general, Brandis, had co-sponsored a cabinet submission recommending a referendum to guarantee a Voice in the Constitution. Brandis's support aligned with my understanding of his office's position: I had met with a very senior member of Brandis's team the previous year, together with some Indigenous colleagues. We were told a constitutional Voice was the 'preferred approach' of the attorney-general's office because it was the most constitutionally sound way of achieving constitutional recognition. However, Turnbull reportedly led opposition to the idea in cabinet, arguing the Voice was 'too ambitious' and calling instead for a symbolic solution. The cabinet was split: some wanted to avoid a partisan fight on the issue, others wanted Labor to explain how the Voice would work, given Bill Shorten had announced Labor's support.[2]

Seeking a way to 'pull it out of the fire', Noel explained to Scullion his alternative strategy of deferring a referendum until after the Voice was legislated. Scullion said he would 'see what he could do', but Noel heard nothing more from him or Turnbull.[3] It demonstrated, once again, the Coalition's preference for obstinate refusal rather than compromise or collaboration with Indigenous leaders. This experience probably informed Noel's later view that it would be a mistake to legislate a Voice before holding a referendum. Legislating first was unlikely to garner Coalition support for a referendum and would reduce the likelihood of constitutional enshrinement ever being achieved.

Thinking back on this history, I am reminded what a close-run thing it was in 2017. Just the year before, our conservative ally Julian Leeser had become a Liberal MP. Given the split in the cabinet, and Brandis and Scullion's reported support, some leadership and courage from the prime minister might have tipped the scales in Indigenous peoples' favour. Turnbull could have made the positive case, stared down the howls of Banquo's ghost and refined and developed the reform requested by the Uluru Statement. Led by a supportive Coalition government, the Voice referendum would have been far more likely to succeed.

Turnbull instead chose to reject the Voice, in an effort to prevent Abbott from using it as a stalking horse on his prime ministership. His rejection dealt future chances of bipartisanship a killer blow. For how could any future Liberal leader, let alone a leader dealing with a right flank headed up by Peter Dutton, position themselves as more progressive than the Liberals' wettest leather-jacket-wearing leader without inflaming the party's right? Turnbull's actions meant bipartisanship would be almost impossible to achieve. The mistruths articulated in his statement of refusal – that the Voice would be a 'third chamber' that would undermine principles of equality[4] – would reverberate over the next six years.

The future attorney-general Christian Porter also told us he supported the Indigenous advisory body proposal in 2015, and in a separate meeting described the approach as an 'elegant solution'. Porter endorsed *The Forgotten People*, the collection of essays I co-edited with Freeman making the liberal and conservative case for a constitutionally guaranteed Indigenous advisory body. We thought his support was significant, which is why Freeman and I asked Porter to launch the book in Perth in February 2017. He agreed. In the intervening time, however, Abbott had been rolled as prime minister and the new prime minister, Turnbull, had elevated Porter to the social services ministry. Around the time Turnbull switched from 'Yes' to 'No', Porter also changed his mind. He rocked up to the Perth launch, told us he no longer supported a constitutional Voice and started arguing publicly against it, telling the audience he preferred a purely symbolic model. Participating in the discussion panel, I urged Porter to work with Indigenous leaders to refine the compromise co-devised with his Liberal colleague, instead of just dismissing it – a suggestion that drew applause from the audience but no proper response from Porter. Noel subsequently extended the invitation to Porter in writing, conveying our desire to collaborate to refine the drafting to address any Coalition concerns. Porter never replied.[5] Instead, months later, the minister sent me a menacing personal letter rebuking my public recounting of this behaviour.[6]

When Tony Abbott was prime minister he seemed committed to Indigenous recognition. Abbott was close to Leeser and Freeman, and Noel had put extensive energy into fostering a productive relationship with him. Abbott's imprimatur sanctioned our engagement with constitutional conservatives in 2014, and he was open to the Indigenous body idea. Inspired by New Zealand, however, he thought reserved Indigenous parliamentary seats would be preferable way of empowering Indigenous peoples with a voice. Noel advised him against this option, which he felt was too far-reaching to succeed, but Abbott's office floated it anyway. *The Australian*'s Dennis Shanahan leaked the alternative proposal, which was supported by advocates such as Jacqui Lambie and Michael Mansell, but dismissed it as too ambitious.[7] When our group showed Abbott our proposed drafting for a constitutionally guaranteed Indigenous advisory body in December 2014, the prime minister was encouraging – he even proposed his own off-the-cuff drafting of a shorter amendment.[8] Abbott expressed concern, however, about the difficulty of building consensus within his party.

A few years later, during the First Nations regional dialogues and then after Uluru, Abbott again told me and Indigenous leaders, including Noel, that he wasn't opposed to guaranteeing an Indigenous advisory body in the Constitution. We asked him to help advocate it. But when Turnbull rejected the Uluru Statement in October 2017, Abbott backed him.[9] And, unlike some Liberals, who became more progressive and courageous when they left Parliament (like Turnbull and Julie Bishop), Abbott slid further to the right after he lost his seat in 2019. He became a prolific 'No' campaigner in the lead-up to the referendum.

Then Nationals leader Barnaby Joyce kicked off the 'third chamber' denigration that Turnbull ran with. In 2019, Joyce apologised 'unreservedly' for the mischaracterisation,[10] but rather than backing a constitutional Voice, he pushed for regional Senate seats as an alternative way of empowering Indigenous voices without a referendum. Bridget McKenzie of the Nationals also changed her mind. In 2014, she sat on Ken Wyatt's Joint Select Committee and heard our advocacy about an Indigenous advisory body. Back then she was amenable to our approach, describing it as a way of bringing Samuel Griffith Society types together with the Indigenous activist types of Redfern.[11] She got it. But when the idea became paired with talk of treaties and framed as an Indigenous proposal after the Uluru Statement, her enthusiasm dwindled. She ultimately advocated 'No' with the Nationals.

We had dozens of meetings with Coalition members over several years. Often, we left these meetings feeling buoyed. But many who expressed support for a Voice in the early days, viewing it as a conservative proposal, became 'No' campaigners against 'Albanese's Voice' in 2023.

~❦~ ~❦~ ~❦~

After the Turnbull government's 2017 rejection of a Voice, the shifting political landscape nonetheless created space for optimism. The 2019 election got rid of some dead wood and brought in fresh blood. Selling out on major policy agendas did not stop the right coming for Turnbull – he was rolled regardless. Scott Morrison defeated Peter Dutton and Julie Bishop in a leadership spill and became the new prime minister going into that election. Turnbull resigned from Parliament and was replaced in Wentworth by Teal independent Kerryn Phelps in the ensuing by-election. Abbott lost his seat to Teal independent Zali Steggall. All the Teals were passionate Voice supporters.

Meanwhile, Andrew Bragg entered Parliament as a new Liberal senator for New South Wales. Bragg had championed same-sex marriage and supported a constitutional Voice. Bridget Archer was also elected in Tasmania and she was a Voice backer too. Porter resigned from the front bench in 2021 and from Parliament the following year, after historical rape allegations were publicised, creating space for a new fresh-thinking attorney-general. There was hope these shake-ups might enable Julian Leeser to take a more senior role: his assent to a position of greater influence could be a game changer for our cause.

Depressingly, Scott Morrison seemed no better than Turnbull on the Voice. Soon after winning the leadership contest, he perpetuated the 'third chamber' misnomer. 'They can dress it up any way they like but I think two chambers is enough,' he told Radio National. 'I share the view that I don't think that's a workable proposal.'[12]

But hopes were raised again after the Coalition won the 2019 election. Money had been allocated for a referendum and a Voice co-design process, and Morrison said he was committed to Indigenous constitutional recognition.[13] The prime minister appointed Ken Wyatt as the first Indigenous Minister for Indigenous Australians and kicked off the Indigenous Voice Co-Design Process, which Wyatt presided over. In a speech to the National Press Club in Canberra, the new minister announced the Morrison government was 'committed to recognising Indigenous Australians in the constitution' and 'working to achieve this through a process of true co-design'. Wyatt confirmed that all options for a Voice would be considered, and specifically confirmed that a constitutionalised Voice was on the table for discussion.[14] But he had evidently not sought approval from the prime minister's office. As journalist Rick Morton described:

> Wyatt had scarcely left the stage ... when the wheels of rejection began to turn. The prime minister's office started briefing journalists and explicitly ruled out one of the options Wyatt had just publicly backed.
>
> The prime minister's advisers, and later Morrison himself, made it clear: there will be no mention of a Voice to Parliament in the constitution under the current government.[15]

A month later, Wyatt capitulated. 'I want to be very clear – the question we put to the Australian people will not result in what some desire, and that is an enshrined Voice to the Parliament,' he said.[16] History was repeating itself. In 2014, Wyatt had tried through his Joint Select Committee process to push variations of a racial non-discrimination guarantee, only to be forced to abandon the reform due to a resistant party and leadership. In 2019, he tried to push the alternative middle ground proposal developed with constitutional conservatives then endorsed by Indigenous people through the Uluru Statement – a constitutional Voice – but the prime minister's office blocked him. Wyatt was the minister in charge of this issue, but he had no real power within an obstructive party. This disproved the argument propounded by Turnbull and countless other Voice opponents that Indigenous people did not need a constitutional Voice because they had Indigenous parliamentarians to advocate their interests. The political reality is that Indigenous politicians are often prevented by restrictive party politics from effectively prosecuting Indigenous rights. No wonder Indigenous Australians were calling for an independent, constitutionally guaranteed Voice *to*, rather than *in*, Parliament.

Noel and I were not the only ones trying to persuade politicians. The 'Yes' campaign was prosecuted by several groups.

My 2018 book, *Radical Heart*, attracted the attention and enthusiasm of philanthropists Henry and Marcia Pinskier in 2021. They generously donated funding for me to establish the Radical Centre Reform Lab at Macquarie University's Law School, where I was a senior lecturer. Our small team focused on educating multifaith and multicultural communities about the Voice. Our work had impact, but we were a minor player.

I also continued to work with Noel and CYI, as the campaign group From the Heart (later rebranded Yes23) took the reins of the

Voice campaign. Headed up by Indigenous advocate Dean Parkin as campaign director, From the Heart was overseen by Australians for Indigenous Constitutional Recognition (AICR). The board of AICR included Noel, Liberal adviser and pollster Mark Textor, Thomas Mayo, plus other heavy hitters such as former Howard adviser Tony Nutt, AFL general manager of inclusion and social policy Tanya Hosch, Reconciliation Australia's Karen Mundine, former Labor government adviser Lachlan Harris, with Gilbert + Tobin law firm founder Danny Gilbert and Indigenous filmmaker Rachel Perkins as co-chairs.

Noel had started working with Textor, of the lobbying, polling and consultancy firm Crosby Textor, hoping his guidance and connections would help win over the Coalition. Textor believed Morrison was persuadable, despite his negative remarks in the media. The post-pandemic era was the perfect time for reform that transcended ideological divides, because of the 'national "whatever it takes to fix this" mood', Textor enthused in 2020:

> National cabinets, non-traditional economics, a proposal for a new accord, are examples of casting aside ideological stances in favour of structures that get real results – and this offers great hope for a new approach to solutions that close the gap between Indigenous and non-Indigenous Australians ... [T]hat is what a Voice to Parliament is all about – listening to the voices of our experts who are Aboriginal and Torres Strait Islanders in their communities.[17]

Given Textor's Coalition relationships, Noel and other Voice advocates began to hand over to Textor to advise on the best way to obtain Coalition support – although Noel still made independent efforts too.

Then there was the Uluru Dialogue, run out of the Indigenous Law Centre at the University of New South Wales (UNSW), under Megan Davis and Pat Anderson, who were also working hard to persuade politicians and engage with the public. The Uluru Dialogue described itself as representing 'the cultural authority of the Uluru Statement from the Heart'. Its advocacy was characterised by steadfast defence of the Indigenous mandate created by the Uluru Statement, an approach epitomised by the hashtag #StayTruetoUluru.

Finally, there was Uphold & Recognise, established by Leeser and Freeman to prosecute conservative arguments for a constitutional Voice. I worked closely and informally with U&R for many years, but the beginnings of a fracture emerged in 2020, when it began pushing watered-down constitutional drafting that Noel and other key Indigenous leaders did not agree with.

# 6
# ON CONSTITUTIONAL COMPROMISES

Frank Brennan propagated the myth that Voice proponents and the Labor government adopted a 'crash or crash through' approach to the referendum, devoid of pragmatic compromise.[1] In this chapter, I dive deeply into some of the many constitutional compromises hammered out by Voice advocates in pursuit of bipartisanship and referendum success. This was a referendum replete with compromises, but they were all one-sided. Indigenous people made all the concessions. The Coalition never shifted to meet Indigenous people in the middle.

The media sang from Brennan's hymn sheet. Peter van Onselen, writing in *The Australian* on referendum day, claimed that those championing the constitutional change 'made the mistake of deciding they didn't need to work cooperatively or incrementally with sceptics, believing instead they could bulldoze their way to success'.[2] David Crowe a few days later wrote that Albanese and Indigenous leaders 'could not compromise with those who opposed them, even when the past century has shown that a referendum will fail without bipartisan support'. The lesson, according to Crowe, was that 'a "Yes" vote is only possible for leaders who compromise more than they would like', which was 'true for Indigenous leaders as much as party leaders'.[3]

The 'no compromise' narrative is inverted. As we have seen, the Voice was born out of compromise with constitutional conservatives in 2014. Indigenous leaders stepped 'to the right and up', abandoning a racial non-discrimination guarantee that would have worked wholly through litigation (to which conservatives objected) to embrace a constitutionally guaranteed Indigenous advisory body that would work through political processes. Noel in his 2022 Boyer Lectures described this compromise as addressing 'the objection of justiciability: the opposition of constitutional conservatives and the political right to diminishing parliamentary supremacy'.[4]

The words negotiated with constitutional conservatives in 2014 were published by Twomey in 2015:

> 60A
> (1) There shall be an Aboriginal and Torres Strait Islander body, to be called the [insert appropriate name, perhaps drawn from an Aboriginal or Torres Strait Islander language], which shall have the function of providing advice to the Parliament and the Executive Government on matters relating to Aboriginal and Torres Strait Islander peoples.
> (2) The Parliament shall, subject to this Constitution, have power to make laws with respect to the composition, roles, powers and procedures of the [body].
> (3) The Prime Minister [or the Speaker/President of the Senate] shall cause a copy of the [body's] advice to be tabled in each House of Parliament as soon as practicable after receiving it.
> (4) The House of Representatives and the Senate shall give consideration to the tabled advice of the [body] in debating proposed laws with respect to Aboriginal and Torres Strait Islander peoples.[5]

The amendment addressed conservative concerns but still established four constitutional guarantees for Indigenous people: Parliament must establish the body, the body must have the function of providing advice to Parliament and the executive government, the body's advice must be tabled in Parliament, and the Houses must consider the body's advice.

However, Turnbull's 2017 rejection necessitated a 'second pivot' to address the new 'third chamber' scare campaign. As Noel explained, this second compromise was put forward in the 'more streamlined' drafting he submitted with Megan Davis and Pat Anderson to the Leeser–Dodson Committee in 2018. It made the ask smaller by omitting the tabling procedure and consideration requirements, and, after further refinements, evolved into the wording proposed by Albanese in 2022.[6]

There are two points to make about Noel's remarks in his Boyer Lectures. First, for years he and I described the proposed constitutional amendment as 'non-justiciable'. In retrospect, given the unexpected furore that ensued some eight years later about the potential procedural justiciability of the Voice's advice to the executive government, 'non-justiciable' might not have been the best term to use. What we meant to convey with the term was the fact that the proposed Voice amendment would not empower the High Court to invalidate laws and policies relating to Indigenous peoples for failure to comply with some far-reaching, judicially interpreted principle, as would have occurred under a racial non-discrimination guarantee. This was the key concern the conservatives expressed at the time, which we addressed through our collaboration. The new approach of a constitutional Voice upheld parliamentary supremacy. There was no veto, and no scope for the High Court to invalidate laws and policies for any failure to follow the Voice's advice. The key shift was from judicial power to strike down laws and policies relating to Indigenous peoples, to Indigenous advisory input into the making of those laws and policies.

We were not back then grappling with disputable arguments that would be raised eight years later in 2022 – and which were only raised once this became known as 'Albanese's amendment' – about procedural fairness implications potentially arising in relation to advice to the executive. That was another kind of judicial review, which did not undermine parliamentary supremacy but only insisted on fair processes being employed in government decision-making. That administrative law issue was not raised by our conservative collaborators in 2014 or over the intervening eight years. Rather, constitutionally sanctioned engagement with government was seen by all as necessary and important. It therefore remained in the plethora of offshoot amendments that flowed from the original drafting.

The second point relates to the 'second pivot' Noel describes – the additional compromise Indigenous leaders made in response to Turnbull's rejection of the Voice in 2017. This was in fact one of multiple further concessions Indigenous people and other Voice advocates made in pursuit of bipartisanship. Admittedly, these subsequent compromises were sometimes poorly timed and executed, and undersold, and therefore undervalued. Some were formulated in silos: via good-faith but isolated intellectual attempts to accommodate Turnbull's mendacious objections to a constitutional Voice.

The central problem was that Turnbull's 2017 rejection mischaracterised and dismissed the concept of a Voice, without critiquing the specific wording of any proposed amendment. Recall that the original words published by Twomey in 2015 did not form part of the Referendum Council's report or Turnbull's statement of rejection. Rather, his rejection was anchored in pseudo-principle and was primarily driven by politics. The subsequent constitutional compromises made by Voice proponents were thus well-meaning, but premature. Trying to address the bogus 'third chamber' complaint via constitutional adjustments was trying to answer a bad-faith political play with good-faith legal manoeuvring. Voice advocates hoped the perfect drafting refinement might allow the Coalition to demonstrate that its objections had been addressed, enabling it to come on board without losing face. But the blockage was political, not legal.

There was a connective piece missing in the development of the subsequent drafting compromises: negotiation. This was not the fault of Voice advocates, but a failure of official process. The fact that neither the Coalition during its five years in power after the Uluru Statement nor Labor in 2022 convened an official negotiation process between Indigenous people and the spectrum of politicians (particularly Coalition politicians) was a serious omission – probably deliberate on the part of the Coalition, which didn't want to progress consensus on a Voice. But a negotiation process to settle bipartisan and Indigenous agreement on the amendment should have been Labor's first step once elected. Such negotiation could have run concurrently with a bipartisan process to finalise the operational details of a Voice, to be legislated after the referendum. Sure, the Coalition might not have come to the table or might have played a spoiler role throughout. But some innovative engagement mechanism – outside the humdrum of ordinary partisan politics and committees – should have been attempted.

I do not agree that a constitutional convention was the answer, as the Liberals argued, albeit very late in the day: why didn't they convene a convention when in government? Constitutional conventions are adversarial. In the republic debate, this mechanism consolidated and amplified division. Look how it platformed long-term rivals Abbott, a monarchist, and Turnbull, a republican. It helped their political careers but did not foster republican consensus, bipartisanship or referendum success. The Voice referendum did not need more rancorous debate to spotlight political egos – there was enough of that in Parliament. What was needed was a sui generis negotiation process to facilitate bipartisan and Indigenous agreement.

In 2021, CYI proposed a formal negotiation process between Indigenous people and political representatives to finalise the constitutional amendment.[7] I envisaged that the Indigenous negotiating team could be the Indigenous Referendum Working Group, or a subgroup thereof, as appointed by the government.[8] If desired, additional or alternative representatives could also have been appointed as negotiators by the Working Group, on the basis of application and merit. The political representatives in these negotiations could include the prime minister, the Indigenous affairs minister and the attorney-general, with equal participation by the Opposition, as well as minor parties and independents, to facilitate multi-party support for the agreed constitutional change. A retired judge could have been engaged to oversee and mediate the negotiations. Supported by expert advisers on all sides, the negotiations could have used the government's 2022 draft amendment as a starting point from which to discuss, refine and agree on the amendment to be put to a referendum.

Additionally, perhaps preceding these negotiations, a second series of broader deliberative dialogues could have been convened soon after Indigenous people issued the Uluru Statement, to enable the Indigenous representatives to explain, discuss and flesh out their proposal in collaboration with their non-Indigenous fellow citizens. Rather than the Coalition government simply vetoing the Indigenous call for a Voice and verballing the Australian people's opposition (in contradiction to polls at that time showing around 60 per cent support),[9] it could have supported Australians to more deeply engage with and shape the Indigenous Voice idea – to test and grow the public's appetite for and understanding of the proposal.

These broader dialogues could have enabled the Indigenous delegates to explain to a representative cohort of non-Indigenous Australians why they preferred this practical form of recognition to symbolic recognition, discussing the pros and cons of this solution versus others that had been on the table. This would have better enabled non-Indigenous people to come on the transformative journey. The discussions could have delivered the same civics and legal education that was provided during the Indigenous regional dialogues, and, with the assistance of legal experts, Australians could have collaboratively refined the draft constitutional amendment. Like the 'deliberative mini-publics' utilised in Ireland, these dialogues could have involved randomly selected members of the public, rather than politically selected participants, to help break through partisan divides.[10]

Such a process might have facilitated deeper cross-cultural understanding and empathy, which was arguably deficient in the Voice debate due to the lack of non-Indigenous engagement with Indigenous communities. As Noel explained in 2022, the Voice referendum was unlike the same-sex marriage plebiscite because there was not the same 'requisite empathy of love to break through the prejudice, contempt and, yes, violence, of the past. Australians simply do not have Aboriginal people within their circles of family and friendship with whom they can share fellow feeling.'[11] Properly publicised and promoted, cross-cultural dialogues might have helped bridge this empathy gap, by demonstrating how understanding across divides can be forged through dialogue. That, after all, was what an Indigenous Voice was all about. Such a process might have assisted with broader uptake of the proposal, which then would have benefited from both Indigenous and public deliberation, helping counter perceptions that the agenda was driven by political elites. A bipartisan negotiation process could have followed, to facilitate political and Indigenous agreement on the final drafting.

These are just some ideas for how Indigenous, bipartisan and broader community buy-in could have been better facilitated. The Coalition, when in power, evidently had little interest in devising such processes, notwithstanding the 2018 Joint Select Committee's recommendation for further work to be done on the Voice constitutional amendment. However, Albanese's Labor government should have instigated a negotiation process to try to facilitate bipartisan agreement. Had the Coalition refused to participate or played spoiler, its obstructive role would then at least have been better exposed.

In the absence of an official negotiation process, civil society searched for constitutional compromises independently. These follow-up compromises, formulated by the disparate elements of the 'Yes' side, were inevitably unilateral: Coalition opponents were not involved. These were not constitutional solutions anchored in a negotiated deal with objectors, as had been the case in 2014. Therefore, they turned out to be pivots without political pay-off. Key antagonists felt no ownership of the resulting revisions, if they noticed them at all.

This is my key takeaway from over twelve years of working on constitutional recognition. You cannot compromise unilaterally, no matter how diligently you think you are addressing another's expressed objections. A real radical centre only emerges from genuine dialogue between parties defending divergent interests. Consensus is only built if the objectors help discover, or at least feel they have helped discover, the negotiated solution. The opponents need to touch and taste their win: they need their power personally confirmed. Having them in the room to co-devise the solution is the only way to get their buy-in. Hence the process of creating a compromise is just as important as – perhaps more important than – its substance, because shared ownership is built through inclusion. Likewise, however, if the purported compromise is just a weakened position that tries to address conservative objections but lacks Indigenous support, then it is not a compromise at all – it is a unilateral sellout that goes nowhere because it attracts Indigenous opposition.

Finally, for genuine dialogue and synthesis to occur, both parties must be prepared to engage honestly and in good faith on substantive principles and policy. Conversations need to mean something, and the players need to act in accordance with their commitments. From our experience, this condition was mostly missing on the Coalition side, which is perhaps why good-faith negotiation never eventuated. And when Labor won government in May 2022, no amount of compromise by Indigenous leaders was likely to have changed the fact that the Coalition under Peter Dutton decided to use the referendum to hurt Albanese. Yet Indigenous people did compromise, even then.

◈ ◈ ◈

After Turnbull's rejection in 2017, the various pro-Voice groups articulated further constitutional compromises that might bring the

Coalition on board. On one side of these efforts, drafting variations were overseen by constitutional lawyers at UNSW, under Megan Davis's leadership. Davis and other UNSW experts, together with Noel and Pat Anderson, put forward revised drafting via a submission to the 2018 parliamentary committee. It read:

(1) There shall be a First Nations Voice.
(2) The First Nations Voice shall present its views to Parliament and the Executive on matters relating to Aboriginal and Torres Strait Islander peoples.
(3) The Parliament shall, subject to this Constitution, have power to make laws with respect to the composition, functions, powers and procedures of the First Nations Voice.[12]

It was shorter and simpler than the original drafting. The tabling procedure and the requirement that the Houses consider the advice were omitted, making it much more modest. Instead of four constitutional guarantees for Indigenous people, there were now only two: the guarantee that the Voice be established and that it be able to 'present its views'.

The shift from 'providing advice' to 'present[ing] its views' probably sought to address the worry that some Indigenous people felt 'advice' was too weak. However, the 2018 submission clarified that the Voice's power to 'present its views' imposed 'no concomitant obligation on the Parliament' to follow or implement those views, consistent with the understanding that the Voice would have no veto.[13] The views presented would therefore be advisory, if even it was not called 'advice'. I wondered how opponents might exploit the new phrase. 'What did "present its views" mean?' they might ask. Did it require a physical or verbal presentation? Would the High Court have to decide? To me, 'advice' felt more clear and familiar.

The drafting abandoned the term 'Aboriginal and Torres Strait Islander' and instead referred to 'First Nations', using the language of the Uluru Statement. The amendment also no longer referred to a 'body'. Instead, reflecting the Uluru Statement, it talked about a 'First Nations Voice'. Switching from a boring old advisory body to a 'First Nations Voice' arguably made the reform sound more mysterious. A 'body' was an unremarkable, institutional word. A 'Voice' suited the evocative poetry of the Uluru Statement, but it was not particularly constitutional language. Nor was its meaning readily understood. Throughout the campaign, pollsters would say many Australians thought the 'Voice' was a TV show. After the Uluru Statement, however, the title stuck. Law professor Gabrielle Appleby published a refined version of the 2018 UNSW drafting in 2020, clarifying that a Voice would be a body. It returned to the original formulation of the opening words, this time specifying: 'There shall be a body, to be called the First Nations Voice.'[14]

Notwithstanding these shifts in terminology, the deletion of the tabling procedure and consideration requirement made the constitutional ask significantly smaller. Indigenous people were conceding ground. But what were they getting in return? Their concessions did not cause the Coalition to reconsider its opposition, although Voice supporter Andrew Bragg noted in his 2021 book that the 2018 version was 'simpler and cleaner' because it ditched the 'problematic' tabling procedure.[15] If other politicians noticed Indigenous people bending over backwards, they didn't indicate that they cared.

❧ ❧ ❧

What about the compromises non-Indigenous people made to try to force Indigenous people to concede more than they wanted to? These did not cut through either.

Freeman and I worked together, with Twomey's guidance, to explore 'pivot' variations of our original 2014 drafting, not to address any legal or technical objections but to address the amorphous political problem of Morrison's apparent opposition (which followed Turnbull's) to the concept of a constitutionalised Voice. Perhaps a refined and simpler Voice amendment could win Morrison's support, the idea being that any revised drafting would only move forward with Noel's approval, as had been the case in 2014. But after I received advice that Noel felt this revised version was too weak and asked for it not to be published, Freeman's group, U&R, ran with it anyway. Twomey published the weaker amendment, clarifying that she preferred the original drafting as published in 2015, because it was 'simple, clear and fair' and would 'avoid the interference of courts by making the consideration of advice a matter of internal parliamentary affairs'.[16] That 2020 drafting variation read as follows:

> The Commonwealth shall make provision for Aboriginal and Torres Strait Islander peoples to be heard by the Commonwealth regarding proposed laws and other matters with respect to Aboriginal and Torres Strait Islander affairs, and the Parliament may make laws to give effect to this provision.

This proposal did not guarantee the existence of an Indigenous body and lacked the endorsement of key Indigenous leaders. However, U&R began lobbying the government with the weaker drafting, which risked undercutting Indigenous people being able to bargain for themselves. By offering a weaker and weaker amendment without Indigenous backing or any offer of bipartisan support in return, the parameters for constitutional discussion might get dragged lower and lower too early in the discussion. Indigenous people might be forced to accept less and less for no political gain. This was the anxiety Noel and I harboured, which I tried to communicate, but U&R pursued its own strategy. Absent an official process to facilitate direct negotiation, it became a compromise free-for-all.

Two days after the publication of that revised 2020 drafting, Noel, Davis, Anderson and Indigenous leader Roy Ah-See issued a joint media release cryptically rebuking non-Indigenous people attempting to negotiate a watered-down Voice amendment without Indigenous agreement.[17] 'Those seeking to pivot away from the Uluru Statement to a compromised position do not have the authority either from the delegates at the Uluru Dialogue, First Australians at large or by general public opinion,' Noel said in the release. 'Let us be clear, such calls have no moral, organisational or political justification.' Davis said there was 'no mandate or compelling need to depart from the historic consensus that was reached' via the Uluru Statement, while Ah-See argued that Morrison had 'left open the possibility to enshrine a Voice to Parliament in the constitution', which meant those 'proposing alternatives to this are jumping at political shadows that don't exist'. The release cited research by Crosby Textor that showed 56 per cent of Australians would vote 'Yes' to a constitutional Voice, while 17 per cent would vote 'No'.

To anyone not following the debate closely, it must have appeared confusing. 'Yes' advocates were arguing publicly about Voice drafting without any official words on the table and with little apparent government interest in pursuing a constitutional Voice. But few were paying attention. Though U&R continued to promote its proposal,[18] its variation gained little traction, other than Liberal senator Andrew Bragg endorsing it in his 2021 book. The fact that the only Liberal to specifically advocate it was someone already on record as supporting a constitutional Voice is instructive. Offering up the weaker variation didn't entice anyone from the Coalition to switch from 'No' to 'Yes'. It just encouraged a strong 'Yes' person to prefer something weaker.

Had U&R's revised drafting gained traction, I'm sure it later would have been characterised by opponents as a broad and litigable 'right to be heard', inducing the same procedural fairness anxieties inflamed in relation to the Voice's ability to advise the executive in the other drafting variations (because 'the Commonwealth' could include executive governments across the nation). But while this 2020 revision created rifts on the 'Yes' side, it did not lure the Morrison government to the table for constitutional talks with Indigenous leaders, as had been U&R's hope. It was another intellectual compromise formulated in a silo, with no Coalition involvement – and no Indigenous buy-in either.

⁕ ⁕ ⁕

Danny Gilbert developed another adaptation of the original drafting in consultation with former High Court chief justices Robert French and Murray Gleeson. The judges' involvement was initially meant to be a secret. Gleeson, in particular, did not want his name mentioned, and never publicly backed the wording he had privately endorsed. After his 2019 speech at Gilbert + Tobin advocating a constitutional Voice, he apparently decided not to make any more public comments.[19] The suggested wording was as follows:

> In recognition of Aboriginal and Torres Strait Islander peoples as the First Peoples of Australia:
> (1) There shall be a body, to be called the Aboriginal and Torres Strait Islander Voice.
> (2) The Aboriginal and Torres Strait Islander Voice may make representations to Parliament and the Executive Government on matters relating to Aboriginal and Torres Strait Islander Peoples.
> (3) The Parliament shall, subject to this Constitution, have power to make laws with respect to the composition, functions, powers and procedures of the Aboriginal and Torres Strait Islander Voice.

This version was never officially published, just shared privately with politicians. It ditched the term 'First Nations' and reverted to 'Aboriginal and Torres Strait Islander', which was more palatable to conservatives and, according to research, more palatable to voters too. It also added a line of recognition at the start of the provision, and instead of saying the Voice 'shall have the function of providing advice' or 'shall present its views', it said the Voice 'may make representations'. This was a legal improvement, making the amendment more modest. Instead of the mandatory 'shall', the discretionary 'may' indicated that representations were not compulsory. This eliminated any theoretical uncertainty about whether laws and policies relating to Indigenous peoples could be made without the Voice presenting its views.

I later came to understand that the word 'advice' was abandoned to avoid any possible implication that 'advice', by convention, should be followed, just as advice from ministers to the governor-general by convention should be followed. This change made triply sure that the Voice's input would be non-binding. While I later advocated this correct legal explanation, privately I worried about dropping the term. 'Advice' is a word everyone understands, while 'representations' could sound ambiguous to laypeople.

Greg Craven, during his testimony to the 2023 Joint Select Committee, at the height of his last-minute attacks on the government's drafting, suggested that 'representations' was somehow scarier than 'advice'. He provided no sound reasons for this claim. '"Representations" is a much more fundamental sort of thing,' he said. 'A representation is something that comes from someone with their own power, in a sense. If I give a representation to you, it's quite different from giving advice to you.'[20] Make of that what you will.

Senator Jacinta Nampijinpa Price also highlighted the omission of 'advice' in her scare campaign, arguing in a speech to the National Press Club in September 2023 that the Voice was not an advisory body, as the 'Yes' case claimed, because 'nowhere in the question that will be put to Australians … do the words "advice", "advise" or "advisory" appear'.[21] This argument was nonsense but went unchallenged by attendees of the event. Journalist and long-time Voice supporter Chris Kenny succinctly refuted Price's assertions, explaining that 'representations' was more legally modest than 'advice'.[22] Twomey had also clarified this in her submissions to the 2023 parliamentary committee months earlier, as had Julian Leeser in a speech to Parliament in May 2023, saying '"advice" implies mandatory consideration, whereas "representation" only implies receipt'.[23] I also explained the more modest legal implications of 'representations' repeatedly,[24] but I don't know if such explanations resonated.

Of course, if the word 'advice' had been used instead, 'No' proponents would no doubt have fearmongered about the arguable legal implication that 'advice' should by convention be followed (like with the governor-general), but this would have been an esoteric and legalistic argument, contrary to the ordinary understanding of 'advice'. We can only speculate as to which word would, on balance, have been less susceptible to lies and attack.

⁂

There is no doubt these further compromises made the drafting more moderate and succinct than the original 2014 compromise. Instead of four constitutional guarantees, there were now only two – the guarantee that the body be established and that it 'may make representations' – and the non-binding nature of the Voice's representations had been legally reinforced. Indigenous people were giving ground.

In retrospect, they were giving ground too early. It would have been strategically better to start with the original, more ambitious wording, saving the additional compromises for future negotiations, when pressure to make big concessions would be applied. The tabling and consideration requirements in the original drafting could have been good criticism absorbers, and obvious targets for Voice opponents. When pressure was applied, Indigenous leaders could have agreed to remove these elements to let opponents have some big wins, so hopefully the bargaining might have resulted in something Indigenous leaders already found acceptable – an advisory Voice amendment with no tabling or consideration requirements. With those elements pre-emptively removed, however, Indigenous people might be left with minimal room to manoeuvre when faced with real oppositional heat. Multiple concessions would already have been made: there would be little left to remove without gutting the provisions completely.

Noel preferred to be proactive. He felt the tabling procedure was susceptible to criticism – that it facilitated the 'third chamber' misnomer – so best get rid of it. His willingness to make such concessions demonstrated his and others' preparedness to shift to address conservative concerns. It showed flexibility. Even though a constitutional Voice was a compromise to begin with, Indigenous people made more and more concessions to try to address right-wing objections and attract Coalition support.

Noel believed any reasonable person would see that the revised amendment was a simple and even more modest constitutional change. While I feared opponents would not be reasonable, I deferred to his judgement. Besides, the ship had sailed: the UNSW variation and many others were public, and they had ditched the tabling and consideration requirements too. We began sharing the Gilbert, French and Gleeson drafting with Labor and Coalition politicians.

# 7

# FLIP-FLOPPERS

All that manoeuvring to develop additional compromises did not bring Morrison to the table. The Liberal Party's position on Indigenous constitutional recognition went backwards. Although Morrison had repeated the 'third chamber' misrepresentation after seizing the prime ministership in August 2018,[1] the Liberals' policy platform ahead of the May 2019 election supported the 2018 Joint Select Committee's recommendations for a Voice co-design process, to be followed by 'deliberate and timely' consideration of 'legislative, executive and constitutional options' to establish an Indigenous Voice. The government had committed $7.3 million for the Co-Design Process and set aside $160 million to hold a referendum. The governor-general's speech at the opening of Parliament on 2 July 2019 pledged to 'find consensus on a way forward for constitutional recognition of Indigenous Australians' and 'develop ground-up governance models for enhanced, inclusive and local decision-making on issues impacting the lives of Indigenous Australians'. Morrison's February 2020 Closing the Gap speech reiterated the Liberals' election commitments. But the situation deteriorated.

U&R began pushing its watered-down constitutional drafting from July 2020,[2] eliciting public pushback from Indigenous leaders, and lobbied the Morrison government to consider its weaker approach at least into early 2021.[3] Rather than enticing Morrison, these efforts and the resultant divisions on the 'Yes' side in fact might have given the PM new excuses for inaction. In March 2021, Morrison claimed there was 'still no clear consensus proposal at this stage which would suggest mainstream support in the Indigenous community or elsewhere'.[4] He said it had never been Liberal policy to hold a referendum on a constitutional Voice and softened his commitment to symbolic constitutional recognition.

Despite Morrison's remarks, advocates retained hope that Liberal support for a constitutional Voice was growing. Senator Andrew Bragg, a self-described 'constitutional conservative', had vocally supported a constitutional Voice in his maiden speech to Parliament in 2019. Making a compelling Liberal case for a constitutional Voice as a modest proposal, Bragg contradicted Turnbull. 'A First Nations Voice would not be a third chamber,' he declared. 'Further, the campaign that "race has no place" in the Constitution may sound good, but ... our Constitution already contains race in several places.' Bragg argued that the 'issue of proper recognition in the Constitution will not go away' and if the Voice failed, then 'more radical concepts could be proposed, such as reserved seats for First Peoples, as already exist in New Zealand and the U.S. State of Maine'. Almost every comparable nation recognised its First Peoples in some form, he noted.[5]

In May 2021, Liberal South Australian premier Steven Marshall endorsed Bragg's arguments for a Voice at the launch of the senator's book *Buraadja* and promoted his efforts towards a state-based Voice in South Australia. 'This issue can often be divisive, so it is very, very helpful to see someone from the Liberal Party taking a leadership role and arguing from our side of politics,' Marshall said.[6]

Then, in June, the Liberal NSW premier Gladys Berejiklian launched Bragg's book in Sydney and came out unequivocally in support of a Voice. 'Leadership isn't necessarily about having a title; it's about having the courage and conviction to make change,' she said, calling for political unity.[7] Bragg indicated that the party room was becoming more supportive of constitutional change, particularly among newcomers to parliament.

Notably, these Liberal leaders did not appear to support the Voice because of the weaker constitutional drafting Bragg preferred – Bragg discussed many options in his book and noted all variations should be kept on the table. He also noted that the original Voice constitutional drafting had been endorsed by former chief justice Murray Gleeson, which provided 'assurance the system will not be imperiled'.[8] Rather, these new supporters seemed moved by Bragg's compelling arguments and the fact that their Liberal colleague was making them.

In August 2021, Treasurer Josh Frydenberg launched Bragg's book at an online event. We were encouraged by Frydenberg's remarks, which did not endorse Bragg's arguments for a constitutional Voice but indicated openness.[9] Noel wrote to Frydenberg asking for a meeting, and we met with him over Zoom in September. We explained the proposal's conservative genesis and urged the Coalition to take ownership of the idea. After listening to our arguments, Frydenberg told us he liked the Voice proposal. He advised us not to push the government too hard before the 2022 election but noted that Scott Morrison was open to the Voice – he just needed more support within the party. Frydenberg challenged Noel to meet with all the Coalition parliamentarians to tell the conservative story of the Voice, as we had done in our meeting with him. If we helped rally the party room, he could then facilitate a meeting with the prime minister. We took Frydenberg's advice seriously; it aligned with Mark Textor's advice to Noel that Morrison was persuadable. Noel subsequently wrote to every member of the federal Coalition asking to meet.

It was mainly Liberal moderates who agreed to meet with us. Most of the party's right ignored our requests, which indicated resistance on the party's conservative flank. (Noel did get a very warm response from Michaelia Cash but was never able to lock in a meeting.) One parliamentarian explained that most conservatives in marginal seats were worried about retaining them. They were neither concerned with nor interested in the issue, and some Voice opponents determined their preselection, making advocacy very difficult.

We met the Liberal South Australian senator Ann Ruston, who was very supportive. Ruston was on Ken Wyatt's 2013 parliamentary committee and told us the issue of Indigenous constitutional recognition was of critical importance to her. She said she was keen to help and urged us to keep up our educative meetings with MPs. She said many Coalition MPs still didn't understand the Voice's history, the processes undertaken or what the Voice was (and wasn't). She said the 'third chamber' mischaracterisation was still widespread and needed to be refuted.

We met David Coleman MP, member for Banks in south-west Sydney. He, too, was generally positive, having talked to Bragg on the topic. He wanted to ensure the Voice would have no veto power and would be not a third chamber – he noted that many MPs were still worried about this – but understood this was not what was being proposed.

John Alexander, former professional tennis player and Liberal member for Bennelong, was very supportive. 'It's extraordinary it hasn't happened yet,' he said. 'Recognition is an obvious no brainer.' He thought the Voice idea was sensible. He wanted to get a group to approach the PM and ask him to take action – perhaps he was emboldened by his imminent retirement before the 2022 election. Alexander had previously backed Wyatt's ill-fated push for a constitutional Voice. 'Only by walking together and engaging can we uncover pathways to a better future,' he had declared in 2019. 'I'm with Ken on this, he has my full support for the process he has initiated, and I hope it can conclude with a successful referendum vote and form of "voice" we can all be proud of.'[10]

On 14 October 2021, we had a group Zoom meeting with several Liberals: James Stevens, Andrew Bragg, Julian Leeser (though we engaged with him separately as well), Katie Allen, Andrew Laming, Dave Sharma, Tim Wilson, Celia Hammond, Matt O'Sullivan and Angie Bell. Leeser, Bragg and Western Australian MP Hammond were openly supportive. The following year, Hammond declared publicly: 'I support a referendum to enshrine a First Nations voice to parliament in our Constitution in the next federal term ... I believe this has broad community support.'[11] But Hammond lost her seat of Curtin to Teal independent Kate Chaney in the 2022 election. The positions of others in the meeting were unclear.

We had a productive meeting with Greg Hunt, the health and aged care minister. After listening to our arguments, he said his understanding had increased but he would not commit yet. He said he had noted the lack of an Indigenous representative body to engage with Indigenous communities during the Covid vaccine rollout – a practical problem in need of a solution. He could see how the Voice would have helped.

We met Linda Reynolds, who had become very supportive. She remembered our briefings years earlier and was glad to see consensus had progressed. 'This is something I am willing to support,' she said.

The Victorian MP Russell Broadbent had also shifted after years of engagement. He was now supportive, and even passionate, about the Uluru Statement. He told us he wanted the government to hold a referendum on the Voice: Howard had committed to recognition in 2007 and it should have been done by now. He was keen to help.

We engaged the Nationals as well. In October 2021, we met with former party leader Michael McCormack. By this time, he was on the back bench, having lost the leadership to Joyce in June. McCormack loved the 'Nixon to China' line in Noel's letter. He said he was very supportive of a constitutional Voice and happy to help in whatever way he could. Incredibly, he thought we would find broad support in the National Party. McCormack said he would try to arrange an opportunity for us to brief the Nationals party room. It never eventuated.

We also had a meeting with Nationals MP Mark Coulton, whom I had met several times in previous years. This engagement paid off: he was very supportive. Coulton said he had many Aboriginal people in his electorate, and while there were some dissenters, the majority were saying the Voice was the proposal they wanted. He felt it was the next step after the apology. 'I will back it, as it is what the people want,' he said.

In November, we met Nationals member David Gillespie. He said the proposal had piqued his interest and hadn't crossed any red lines. As he was a 'proud conservative', the constitutionally conservative arguments resonated with him. The Nationals Victorian MP Anne Webster was also a self-described conservative who had a Julian Leeser–type perspective on constitutional reform (after we explained what that was), but this was the first time she had heard about his role in this proposal. Both she and Gillespie were very interested in the conservative origins of the Voice.

These are just some of the conversations we had with right-wing politicians. As in previous years, however, most who expressed support privately did not publicly back the Voice in 2023. They stood with their parties in opposition. Once Labor won government, Ruston told Parliament the 'prime minister's Voice' would 'wrap government … in a whole new level of complexity' which could 'render the government inert'.[12] Coleman joined efforts to hammer Albanese for failing to answer the onslaught of 'detail' questions.[13] And two days after the referendum defeat, Reynolds stood up in Parliament to congratulate Western Australians for comprehensively rejecting the Voice in response to an 'emotionally manipulative' 'Yes' campaign that lacked detail.

Tim Wilson had been publicly encouraging about a constitutional Voice on several occasions in previous years, putting a liberal spin on the idea.[14] He wrote an essay promoting Indigenous recognition in *The Forgotten People*, the 2016 essay collection I co-edited, and later penned another essay proposing constitutional recognition of local Indigenous voices. Turnbull probably blocked him from publishing this, but Warren Mundine, working with U&R, in 2017 published a similar essay in his name instead.[15] Two years later, however, Wilson said it would be 'deeply problematic' to constitutionally enshrine the Voice,[16] and in 2021 he suggested a constitutional Voice would lack legitimacy.[17] After he lost his seat to Teal candidate Zoe Daniel in the 2022 election, he did not actively promote a 'Yes' vote from outside Parliament. In 2024, Wilson was preselected as the Liberal candidate for Goldstein once again.

Broadbent provides perhaps the most depressing example of right-wing flip-flopping. After early resistance, Broadbent turned passionate Voice supporter,[18] later emphasising his Christian duty to advocate a 'Yes' vote. In *Statements from the Soul*, a collection of essays showcasing multifaith advocacy for the Voice referendum and edited by me and Damien Freeman, Broadbent explained that his 'Yes' stance was anchored in his religious beliefs:

> How do my convictions and experiences as a Christian inform my commitment to implementing the Uluru Statement from the Heart?
>
> The first thing that comes to mind is three of the ten commandments given by God to Moses at Mount Sinai in the Book of Exodus:
>
> *You must not steal.*
> *You must not murder.*
> *You must not testify falsely against your neighbour.*
>
> These commandments were broken by the British government when its fleet of ships arrived to take possession of this country. Custodians of the land were killed and subsequently the claim of terra nullius (land belonging to no one) was made...
>
> The First Peoples have shown deep mercy and a pure heart in writing the Statement, inviting all Australians to walk with them and share in this gift of great grace and truth.
>
> They are peacemakers in the face of appalling discrimination and oppression...
>
> The invitation is one that must not be ignored but embraced in its fullness. It is a line in the sand for which we should be grateful, very grateful indeed. I believe it presents a defining moment in

history for Australia. We walk together or we continue to stumble blindly, ignorant of the gift of a new way being offered. We fail to take up the invitation at our peril …

The acceptance and implementation of the Uluru Statement from the Heart in its fullness is fundamental to the future of this country. Anything less will impoverish that future.

I am committed to doing all I can to see the Statement adopted. Whatever it takes.[19]

In February 2023, Broadbent's office helped disseminate copies of the book containing his essay to Coalition parliamentarians. But like many Liberals who supported the Voice, Broadbent probably faced backlash from his party. According to the co-chair of Liberals for Yes, Kate Carnell, such pressure was common. She described her 'frustration' at the number of Liberals who privately said they intended to vote 'Yes' but would not campaign because of pushback from their branches and threats to their preselection.[20] This dynamic appears to have affected Broadbent. In April 2023, he told ABC Gippsland he would vote against the federal party's opposition to a Voice. Then in June, he faced a preselection challenge in his seat of Monash.[21] By September, Broadbent had changed his position: he said he would no longer advocate the Voice, because an Indigenous woman in his electorate told him not to support it.[22] Apparently, that woman was more authoritative than a national consensus of Indigenous people, and more authoritative than Moses. Or maybe the tablets of stone had been edited with caveats relating to Indigenous peoples and preselections. After the referendum defeat, in November 2023, Broadbent lost his preselection battle and defected from the Liberal Party to sit on the crossbench.[23] Like Turnbull, he got chucked regardless. Maybe he should have just stuck to his convictions.

Leeser, Bragg and Bridget Archer were the only federal Liberals to vocally back the Voice despite Dutton's opposition, with Leeser resigning his shadow cabinet position to advocate 'Yes'. But even Leeser and

Bragg equivocated at times in favour of hammering the Labor government. Both advocated watering down the amendment and raised concerns about the substance and process of the referendum. Their criticisms created excuses for the Coalition's opposition and damaged the Voice's prospects.

With the exception of Andrew Gee, who resigned in protest from the National Party when it decided to oppose the referendum, all the Nationals who had expressed private support for a Voice stood behind David Littleproud and Jacinta Nampijinpa Price in late 2022 to advocate a 'No' vote.

~ ~ ~

The flip-flopping of Indigenous businessman Warren Mundine was particularly dramatic. In 2017, Mundine published an essay with U&R arguing for the constitutional empowerment of local and regional First Nations voices. Extracts were published in *The Sydney Morning Herald* and *A Rightful Place*, an essay collection I edited. His essay proposed a constitutional amendment to guarantee local Indigenous communities are heard in their affairs. It examined the proposal for a constitutionally guaranteed Indigenous advisory body, soon to be endorsed by the Uluru Statement, explaining that 'the right to have a say' was 'understandably important to Indigenous Australians aspiring to a better future'. Appearing at a Melbourne University forum with Noel and Tim Wilson in May 2017, Mundine backed a constitutionally guaranteed Indigenous advisory body:

> We need to have a Voice. We need to be heard. We need to be seen. But we also need guarantees that we just don't have bodies set up and then they're destroyed by governments at government's will – we actually have bodies that are fully recognised, and have the force of law and constitutional law behind them.

Mundine noted that any such body needed to be anchored in local Indigenous communities. Noel and many Indigenous leaders agreed with the importance of local and regional voices underpinning a Voice – an insight later taken up by the Coalition government in its 2021 Indigenous Voice Co-Design Process report and reflected in the Labor government's Voice design principles, which explained that the national Voice would be chosen by local communities.

In 2023, however, Mundine opposed the Voice referendum and led the 'No' case alongside Senator Jacinta Nampijinpa Price. Yet Mundine himself had been chairman of the Abbott government's Indigenous Advisory Council, a hand-picked advisory body that did little to empower local and regional Indigenous communities or improve practical outcomes in Indigenous affairs. The fact that he later opposed an advisory body whose members were to be chosen by Indigenous communities demonstrated the hollowness of Mundine's ultimate position. But flip-flopping was normal for Mundine, a former ALP president turned Liberal candidate. His position-shifting was more about career tactics than changeable convictions. In 2023, he was vying for a spot on the Liberals' NSW Senate ticket, so appealing to the Liberal base and slamming Labor must have seemed like a good career move.

Mundine's chances at the Senate were destroyed, however, when he proclaimed his longstanding support for treaties during the referendum campaign, to the ire of Liberal preselectors.[24] His remarks contradicted the 'No' case. Right-wing 'No' opponents had been arguing that voting 'Yes' to the Voice would open the door to terrifying treaties. Mundine unexpectedly contended the opposite: he said treaties would be more likely if the Voice failed, echoing arguments made by left-wing opponents of the Voice, such as Lidia Thorpe, who wanted treaties to precede the referendum. His claims were bogus. If the Australian polity could not endorse a non-binding advisory body for Indigenous people, how was it going to get behind treaties, usually framed by the right as more ambitious and scary? Predictably, following the failure of the

Voice referendum, commitments to treaty processes are being wound back by Liberals in some jurisdictions,[25] and the federal Labor government seems scared to pursue a Makarrata Commission.

It must have been difficult for Mundine. There were reports of him having to fire staff at his 'No' outfit for making racist remarks.[26] He had to associate with 'No' campaigner Gary Johns, who in a 2022 book called for Indigenous people to undergo blood tests to receive welfare payments, and once described Indigenous women as 'cash cows'.[27] He had to put up with his colleagues condemning as 'apartheid' the Voice proposal he once advocated.[28] Yet when I debated him at events, it always seemed Mundine was more in favour of a Voice than against it. He sounded conflicted. At one point, Mundine said he was suffering serious mental health issues and had contemplated suicide. He said it was because of racist attacks from left-wing 'Yes' advocates, encouraged by the prime minister who had started the divisive Voice debate.[29] Sean Gordon, the Indigenous Chair of U&R and later co-chair of Liberals for Yes, took a contrary view: 'I would encourage Warren, for the sake of your mental health ... Don't engage with these type of groups [that are] already voting "No".'[30]

*~ ~ ~*

Although Noel met with as many Coalition politicians as he could in the lead-up to the 2022 election, he never personally met with Morrison, as he had with conservative prime ministers before him. Textor became the main conduit between the prime minister and the From the Heart campaign (later Yes23), for which he was a key adviser, and between the prime minister and Noel. While our other conservative colleagues urged Noel to meet Morrison directly to try to garner an election commitment that might keep bipartisan support for Indigenous constitutional recognition alive (even if it was just a commitment to pursuing the next steps towards a referendum), From the Heart resisted this approach. Noel felt he and the campaign had to display a united front in engaging with the PM.

Before the 2022 election, From the Heart released an advertisement to demonstrate public momentum for a Voice. Dean Parkin said this was the first time the Indigenous community had taken charge in such a way during an election campaign. 'An Indigenous-led cause is putting out a very serious television commercial during an election campaign to elevate our issues to the national agenda,' he told *The Sydney Morning Herald*.[31] The ad, which was voiced by advertising expert Ted Horton, did not include any visual imagery. It was a black screen. According to Horton, who like Textor had formerly worked on Howard's campaigns, this was to keep the message simple and apolitical. 'I didn't want anything that could get in the way of the very simple and sole message of whether we do or don't formally recognise Indigenous Australians,' he explained. 'There comes a time when we just have to make a decision: yes or no. It can't go on forever.'

The text of the ad was arguably unhelpful given the debate playing out about whether to legislate the Voice first. Noel by now opposed legislating first, as did most Voice advocates, because we realised that if the Voice was legislated into existence, the political pressure for a referendum would dissipate, and the body and its Indigenous representatives would become a target for 'No' campaigners. If it was legislated first, the institution would likely never get into the Constitution: a Voice would already exist and the main argument for a constitutional guarantee – the absence of a Voice – would have been eliminated. Oddly, From the Heart decided to reference this complex issue in its ad, which highlighted the fact that legislating was an option. 'We could ask the government to legislate it,' the voiceover reasoned, 'but we would rather the Australian people vote for it. Just think how much more powerful it would be if the recognition hoped for by Indigenous Australians was achieved with the support of all Australians.'[32] Including this argument contradicted advice from pollsters, who warned against discussing the legislation-first issue because it was confusing and turned people off. Reminding politicians of the legislate-first option was also unlikely to entice the Coalition to support the referendum – it would more likely do the opposite. The ad now seems to have been taken offline. News stories that mention it have a blank space where the video once played.

Parkin and Textor had apparently briefed the PM about the ad prior to its release. However, its launch created media focus that brought Morrison's position to a head, right before the election. On the day it was released, Morrison was asked by a journalist whether he would commit to a Voice referendum. 'Why would I?' Morrison replied. 'It's not our policy to have a referendum on the Voice, so why would I be doing that?'[33] The May 2022 election became the first in over fifteen years lacking bipartisan commitment to a referendum on Indigenous constitutional recognition. The Liberal election platform said nothing about Indigenous constitutional recognition, though it did commit to establishing local and regional voices. Despite advice from right-wing political experts, the 'Yes' side could not persuade the Coalition at this crucial juncture. The Liberal Party's position had degenerated, contrary to the positive indications received in our meetings.

⋄ ⋄ ⋄

Morrison's public remarks were at least consistent. Turnbull's were not. Having privately supported the advisory body idea in 2015, then publicly rejected the Voice as a 'third chamber' in 2017, after he left Parliament and the referendum drew nearer Turnbull changed his mind again. The man who did more damage to the Voice referendum than perhaps any politician in Australia suddenly became a 'Yes' campaigner – well, sort of. His advocacy was double-edged. Even after he had ostensibly switched from 'No' to 'Yes', Turnbull presented 'No' arguments flimsily clothed in a promise that he would be voting 'Yes' because it was the right thing to do. In my view, this was actually stealthy 'Yes'/'No' advocacy – a subtle artform perfected by Frank Brennan (more on that later) – through which a purported Voice supporter politely trashes the Voice proposal by raising serious misgivings to furnish Australians (and the Coalition) with reasons to say 'No', while simultaneously claiming moral exoneration by urging they nonetheless vote 'Yes'.

Take Turnbull's opinion piece in *The Guardian* in August 2022, explaining why he had decided to vote 'Yes'. Turnbull conversely argued that 'all of the offices and institutions in our constitutional democracy should be open to any Australian citizen' and that the Voice would be 'inconsistent with those republican, egalitarian principles'. Hardly a compelling case for an Indigenous Voice: his message was still infused with IPA (Institute of Public Affairs) rhetoric, just like his rejection of the Uluru Statement in 2017. Turnbull also claimed the Voice was 'a much more substantial change to our constitution than was envisaged in the 1999 republic referendum', which was bound to scare off undecided voters. Yet the republic referendum had put forward sixty-nine changes to the Constitution, while the Voice involved one modest change, as Leeser repeatedly pointed out on the campaign trail.[34] Even Howard, who opposed the Voice, agreed with Leeser on that front, noting that, as prime minister, he had 'allowed and promoted a conscience vote on the republic' because it was 'far more fundamental to the structure of our Constitution' than an advisory Voice.[35] Yet after raising those and more misgivings about this potentially very powerful and untested Voice – 'It could well be a wild ride,' he warned – Turnbull nonetheless urged that 'after centuries of dispossession and disempowerment', we should accept the Uluru Statement's 'offer of reconciliation'.[36]

This was 'Yes'/'No' equivocation. Turnbull's weak, last-minute efforts could not undo the major damage done in 2017, when, as prime minister of the country, he officially rejected Indigenous people's call for a Voice as a 'third chamber of Parliament' and a breach of democratic equality. His later contributions probably added to the damage.

First, because he was a high-profile former prime minister, he would have drawn focus from 'Yes' advocates unequivocally making the case. Second, as the Liberals' most left-leaning leader, Turnbull coming out late (and prevaricating at that) for a 'Yes' vote would have deepened the resistance of the right, helping frame the Voice as a wet proposal that Peter Dutton should oppose.

Third, Turnbull's embedded criticisms meant his arguments would not have persuaded many soft 'No' or undecided voters to switch to 'Yes'. In highlighting and exaggerating misgivings, he was giving equivocating voters excuses to vote 'No'. The main thing his advocacy achieved was to help salvage his progressive credentials. To his credit, however, Turnbull put effort into ground campaigning and, according to disclosures, donated $50,000 to the 'Yes' campaign.[37] In advocating the Voice, he was joined by Julie Bishop, another Liberal moderate who never publicly supported it when she was in Parliament.[38]

After the referendum's defeat, Turnbull went back to saying the Voice was a bad idea, underscoring the disingenuousness of his short-lived 'Yes' position. 'I always thought the Voice would go down,' he bragged. 'I think it was a mistake putting it to a referendum. The fundamental error was insisting [the Voice] had to be put into the constitution.'[39] Turnbull later reflected that 'the Voice campaign presented a blank canvas on which its opponents could paint whatever apocalypse they liked'.[40] He did not remind readers how he, as prime minister, had filled that canvass with colourful scares. Nor did he admit that he, perhaps more than anyone else, had made bipartisanship basically impossible. Despite this, the media still goes to Turnbull for analysis of the reasons the referendum failed.

☙ ☙ ☙

When Morrison lost the May 2022 election, Dutton took over as Opposition leader. Some said the referendum would have played out differently if Josh Frydenberg had kept his seat and led the party instead. Joe Hildebrand, for instance, argued the Teals contributed to the lack of bipartisanship by ousting moderate Liberals from inner-city electorates and forcing the Liberal Party further to the right. If Frydenberg were Opposition leader, Hildebrand contended, 'the Liberals would be supporting a voice to parliament … and its success would be all but assured'. 'Josh himself told us so,' Hildebrand wrote, pointing to Frydenberg's remarks at the August 2021 launch of Bragg's book.[41] Ken Wyatt later expressed a similar opinion.[42]

I think this view is perhaps naive. First, Frydenberg did not endorse a constitutionally guaranteed Voice when he launched Bragg's book. He stopped short and instead called for 'compromise' and 'consultation'.[43] Second, even when a moderate (Turnbull) was leader of the Liberals, he rejected the Voice. So how do we know Frydenberg would have had more courage? Any moderate leader would be under pressure from the right, which would make it difficult to lead on the issue. After Turnbull's rejection, it would have been even harder for a progressive leader to take a contrary public stance – it would have meant positioning themselves further to the left than Turnbull. Third, while Frydenberg privately told us he liked the idea of a Voice, so did many Liberals and Nationals who later adopted a contradictory 'No' stance. It is likely Frydenberg would have toed the party line. He did not publicly contradict Turnbull or Morrison in their rejections of the Voice. He was part of the cabinet decision to reject the idea in 2017. And, unlike Turnbull and Bishop, Frydenberg did not become a 'Yes' campaigner when he left Parliament after the 2022 election. So why the confidence that he would have supported Labor's referendum as Opposition Leader?

The fact is, Peter Dutton became leader. Like Abbott, Dutton would have been the perfect right-wing leader to push this issue forwards. He could have distinguished himself from Turnbull, who never understood the political importance of the fact that the proposal was conceived by Indigenous people in cooperation with constitutional conservatives. Dutton could have championed the Voice from a conservative perspective and would have been more effective in bringing the Coalition along than Turnbull could have been. Plus, as Noel reminded me, Dutton was pragmatic in a way that neither Turnbull nor Abbott appeared to be. Dutton came up with the plebiscite as a middle path to resolve the issue of same-sex marriage. Noel was hopeful Dutton might understand how the Voice could also be a middle way for achieving Indigenous recognition.

Noel met with Dutton in November 2021. His concerns in that meeting were pragmatic: Dutton indicated the Liberals could not go to the election with a commitment to constitutional change because Pauline Hanson and other right-wingers would oppose it, but he was otherwise open to a referendum. These remarks probably influenced Noel's ultimate decision not to push Morrison for a 2022 election commitment. In December 2022, a year later, Noel met with Dutton again. Noel reported that the meeting was very warm. He said Dutton could not have been more open to the idea of a constitutional Voice. Dutton even told Noel he didn't buy the argument that this would 'divide Australia by race'. He had no issue with the proposal on those grounds.

The Empowered Communities Indigenous leaders engaged with Dutton too, and in February 2023 invited him to visit them on country. Later that month, Dutton travelled to north-east Arnhem Land to meet Yolngu leaders. After visiting the Dhupuma Barker school at Gunyangara, which had achieved a 100 per cent attendance rate after Yolngu people were given greater control over local education, Dutton remarked that 'the right voice from the right people can be a positive influence'. However, he said Labor's Voice proposal lacked detail.[44] We know what Dutton's ultimate position became.

# 8
# ALBANESE'S VOICE

Dutton's appointment of Julian Leeser as shadow attorney-general and minister for Indigenous Australians suggests he was initially open to the Voice referendum but later changed his mind. Leeser's promotion made me ecstatic. Imagine: the constitutional conservative we had worked with eight years ago to co-develop the idea of a constitutionally guaranteed advisory body was now being given carriage of this issue by the Coalition. Dutton must have known Leeser's history – why else would he be appointed to these positions? We hoped our collaboration with conservatives would now start to pay off. Leeser was well positioned to make the conservative case in his party. He had opposed every other attempt at constitutional change – a republic, a bill of rights and constitutional recognition of local government – but was a co-creator and long-time supporter of the Voice. He understood that this reform would empower Indigenous voices while upholding the Constitution.

∽ ∽ ∽

In July 2022, at the Garma Festival of Traditional Cultures in north-east Arnhem Land, Prime Minister Albanese released a draft constitutional amendment for further consultation.[1] It was the version developed by

Gilbert in consultation with French and Gleeson. This was the first time any government had officially released draft wording for a constitutional Voice. The prime minister explained:

> Our starting point is a recommendation to add three sentences to the Constitution, in recognition of Aboriginal and Torres Strait Islanders as the First Peoples of Australia
>
> > *There shall be a body, to be called the Aboriginal and Torres Strait Islander Voice.*
> > *The Aboriginal and Torres Strait Islander Voice may make representations to Parliament and the Executive Government on matters relating to Aboriginal and Torres Strait Islander Peoples.*
> > *The Parliament shall, subject to this Constitution, have power to make laws with respect to the composition, functions, powers and procedures of the Aboriginal and Torres Strait Islander Voice.*
>
> These draft provisions can be seen as the next step in the discussion about constitutional change.
>
> This may not be the final form of words – but I think it's how we can get to a final form of words.
>
> In the same way, alongside these provisions, I would like us to present the Australian people with the clearest possible referendum question.
>
> We should consider asking our fellow Australians something as simple, but something as clear, as this:
>
> > *Do you support an alteration to the Constitution that establishes an Aboriginal and Torres Strait Islander Voice?*[2]

There were several surprising things about the announcement. First, it took us by surprise, though this was the amendment Noel and Danny Gilbert had been advocating.

Second, the PM incorporated the first preambular line of recognition from the Gilbert, French and Gleeson version into his speech, rather than announcing it as part of the proposed amendment. I assume this was a mistake.

Third, the draft words were released with no explanation of their meaning or history. There was no basic one-page legal explainer provided to dampen the fear campaign that would inevitably ensue, and no explanation of how these words had evolved from an earlier and more ambitious provision developed by Indigenous leaders in collaboration with conservatives like Leeser.

Fourth, although the PM said the words were a starting point for further consultation, he did not indicate what the consultation process would be. The next steps were unclear.

Fifth, the proposed referendum question was at odds with the *Referendum Machinery Act*, which requires referendum ballot papers to reflect the title of the proposed law to change the Constitution. It was strange that the prime minister's office had publicly announced a draft question that didn't comply with the relevant legislation.

Finally, the prime minister made the announcement without any Liberals or Nationals by his side. Seated around him on the panel were the Indigenous Labor MPs. Leeser, who was now in charge of this issue for the Coalition and had travelled up to Garma, was not visible – though he had advocated a constitutionally guaranteed advisory body longer than anyone in Labor. Although Albanese acknowledged Leeser in his speech, it was a missed opportunity to demonstrate bipartisan co-ownership. The government could have framed this as Leeser's Voice as much as Albanese's. To get creative: it could even have positioned it as Labor coming on board with Leeser's co-developed concept, as resoundingly embraced by Indigenous Australians (which was the truth). It would have been harder for the Coalition to attack a proposal co-devised with their shadow minister.

However, Albanese had claimed the Voice for Labor on election night and his Garma announcement underscored that message. Maybe this was understandable after five years of Coalition leaders rejecting a constitutional Voice. But commentators immediately began referring to 'Albanese's Voice',[3] which goaded the Opposition. The drafting became known as 'Albanese's model'.

I am unsure how well key Labor players understood or remembered the extent of conservative involvement in the Voice's development. Perhaps the tactical utility of this history was overlooked. When Noel and I months later published an opinion piece reminding everyone that the same con cons, who by then were raising complaints about 'Albanese's model', had in fact co-devised the original 2014 drafting from which the government's proposal was directly descended,[4] Albanese reacted as if this was valuable new information. The PM told radio listeners in March 2023 that 'people like Julian Leeser helped with the wording, if you go back many, many years where this has been kicked around'.[5] But this explanation came seven months after the Garma announcement, during which time opponents deployed an open slather attack on Albanese's draft words without any of that historical and political context. Had Leeser's co-ownership been promoted from word go, the tone of the debate might have been different.

The modest constitutional change became inadvertently framed as more ambitious and potentially scary than it was. Indigenous journalist Bridget Brennan, speaking on a televised panel at Garma, argued that the Voice needed to be 'feared and revered'. 'It has to be about reparations,' she said, expressing her hopes for the reform but some scepticism about its limited power.[6] While she noted Parliament would have 'ultimate supremacy' over the Voice, opponents nonetheless capitalised on her comments. By Wednesday, Pauline Hanson was arguing that Albanese's Voice would open the door to reparations – a theme the conservative lobby group Advance amplified throughout the campaign.

When journalist David Speers asked the prime minister whether policymakers would listen to the Voice on practical issues such as alcohol bans in the Northern Territory, Albanese replied that only a 'brave government' would disregard its advice.[7] This should have been acknowledged as an important concession to the right. The Labor government had previously ignored the advice of local Indigenous communities in winding back alcohol restrictions that most conservatives would also have preferred to keep. The PM was admitting the government had got it wrong and was demonstrating how an Indigenous Voice could enable better – and in some cases more conservative – decisions to be made in future. Albanese was in fact making the same argument former Liberal Party vice-president and conservative Voice supporter Karina Okotel had compellingly made the previous month,[8] just with less careful language. But opponents twisted Albanese's incautious use of the word 'brave' to exaggerate the Voice's potential power. 'Only a "brave" government would defy it,' Paul Kelly warned in *The Australian*. 'The voice would not be a third chamber, but the media coverage would surely resemble that of a third chamber [because the Voice] would have democratic and moral authority.'[9]

It was irrational: critics of Labor's removal of alcohol bans up north were suddenly fearmongering that the Voice might influence governments to keep the bans in place. Objectors were tying themselves in hypocritical knots, but the word 'brave', negatively framed, conjured an effective scare. If the mighty Commonwealth government needed to be 'brave' to ignore the Voice, that must mean the advisory body would be shockingly powerful. In truth, while Voice advocates hoped a constitutional Voice would carry moral and political weight so its advice could not be easily disregarded, the government and Parliament would still decide whether to follow its advice. The PM thus needed to carefully balance Indigenous hopes for the reform with reactionary fears, which required precise language. 'A sensible government will heed sensible advice from the Voice' would have been a better choice of words. Or 'Its advice could not lightly be ignored'. However, the government's approach did not seem overly practised or careful. The PM's slip-up and Brennan's remarks at Garma left the sense that key lines or traps to avoid had not been widely shared to help guide the public conversation. It gave the impression that the extent of right-wing exploitation of any missteps was not properly anticipated. Yet with experienced political operatives in the prime minister's office, it is baffling that this could have been the case.

Leeser expressed support for the Voice proposal but urged the Labor government to detail how the body would operate to avoid referendum defeat. Right-wing commentator Janet Albrechtsen slammed Leeser for focusing on 'tomorrow's minutiae' – an admission that questions about 'the detail' were properly dealt with after the referendum – rather than mounting an ideological attack. 'The Liberals have for too long sat on the fence about whether a separate race-based body should be entrenched in our Constitution,' she declared.[10] Albrechtsen later revealed she was involved with Advance's 'No' campaign, which was pressuring the divided Liberal Party to oppose the Voice on principle.[11] But while urging opposition on ideological grounds, she also attacked the Voice's constitutional ability to advise the executive – which is illuminating, for how could limiting the Voice's constitutional scope answer the in-principle objections she raised? Albrechtsen nonetheless pursued both avenues. Voice activists had only spoken of a 'voice to parliament' commenting on proposed bills, she fibbed,[12] though it had always been clear the Voice would advise government too. This new legal attack mirrored the false argument Frank Brennan would make, suggesting the two might be working together.

Given the onslaught brewing, the pre-packaged modesty of the announced amendment, with multiple concessions already built in, also made me worry. I mused again that it would have been better to have announced the original drafting. This would have given Indigenous people more scope to make their compromises in the spotlight, in response to oppositional pressure, enabling opponents to feel they'd had some wins while landing the drafting somewhere acceptable to Indigenous people. The original words co-devised with the con cons would also have given Leeser and Craven more direct emotional attachment to and ownership of the government's proposal. It was too late, however. The words were out there now.

Notwithstanding these worries, when the prime minister announced those words at Garma, I was excited and hopeful. It was the first time since 2014 that any Australian government had proposed constitutional drafting to make the Voice a reality, in large part because this was the first time any prime minister had shown genuine leadership on the issue. Albanese put his prime ministership on the line. He spent political capital. You could see his heart was in it. His tears when he spoke about the Uluru Statement were not for show: his emotion and conviction could not be contained. Albanese knew this was the kind of thing that really mattered in the leadership of a nation. He knew how much Indigenous people needed and wanted this reform, and that it was critical to improving outcomes. Ironically, it was only thanks to a Labor prime minister that the compromise Indigenous people forged with constitutional conservatives finally became government policy. It had taken eight years and dogged persistence by Indigenous leaders, but while the Coalition never took ownership of the Voice or put it to the people during their five years in power after the Uluru Statement, Albanese had the heart and passion to run and win the Voice referendum.

What was lacking, however, was the strategy and precision of execution needed to secure victory in the face of a largely hostile Coalition. The new government was mostly focused on governing, and was not attentive enough to the careful steps required to secure this incredibly difficult yet crucial constitutional reform. Winning a double-majority popular vote despite Coalition resistance demanded tenacity, cunning and hard work beyond measure. Getting to 'Yes', knowing referendums always tend to 'No', would require the government's full focus and ingenuity. It required preparation, discipline, slick messaging, and efficient coordination with and between the 'Yes' teams. It required an overriding commitment to doing 'everything that needed to be done to win' – the same vigour L.B.J. brought to civil rights in the United States, and that Paul Keating brought to delivering the *Native Title Act* in 1990s Australia, but even more, because this was constitutional rather than just legislative reform. The required focus and leadership seemed absent. Thinking back, it is difficult to identify a clear 'general' directing the cause within government and applying the requisite energy and attention to the task. If Keating's approach to native title had been thus, Noel reflected later, there would be no *Native Title Act* today.

❧ ❧ ❧

Two months prior to the Garma announcement, at the May 2022 election, Jacinta Nampijinpa Price had entered Parliament as a new Indigenous senator for the Northern Territory. Her influence on the Coalition was decisive. A former singer-songwriter, Centre for Independent Studies fellow and daughter of NT politician Bess Price, the Country Liberal Party senator made her staunch opposition to the Voice a headline political objective.

Price's maiden speech, delivered a few days before the PM's Garma announcement, condemned the 'platitudes of motherhood statements from our now prime minister'. The government had not demonstrated how the Voice would 'deliver practical outcomes and unite, rather than drive a wedge further between, Indigenous and non-Indigenous Australia,' Price argued. 'And, no, Prime Minister, we don't need another handout, as you have described the Uluru Statement to be.' (In fact, Albanese regularly spoke not of a 'hand-out' but of a 'hand outstretched' and a 'hand of healing' which Australians should grasp.)[13] Price contended that Indigenous Australians had not 'come to agreement' on the Uluru Statement. 'It would be far more dignifying if we were recognised and respected as individuals in our own right who are not simply defined by our racial heritage but by the content of our character,' she said.[14] These were classic Institute of Public Affairs lines. She also raised the unrelated issue of welcome to country practices, suggesting the nation had already gone too far in symbolically recognising Indigenous people.

Strangely for someone opposing an Indigenous Voice, Price cited two examples of the government's 'failure to listen' to Indigenous communities: the scrapping of alcohol bans from dry Indigenous communities 'despite warnings from elders', and the removal of the cashless debit card. Price said these examples showed how legislation 'pushed by left-wing elites' had worsened the lives of Indigenous people. Yet these examples were also used by Voice advocates to demonstrate why Indigenous communities needed a constitutionally guaranteed Voice.[15] Having several Indigenous politicians in Parliament did not prevent these decisions being made without adequate Indigenous community involvement.

Price seemed to view the Voice proposal as a personal affront, perhaps because she saw herself as the anointed Voice for Indigenous peoples. This message came through in her maiden speech via her claim that the Voice would cause Australians 'to disregard our elected voices'.[16] Appearing in a Sky News debate alongside Andrew Bolt for the 'No' team, and against Dean Parkin and me for 'Yes', Price argued that the Voice would undermine 'my voice as an Indigenous representative'. She further claimed the eleven Indigenous politicians in Parliament would 'become redundant if this measure is put in place. What is the purpose of us being there?'[17]

Price appeared to think her job as a politician was to represent Indigenous interests in Parliament – when in fact an NT Senator's job is to represent Territorians, only 30 per cent of whom are Indigenous. No parliamentarian – whether Indian Australian, Chinese Australian, Greek Australian or Indigenous Australian – only represents their own ethnicity. They must represent all Australians in their electorates and their political parties.

Both Indigenous and non-Indigenous parliamentarians would therefore benefit from hearing advice from Indigenous communities when making laws and policies about Indigenous affairs, I argued. As Indigenous leaders like East Kimberley elder Ian Trust later observed, Price, as a Territorian, 'cannot know what is best for the Indigenous communities of Far North Queensland, or APY Lands, or down on Yorta Yorta country'.[18] However, Price said she already consulted widely with Indigenous communities, which is how she knew remote communities did not support the Voice. When referendum booth results demonstrated remote communities were overwhelmingly voting 'Yes', contradicting Price's assertions,[19] the senator in Trumpian fashion suggested the AEC might have manipulated those booths.[20]

Price's impact was critical. In late November 2022, David Littleproud and the Nationals made a surprise early decision to oppose 'Labor's Voice referendum'. Nationals leader David Littleproud justified the decision alongside Senator Price, who as a member of the Country Liberal Party sat with the Nationals in the federal party room. Nationals MPs who had told us they supported the Voice in private meetings stood behind them, nodding like sallow-faced lemmings. Attacking the Voice as elitist, Price took aim at Linda Burney, who as minister for Indigenous Australians had been visiting remote communities to discuss how the Voice could operate.[21] 'Minister Burney might be able to take a private jet out into a remote community, dripping with Gucci, and tell people in the dirt what's good for them – but they are in the dark,' Price argued. Burney's office responded that she didn't own any Gucci.[22] The debate was quickly descending into pettiness and vitriol, and the press lapped it up.

As Chris Kenny pointed out on Sky that night, the Nationals' premature position was nonsensical. First, it mischaracterised the Voice as a Labor proposal and a 'leftist plan', when in fact 'this whole proposal was worked up with conservatives for at least the last six years or more'. Second, the Nationals had been demanding more detail on the Voice from Labor, along with many other conservatives, but then chose to oppose the proposal outright before any detail could be given. 'Why the rush?' Kenny asked. Third, the Nationals were arguing against another Canberra bureaucracy, claiming they wanted to empower local Indigenous voices instead. Yet giving local communities a say was 'the whole point of the Voice', as Kenny noted. 'The whole idea' was 'to make sure that grassroots Indigenous Australians get to have a say in issues that affect them'. Kenny also highlighted the oddity of Littleproud platforming Price, who was not even a frontbencher in his own party.[23] Price's prominence was strange – a fact not scrutinised by other journalists.

Political advisers speculated about the reasons behind the Nationals' premature stance. One theory was that Barnaby Joyce was prosecuting a strategy of destabilisation to take back leadership of the Nationals, which Littleproud had won after challenging Joyce's leadership in May 2022.[24] The Voice was a new issue through which Joyce could torment Littleproud and wedge the Liberals. With pressure on his leadership mounting, Littleproud would have been forced to act quickly, which might explain his party's premature opposition in November 2022.

Splits in the Nationals emerged. Andrew Gee, member for Calare, quit the party. 'I can't reconcile the fact that every Australian will get a free vote on the vitally important issue of the Voice, yet National Party MPs are expected to fall into line behind a party position that I fundamentally disagree with, and vote accordingly in parliament,' he said.[25] The barrister turned politician went on to be one of the most coherent and persuasive conservative advocates for the referendum. Former Nationals leader Michael McCormack, who had expressed strong support to us privately, suggested his party might revise its position, depending on the details of the proposal. WA Nationals leader Mia Davies said she remained open to exploring 'the idea of a Voice', noting the party's state conference had passed a motion of support for the Uluru Statement.[26] Advisers suggested the Country Liberal Party was also not happy that Price had taken a position without properly consulting the party: her stance could cost them bush seats with high numbers of Indigenous voters. The CLP didn't declare opposition to the referendum until February 2023.

The CEO of the Central Land Council, Lesley Turner, also contradicted Price's views. Turner said the Indigenous members of the Council strongly supported the Voice. Price's opposition to it, Turner wrote, 'demonstrates perfectly why electing Aboriginal politicians is not enough and why the voices of Aboriginal Territorians need to be heard by the parliament.'[27]

Meanwhile, Indigenous leaders from the Empowered Communities alliance of ten regional, urban and remote Indigenous communities condemned the National Party's 'premature decision', accusing the party of regional Australia of disregarding 'our local and regional Indigenous voices on this issue', and urging it to 'actively help design a voice that delivers practical results, rather than passively predicting failure and playing political games'. They powerfully declared that:

> Senator Jacinta Price does not speak for Indigenous people in our regions in NPY Lands, in the Goulburn Murray, in Far North Queensland, in East Kimberley and West Kimberley, Ngarrindjeri Ruwe and Far West Coast South Australia, in Redfern and La Perouse and Central Coast NSW. Nor do the Senator's views reflect the views of the Yolngu in North-East Arnhem Land ...
>
> The fact that Senator Price does not listen to or heed our regional Indigenous voices underscores why we need a constitutionally guaranteed voice in our affairs: because individual politicians – be they Indigenous or non-Indigenous – are often too

busy grandstanding and politically manoeuvring to work with our communities on improving outcomes for us.[28]

But the voices of regional and grassroots advocates gained little traction in media and social media compared to the negativity of Price, Warren Mundine and Lidia Thorpe for the 'No' side. While media outlets often struggled to find enough Indigenous 'No' advocates to convey the bothsidesism they doggedly pursued, journalists would seek out Indigenous residents of remote communities who knew little about the upcoming referendum[29] to pump up the 'No' angles in their coverage. This was exploitative: most Indigenous people supported a Voice once they had the proper information, and the media were well placed to help deliver accurate information across the continent, instead of amplifying ignorance. However, news outlets were hungry for conflict, driven by social-media incentives. Overwhelming Indigenous consensus did not attract the same clicks or comments as Price's Gucci attack lines and tirades against 'elitism', which delivered negativity and division conducive to online engagement. Price brought from the right the same clickbait energy Lidia Thorpe delivered from the left. The media's pursuit of 'strict balance' in this way morphed into false balance. It meant news outlets 'ended up not doing a good job of covering the referendum debate', as ABC journalist Laura Tingle admitted.[30] (My sense was that the ABC and SBS were also overcompensating for NewsCorp attacks on their allegedly pro-Voice coverage.) It created the perception that Indigenous people were wholly divided on the Voice, downplaying true levels of Indigenous support.

Noel knew how to penetrate this soundbite environment, though his message sometimes contradicted 'Yes' campaign advice to stay positive and conciliatory. He told Radio National listeners that Price was trapped in 'a tragic redneck celebrity vortex' and was being manipulated to 'punch down on other Blackfellas'. Puppeteered by the think tanks that helped propel her into Parliament, Price had 'turned everything around' in the Nationals, whose 'supposed leader Littleproud' was a 'man of little pride': a 'kindergarten kid'.[31] Price retaliated. We don't 'need a crystal ball to know that if you do not agree with the voice to parliament, you will be called names, be accused of racism, bigotry and it will also be suggested that you are incapable of thinking for yourself,'[32] she predicted.

This dynamic would continue throughout the campaign. The 'No' side would regularly contend that the Voice would divide Australians by race, while accusing 'Yes' campaigners of calling 'No' voters racists – even if they said no such thing. 'Australians are saying ... "Why is the PM yelling at me that I'm not smart enough to understand it, or that I'm racist because I don't support the Voice?",' Dutton told the media in 2023.[33] Albanese had called no one racist, as *AAP Factcheck* pointed out,[34] but the lie proliferated on social media. Perhaps the PM should have sued Dutton for defamation, just as Dutton sued the refugee activist who tweeted that Dutton was a 'rape apologist'. If Dutton had succeeded with his bizarre idea to establish a public fund to support defamation actions by politicians, Albanese's legal costs might have been covered.

The politics were such that Voice advocates could not respond. They could not deny such assertions without amplifying the false charge, nor could they prove opponents correct by identifying racism when it was palpable. As Noel pointed out, the 'No' campaign was 'free to talk about racism' while the 'Yes' campaign was 'snookered from calling it out'.[35] This all worked in favour of 'No' campaign cut-through. Meanwhile, political advisers would remind 'Yes' campaigners that they had to stay positive: they had the harder job of making an inspiring, rational and truthful case for reform. Getting exposure was thus a challenge because sensible reform is nuanced: it is not easily reduced to a slogan, falsity or soundbite. The 'Yes' campaign had to coherently and calmly sell this reform in an environment of noisy polarisation and unfair media coverage. Securing bipartisan support was therefore crucial. If the Coalition had supported the Voice, much of the division and controversy could have been eliminated. The public would have felt reassured rather than frightened by the partisan fight. But the Nationals' early opposition made the possibility of bipartisanship even more remote.

# 9
# WHERE IS THE DETAIL?

Peter Dutton said the Liberals were leaving their position open for the moment. To his credit, Senator Bragg got on TV to encourage his party not to follow the Nationals' opposition. But Dutton was still complaining about the lack of detail from the Labor government. The Liberals were waiting for that detail before deciding whether to support Albanese's referendum, he said.

This was a stalling tactic while Dutton weighed his options. After all, future Parliaments could legislate whatever Voice details they liked. A Liberal government might completely redo detail implemented under Labor. Detail was therefore not relevant to whether Dutton supported the proposed constitutional amendment, which put the Parliament – of which Dutton and his party were a part – in charge of the detail.

Ken Wyatt argued the detail excuse was rubbish. 'Just learn to read,' he said.[1] Wyatt had twice brought the cabinet a detailed Voice proposal while a member of the Morrison government. All Coalition ministers had been given the detail, but they ignored the hefty Indigenous Voice Co-Design Process report, which was the product of 115 community consultations, 120 meetings and more than 4000 submissions.[2] Yet the claim that Labor's Voice referendum 'lacked detail' took off, propelled by high-profile politicians such as Dutton, Price and, unfortunately, Leeser. It was an effective obfuscation.

Back in March 2021, while the Coalition's Indigenous Voice Co-Design Process was underway, Noel gave a speech at the National Museum urging the Morrison government to finalise and release the details of the Voice, to be legislated after a successful referendum:

> Let us complete the legislative design of the Voice, and produce an exposure draft of the Bill so that all parliamentarians and the members of the Australian public can see exactly what the Voice entails.
>
> Let us set the Bill aside and settle on the words of constitutional amendment that recognises Indigenous Australians and upholds the Constitution, and put the amendment to a referendum of the Australian people at the next best opportunity.[3]

The 2021 Co-Design report, published in December, recommended a national voice anchored in local and regional voices. Morrison claimed he would start work on establishing local and regional voices, but there was resistance to implementing a national voice.[4] However, work was not progressed before the May 2022 election.

When Labor won that election with a mandate to implement the Uluru Statement, it announced it would finalise the Voice detail. Senator Patrick Dodson planned to develop an 'exposure document' setting out the key design elements of the Voice in preparation for a referendum, probably in 2023. Dodson wanted it ready before Christmas 2022. 'It's natural for people to want to know something about what this going to look like,' he said.[5]

Then time began to run away. It was only in September 2022 that the government appointed the Referendum Working Group. On 29 September, the group released its Design Principles for the Voice:

- The Voice will give independent advice to the Parliament and government.

- The Voice will be chosen by Aboriginal and Torres Strait Islander people based on the wishes of local communities.
- The Voice will be representative of Aboriginal and Torres Strait Islander communities, gender balanced and include youth.
- The Voice will be empowering, community-led, inclusive, respectful and culturally informed.
- The Voice will be accountable and transparent.
- The Voice will work alongside existing organisations and traditional structures.
- The Voice will not have a program delivery function.
- The Voice will not have a veto power.

These high-level principles did not appease Coalition demands for detail. In late 2022, Leeser outlined seven questions he wanted the Labor government to answer:

- Who will be on the Voice?
- How will these people be chosen?
- What powers and functions will it have?
- How will it represent the diverse communities that make up our Aboriginal and Torres Strait Islander peoples?
- How will it address the real issues that affect people's lives every day in communities?
- Will regional and local bodies exist?
- How will the government ensure the body hears from voices who don't already have a platform in Australian public life?[6]

These questions had simple answers distillable from the 2021 Co-Design Process report, but Labor's election platform made no mention of the co-design work carried out under the Coalition.

The government seemed unable to respond effectively. If this was partly a partisan blockage, progress might also have been hampered by divergence within the Indigenous leadership. The Uluru Dialogue was critical of the Co-Design Process convened by Marcia Langton and Tom Calma, and resisted suggestions that its detail should form the basis of the Voice's design. Although Megan Davis had been appointed to every major committee progressing Indigenous constitutional recognition since 2011, she had not been appointed to the Co-Design Process, which, she argued, failed to centre Indigenous peoples as 'active participants'.[7]

Whereas Voice advocates like Noel and Langton, who were involved in the Co-Design Process, pointed to the final report as evidence that the detail had already been delivered,[8] Davis contended it could not provide the right framework, not least because 'it was designing a voice to government, not a voice to parliament'.[9] The critique partly rebuked the Coalition's shift in nomenclature – the adjusted title of 'Voice to Government' that the Co-Design Process adopted. In substance, however, the report detailed mechanisms for the Voice to engage with both Parliament and government, just as iterative constitutional amendments since 2014 always envisaged the Voice's ability to advise both.

Others also criticised the Calma–Langton approach. During the September 2022 Sky News debate, Parkin suggested the Voice would not be anchored in local and regional voices, contrary to Calma–Langton. 'Minister Burney has talked about this being elected,'[10] he said. Indigenous lawyer Teela Reid, who sat with Parkin and Davis on the Referendum Working Group, was also critical of the Co-Design Process report's focus on regional groupings rather than First Nations.[11]

The Uluru Dialogue subsequently added a constitutional prong to its argument against developing the legislative detail prior to the vote. Gabrielle Appleby and Eddie Synot, of the Indigenous Law Centre at UNSW, contended that releasing a legislative model before the referendum could mislead voters into thinking they 'are voting on the detail of the model, and not the actual constitutional provision'. It could mean future Parliaments 'would be reluctant to disturb the model that was passed with the referendum'.[12] Appleby further suggested that releasing a fully formed legislative model prior to the referendum could 'de-facto entrench' that model, which might even 'operate at a legal level, with that detail possibly constraining the future interpretation of the voice'.[13] Davis echoed these arguments in January 2023.[14]

A better strategy would have been to emphasise the three years of detailed design development already completed under Wyatt. The Coalition owned that work, which meant a successful referendum would have precipitated legislation of a model that should have had Coalition support. But while we hoped the Labor government would endorse Calma–Langton to give the Coalition more ownership of the direction, this risked a negative reaction from some Indigenous leaders, which could affect Indigenous backing and undermine public support. Labor decision-makers must have felt stuck.

༄ ༄ ༄

Dodson did not deliver his exposure document by Christmas 2022. The questions about detail kept coming in the new year.

On 7 January 2023, Dutton wrote to Albanese, accusing him of 'playing clever and tricky political games by withholding detail and rushing the referendum'. The letter listed fifteen questions on detail, more than double Leeser's list of seven the previous year. Who would be eligible to serve on the body? What would be the prerequisites for nomination? Would the government clarify the definition of Aboriginality to determine who could serve on the body? How much would it cost taxpayers annually? If needed, could the body be dissolved and reconstituted in extraordinary circumstances? How would the government ensure that the body include those who still need to get a platform in Australian public life? Would the government rule out using the Voice to negotiate any national treaty? And would the government commit to local and regional Voices, as recommended in the Calma–Langton report? While most of the questions were answerable, some were deliberately antagonistic; the treaty question was a wedge. Labor could not rule out that the Voice would advise on treaties, because this would attract Indigenous opposition, but highlighting Indigenous interest in treaty-making would provide more fodder for right-wing attacks.

Langton argued that the demands for detail were a political tactic: the Coalition was doing everything it could to deceive Australians into believing there was no detail.[15] Her analysis was accurate, which created a conundrum for the government. To answer the Liberals' ever-growing list of questions would be to let the opponents run the debate. Given disagreement among the Indigenous leadership, and the importance to Labor of Indigenous buy-in, deferral of the detail must have seemed like the only viable course.

That conclusion was probably bolstered by perceived lessons from the 1999 republic's failure, which political advisers warned was driven by disagreement on detail. According to journalist Katharine Murphy (who is now a key adviser to Albanese), the lesson of 1999 was 'don't get bogged down in detail', which 'can be weaponised to split the "Yes" case and torpedo a referendum'.[16] The dominant view was that the detail should be determined after referendum victory. There was also the timing issue. Given the time that had passed, the government probably could not build consensus behind the final details of legislative design and deliver a referendum in its first term, especially if Wyatt's Co-Design work could not be utilised without causing public ructions.

Noel began to argue that 'the referendum is about the principle, not the detail'. Dodson reiterated the message. 'The Parliament deals in detail,' he explained. 'That's why we have oppositions and arguments and committees and reviews etc. That's where detail is done.'[17] It was a correct explanation I also prosecuted. As a matter of constitutional reform, deferring detail is ordinary practice. Because disagreement is inevitable, it is usual for constitutions to articulate high-level principles and rules, so the nuts and bolts can be debated, resolved and evolved flexibly via later legislative processes. This shows respect for Parliament.

Politically, however, this did not mollify the Liberals. Yet providing details would not have delivered bipartisanship either, because bipartisanship was not being offered in exchange. While the government's failure to answer Dutton's questions created space for 'No' campaign scaremongering, releasing more detail would have given Voice opponents more material to attack. This had already begun, with Dutton arguing that the Voice would be made up of 'twenty-four academics'[18] and would therefore not be representative. This was a deliberate distortion of the Coalition's own Calma–Langton report and its recommendation that a national Voice have twenty-four members – a model the Labor government had not even adopted.[19] It demonstrated the dishonest critiques that more detail would fuel.

In May 2023, Burney committed to establishing local and regional voices as part of the Voice design.[20] This aligned with what most Indigenous people wanted, as reflected in the Co-Design Process report and the sustained advocacy of many Indigenous leaders, including the Empowered Communities alliance. It was also a concession to the Liberals, but it delivered no pay-off. The Liberals had by then locked in their formal opposition. Dutton did not acknowledge Burney's concession, or the fact that the government's intended Voice design now aligned with Liberal policy. Delivering more detail would not have changed such game playing, but not doing so provided additional excuses for right-wing opposition. It was a no-win situation for the 'Yes' campaign.

# 10

# TOPSY-TURVY WORLD

How is it that some of the constitutionally conservative co-creators of the Voice amendment ended up doing little to defend their own work – and even began maligning the drafting they helped devise? To comprehend the reasons for this, you have to understand how key players over time discarded their constitutionally conservative principles in favour of political tactics. You have to understand that they thought they were cleverly manoeuvring to encourage bipartisanship and referendum success – however misguided their strategies were. You have to understand how some were possessed by a tribal irrationality after Labor won the 2022 election. And you have to understand that some perplexing personalities were involved.

In May 2022, my Radical Centre Reform Lab, together with U&R, coordinated a joint resolution of peak religious organisations calling for bipartisanship on the Voice referendum. The joint resolution was released on the fifth anniversary of the Uluru Statement and was signed by prominent representatives of the Anglican Church of Australia, the Australian Catholic Bishops Conference, the Australian National Imams Council, the Australian Sangha Association, the Executive Council of Australian Jewry, the Hindu Council of Australia, the National Council of Churches in Australia, the National Sikh Council of Australia and the Uniting Church in Australia Assembly. Later, my team coordinated another joint resolution of over 200 multicultural communities in support of the Voice.

The first joint resolution was issued soon after Albanese made his election-night commitment to holding the Voice referendum in his first term. It built on the political and media momentum that announcement created. Rachel Perkins gave an inspiring speech at Barangaroo, and the widespread TV coverage showed the diverse religious leaders offering their support. Several conservative religious leaders came out in favour of the referendum, with opinion pieces making a moral case for the Voice: Archbishop Peter Comensoli, Archbishop Kanishka Raffel, Rabbi Benjamin Elton and Father Antonios Kaldas of the Coptic Orthodox Church. We also asked Greg Craven, as the former vice-chancellor of the Australian Catholic University and one of the conservative co-creators of the Voice proposal, to write a piece underscoring the importance of the religious support and making the moral and conservative case for the Voice.

Craven's piece contained digs at Indigenous leaders who had been downplaying the need for bipartisanship, which was unhelpful to a 'Yes' side striving to be more unified. Craven claimed credit for the original Voice drafting, noting it was 'prescient Indigenous leaders and sympathetic conservative thinkers who first scrawled the constitutional blueprint for the voice. That blueprint, for an ongoing and profound dialogue between Indigenous Australia and our constitutional organs, was carefully considered, refined and adapted by Indigenous leaders and their communities' and 'became a crucial component of the Uluru Statement from the Heart'. However, he also kicked off his 'Labor will not compromise for bipartisanship' narrative. Craven warned that Albanese was adopting a 'take it or leave it approach, where Labor and allied progressives will develop their own model, and present it to Dutton as a fait accompli', destroying any chance for bipartisanship.[1] Labor had only just won the election on 21 May 2022. Yet on 28 May, Craven was publicly chiding Labor for failing to foster bipartisanship – seven days into its stewardship of the cause. His behaviour deteriorated from there.

In the following weeks and months, Craven's frustration with Labor grew. I was warned he was threatening to 'go nuclear' by publicly declaring the referendum dead due to the government's mismanagement. These were my first indications that some of our conservative collaborators might not be able to contain their tribal impulses now the progressives were in charge.

❧ ❧ ❧

Albanese released his draft constitutional amendment at the end of July 2022 but set in place no process for orderly debate. Constitutional personalities fought over the proposed words via opinion pieces and speeches. A damaging free-for-all ensued.

On 13 August 2022, Janet Albrechtsen declared the proposed amendment would spell 'the end of parliamentary democracy as we have known it'. It would empower 'a tiny minority of activists to hold parliament and executive government to ransom' through the 'opportunities for lawfare carefully woven into the Albanese Amendment'. Albrechtsen claimed she had spoken to top silks who agreed.[2]

Craven initially mounted a defence of the Albanese drafting. He dismissed the 'nameless but eminent lawyers' who were 'damning the voice' and rejected the idea of numerous High Court challenges. 'I've been a public, inveterate critic of judicial activism over 30 years, and ... there simply is no playground for judicial usurpation,' he stated.[3]

Meanwhile, U&R had been engaging with conservative barrister Louise Clegg, wife of Liberal shadow minister Angus Taylor. Key con cons thought they could persuade Clegg to participate productively in the drafting debate, which might help get the Liberals on board. Yet they were also prematurely encouraging her to go public with harsh critiques and alternative drafting ideas, instead of first persuading her on the conservative merits of the government's drafting – which was a more modest version of the amendment devised with them in 2014. I could not see the sense in this. Why not convince Clegg of the conservative credentials of the government's draft proposal, which these conservatives had helped embed? Perhaps it was tactical. They wanted a rival proposal to emerge from a right-wing source to facilitate conservative ownership. The problem was the rival proposal they rushed to promote was constitutionally unsound.

On 15 August 2022, Clegg appeared with Craven at the Sydney Institute, where she mounted an attack on Albanese's draft. She critiqued the title of the institution, arguing the word 'Voice' had 'emotive undertones' that did not sit comfortably with our technocratic Constitution.[4] She criticised the drafting for empowering Indigenous people to make representations on all 'matters relating to' them, rather than just on special laws about Indigenous peoples or affairs. 'By deliberately eschewing a narrower path', Clegg argued, the amendment could 'weaponise' Indigenous representations 'about laws of general application (laws that affect all of us) above representations of other citizens'. Clegg predicted this would get 'ugly'. Her contribution helped inflame an ugly and ill-informed debate.

What got lost – and what the con cons did not explain – was that the scope of the Voice had been deliberately drafted broadly to avoid its constitutional remit becoming the subject of litigation. As Twomey repeatedly explained (and as I learned through trial and error in my initial drafting work with Twomey in 2014), narrowing the scope of allowable representations would invite the High Court to resolve what matters the Voice could advise on. By keeping it broad, this became a political judgement. The broad scope was thus a conservative feature of the drafting that had been retained since 2014 for this reason. Clegg, however, proposed that a requirement to hear from the Voice should instead be narrowly incorporated into the conferral of legislative power to Parliament. She proposed an amendment to the race power, section 51(xxvi), to give Parliament authority to make laws with respect to Indigenous people 'for whom it is deemed necessary to make special laws after the parliament has received representations about the proposed laws from a body which represents Aboriginal and Torres Strait Islander people'.

Clegg's alternative amendment would achieve the very things constitutional conservatives had been trying to avoid: litigation and invalidation of laws. First, because only the High Court can conclusively determine which laws are made under which constitutional power, and therefore which laws would require prior representations from the body. Second, because High Court precedent shows that a requirement embedded into one head of power may be applied by implication to other heads of power too, where the other powers are used to legislate about the same subject matter.[5] Third, because Clegg's amendment would give Indigenous people a potential veto over the special laws: if the body refused to make representations, then Parliament's power could not be exercised. Fourth, because laws enacted absent such representations could be invalidated by the High Court. And fifth, because the proposed stipulation that the representations must be from a body that 'represents' Indigenous people would invite the High Court to determine what kind of structure fulfils that criteria, enabling it to invalidate legislation establishing a body that was not considered by the judges to be suitably representative. Our previous work with the con cons had avoided these problems. What Clegg was proposing was far more radical and legally uncertain than the original 2014 drafting devised with Craven and co., and the Albanese amendment derived from it.

Craven did not point out the problems with Clegg's proposal. The con cons instead encouraged Clegg's critique of their own work. They appeared to be abandoning their conservative concerns in relation to Clegg's alternative drafting, in the hope that her proposal would somehow facilitate bipartisanship, while at the same time ignoring (and later denying) the genuine conservative credentials of the government's draft amendment, which they had helped inform. It was topsy-turvy world. Their principles were vacated in favour of political tactics, but the tactics were misguided. Clegg cannot be described as a Voice supporter. As Albrechtsen and others associated with Advance's 'No' campaign revealed after the referendum, Clegg was one of the key people developing the strategy to highlight legal concerns about the drafting. She played 'a pivotal role challenging the rolling waves of "yes" within the Australian legal profession', such that her contribution is praised by 'No' campaigners.[6] Yet here were our conservative allies facilitating and promoting Clegg's arguments, notwithstanding that her attacks were handing the Liberals more excuses to say 'No'. How did they think this would encourage bipartisanship?

Frank Brennan had proposed a similar approach to Clegg's. In January 2022, he also suggested qualifying the constitutional conferral of legislative power to Parliament, to incorporate an obligation to consult Indigenous peoples.[7] He argued that his amendment showed it was possible to 'design the right constitutional hook for the voice without undermining parliamentary sovereignty', but he got that wrong. What Brennan proposed was a constitutional right to be consulted. It had the same problems as Clegg's proposal. Laws enacted in contravention of consultation requirements could be invalidated by the High Court, and Indigenous peoples could just refuse to be consulted, creating a potential veto. Both their proposals would facilitate unpredictable litigation, undermining parliamentary supremacy. Their suggestions presented a striking contrast to the constitutionally conservative approach developed in 2014, which gave rise to the government's draft amendment. The government's approach kept Parliament in charge; the Brennan/Clegg approaches put the courts in charge.

To understand how (unintentionally) ambitious and in fact progressive their rival approaches were, consider the proposal put forward by Megan Davis and Rosalind Dixon in 2016, which advocated an explicitly litigable constitutional duty to consult, because they viewed Twomey's 2015 drafting (as devised with the constitutional conservatives) as too weak. Davis and Dixon noted that, under the Twomey 2015 drafting, Parliament could ignore the body's advice. To remedy this weakness, they proposed that a duty to consult be incorporated into the head of legislative power (just as Clegg and Brennan later did), framing it as follows:

> In exercising its power to make laws under [s. 51(xxvi)], and in all other cases in which laws have a significant or disproportionate impact on Indigenous peoples, the Commonwealth Parliament shall consult with Indigenous peoples in good faith, and through appropriate procedures.[8]

Although more ambitiously and broadly worded, this proposal would also enable laws made without the required consultation to be invalidated, and would give Indigenous people a potential veto, as they could presumably block laws by refusing to be consulted. Davis and Dixon admitted the potential for the invalidation of laws, which was intended, not inadvertent, explaining that a failure to consult could enable Indigenous people 'to challenge the validity of relevant legislation'. Clegg and Brennan, by contrast, were not so self-aware.

By August 2022, Brennan had realised the problems with his January 2022 formulation, so he proposed another:

> There shall be an Aboriginal and Torres Strait Islander voice with such structure and functions as the parliament deems necessary to facilitate consultation prior to the making of special laws with respect to Aborigines and Torres Strait Islanders.[9]

But this too raised issues. It could facilitate unpredictable litigation about which special laws constitutionally required consultation, and the High Court might by implication extend the consultation requirements to other powers too.[10] Additionally, this drafting might restrict Parliament from conferring a broader scope on the Voice, leaving Indigenous people with a body only able to advise on a narrow array of laws enacted under the race power, which is rarely used. (Brennan tried to fix this in his later variations.) Finally, it could again require consultation prior to laws being made, entailing potential for invalidity rulings.

Ironically, Brennan and Craven would later raise fears about a duty to consult being implied in the government's proposed constitutional drafting,[11] even though the government's amendment did not stipulate any consultation requirement, contrary to Brennan's repeated suggestions that it adopt his alternative approach. However, the modesty of the government's proposal compared to Brennan's January 2022 and August 2022 models was implicitly confirmed by the solicitor-general's opinion in April 2023. It noted that the 'deliberate textual choice' not to use the word 'consult' in the government's drafting demonstrated that the powers of Parliament and the executive were not constrained and could not be blocked or held up. Anyone concerned with maintaining parliamentary and governmental supremacy, and avoiding needless litigation, should therefore have been thankful Brennan's 'consultation' models were not adopted.

Albrechtsen publicly endorsed the Clegg and Brennan approaches, which in retrospect is unsurprising given she and Clegg were reportedly associated with Advance's 'No' campaign,[12] and given Albrechtsen's criticisms of the government's drafting echoed Brennan's. She praised their proposals as modest, while denouncing the government's draft as too radical.[13] It was totally back to front. Yet it now seems clearer that – although Brennan and Clegg would likely disagree – the point of these arguments was not to pursue a sensible compromise or encourage bipartisanship: as Albrechtsen later revealed, compromise and bipartisanship were the last things the 'No' campaign wanted.[14] The point, in my view, was to derail sensible debate, discredit the Albanese amendment and create ostensibly legal excuses for Coalition and public opposition.

I alerted U&R that this was fuelling a farcical public debate about the draft words. But U&R wanted Clegg and Brennan to run with their arguments, which they claimed would help bring conservatives into the conversation.

~~ ~~ ~~

The legal debate presented a bizarrely backwards state of affairs, but it created a theoretical opportunity for Indigenous people. Right-wing Voice opponents were endorsing constitutional drafting that they thought was more modest (or which they were pretending to think was more modest), but which in fact would give Indigenous people more legal firepower than what Albanese was proposing. The more radical amendments were being endorsed as sensible and conservative by right-wing players, while the constitutionally conservative approach presented by Albanese was being rejected as too extreme.

While I did not think these more radical approaches were constitutionally desirable (over many years, I had internalised the constitutionally conservative values that our collaborators were now inexplicably abandoning), I could see a potential opportunity for Indigenous people. If Indigenous leaders accepted what Clegg and co. were proposing, they might gain more legal leverage via the courts than if they ran with Albanese's approach – if the problems with the Clegg and Brennan approaches could be kept under wraps, that is (which was unlikely). I rang Noel to explain the topsy-turvy situation. His view was that the deficiencies of the Clegg and Brennan approaches would not be kept quiet. Their inherent problems would be identified and their ideas would be abandoned as unworkable. It was better to stay the course with the Albanese approach, which was modest yet profound.

# 11

# BLACK ROBE RETURNS

The original constitutional drafting devised with Craven, Leeser, Freeman and Twomey in 2014, then published by Twomey in 2015,[1] gave the Indigenous advisory body the function of 'providing advice to the Parliament and the Executive Government'. The reference to the executive was right up front, in clause one. You couldn't miss it. We all agreed with it. In fact, it was Leeser who emphasised the importance of Indigenous people advising the government for the reform to have practical impact. By the time policy positions reach Parliament, they are locked in and difficult to change, Leeser explained. To make a real difference, the body needs to engage on policy development. This is why advice to the executive was there from word go. Over the next eight years, and throughout multiple subsequent variations, our conservative collaborators never raised concerns about it – publicly or privately.

This changed in late 2022, after it became a Labor proposal. The day after Albanese released the drafting at Garma, Albrechtsen raised fears about an alleged 'expansion' of the Voice to allow it to advise the executive.[2] Brennan ran with the misrepresentation that the Voice had been expanded.[3] On 14 November, I was informed that he had been digging up 'stacks of stuff' about how the Voice's representations to the executive could arguably enable judicial review of administrative decisions. Brennan had also no doubt been warning his former

ACU colleague Greg Craven that Albanese's drafting, which Craven had defended as legally sound as recently as August,[4] might not be as sound as he thought it was.

On the same day I was warned about Brennan's investigations into the supposed perils of constitutionally sanctioned Indigenous engagement with the executive, Craven published a new criticism on these grounds. He began abandoning his previous endorsement of the Albanese amendment, and instead began arguing it was legally unworkable. 'The Prime Minister's opening bid words cannot be just anointed', he asserted, suggesting there were 'other models [presumably Brennan's and Clegg's] that should be considered'. 'We know, for example, that the current broad proposal for the voice to consider past and proposed legislative and executive action is very unlikely to gain bipartisan conservative support. It goes way beyond the original idea of a voice vetting new laws.'[5]

Craven's memory is selective. The original Voice drafting devised with Craven in 2014 empowered the body to advise the executive. Either his assertion was a major backflip or a deliberate obfuscation, or he had overlooked the details of the original drafting he co-created and supported for eight long years. In 2014, Craven had advocated a constitutional body 'charged with counselling parliament *and government* on indigenous matters [my emphasis]'. He argued that '*government* would be empowered, not disempowered by [its] timely and wise counsel [my emphasis]'.[6] In a 2021 submission to the Calma–Langton Co-Design Process, Craven and Freeman praised the drafting they had co-created, as published by Twomey:

> We were actively involved in the discussions through which this amendment was drafted. We believed in 2015, and still believe, that it is legally sound. It is a provision that would not undermine the supremacy of Parliament or give rise to uncertainty in the High Court's interpretation of the Constitution.

Even as late as January 2023, the pair explained how their original drafting had provided 'the basis for the Prime Minister's simplified drafting in 2022'.[7]

Yet in November 2022, Craven denied that an ability to advise the executive was ever in the original proposal.[8] Contradicting himself months later, Craven admitted that early drafts he helped develop had 'referred vaguely to representations to the executive'.[9] The 'vagueness' defence was bizarre. How can a proposed constitutional amendment refer to something 'vaguely'? Did we use a tricky faded font or disappearing ink? Did we swipe the professor's reading glasses? No. A proposed constitutional change either refers to something or it doesn't. There are no vague references in legal drafting, only vague lawyers.

Craven was following Brennan. The shift was enabled by Brennan's incorrect claim that the Referendum Council in 2017 only recommended a Voice to Parliament, not to the executive. In fact, the Referendum Council's report envisaged the Voice advising on both laws and policies.[10] According to Brennan, however, Indigenous leaders had belatedly expanded their proposal for a Voice in 2018. They suddenly wanted 'a Voice that could make representations to parliament *and* executive government', he contended.[11] This was a false narrative. There was no such expansion. Indigenous leaders had made the amendment more modest between 2014 and 2018, as explained in Chapter 6. This fact was accepted by Andrew Bragg, whose 2021 book noted the 2018 revision was 'simpler and cleaner' than the original because it dropped the tabling procedure and contained 'fewer words and fewer provisions'.[12]

Brennan seemed especially annoyed that the drafting variation put forward by Noel, Davis and Anderson in 2018 had gained traction even though it was submitted to the parliamentary committee 'months after the close-off date'.[13] He complained about the tardiness of their submission repeatedly.[14] Brennan was like the diligent high school student who always submitted his work on time, miffed at the naughty black kids who got an extension yet still received special praise for their assignment. The griping was adolescent, but Paul Kelly[15] and other journalists adopted Brennan's narrative wholesale.

Brennan's 2023 book includes evidence contradicting his own claim. It quotes Noel explaining the Voice proposal in 2015 as a constitutional change enabling Indigenous Australians to engage with the *'executive government of Australia* and the Parliament [my emphasis]'.[16] It later quotes Noel's 2014 Quarterly Essay, describing the proposed constitutional 'requirement that Indigenous peoples get a fair say in laws *and policies* made about us [my emphasis]'.[17] Brennan's 2023 book fails to quote the original drafting published by Twomey in 2015, which demonstrates that advice to the executive was part of the formulation devised with constitutional conservatives. That omitted technical history disproves his narrative.[18]

Why such manoeuvring to discredit the constitutional drafting? Brennan opposed a constitutional Voice from the start. His 2015 book, *No Small Change*, dismissed the Voice idea[19] in favour of symbolic constitutional recognition, which Indigenous people consistently rejected. He asserted it was 'impossible' to draft a 'technically and legally sound' constitutional Voice,[20] which prompted Twomey to publish the agreed drafting to prove Brennan wrong.[21] That drafting was later endorsed by former chief justice Murray Gleeson. Contrary to Brennan's narrative,[22] Gleeson in his 2019 speech did not *only* endorse a Voice to Parliament. Gleeson said Twomey's proposal, which included advice to both Parliament and the executive, would uphold parliamentary supremacy.[23]

We had to publicly fight Brennan in those early years to keep the proposal alive. Noel condemned the priest 'with his black robes on' butting in to 'determine what is right for our people'.[24] Marcia Langton similarly implored Australians 'to listen to what Indigenous people want. Not Frank Brennan.'[25] Brennan never forgot that pushback. His 2023 book recalls how Langton and Pearson had in 2015 'blown my proposals ... out of the water, making it clear that modest symbolic change was not an option'.²⁶ Yet we even tried to bring Brennan onside in those early years. Together with Leeser, Craven and Freeman, we invited Brennan to talk with us, and in the process convened a bizarre Christian prayer session at the Australian Catholic University in Melbourne, to try to persuade him to cease his public attacks. This was particularly amusing for me, the agnostic cultural Hindu in the group.²⁷ Our prayers did not work.

After Indigenous people issued the Uluru Statement, Brennan claimed he supported a constitutional Voice, but his subsequent advocacy reveals his true position. When Labor got into power, Black Robe returned.

∽ ∽ ∽

Around the same time Craven joined Brennan in denying that advice to the executive was ever part of the original amendment he helped devise, Albrechtsen intensified her fearmongering about anonymous 'constitutional silks' warning of excessive litigation flowing from the proposed constitutional change.²⁸ Former High Court judge Kenneth Hayne defended the government's drafting, arguing that the 'disruptive consequences' being alleged had 'no foundation in the text of the proposed amendment'.²⁹ But Ian Callinan, another former High Court judge, contradicted Hayne. 'I would foresee a decade or more of constitutional and administrative law litigation arising out of a voice, whether constitutionally entrenched or not,' Callinan wrote.³⁰

Brennan's prolific media engagement carefully amplified this furore. In a phone call on 27 February 2023, the prime minister reportedly admonished Brennan for 'feeding the "No" case' and chided the priest's 'politically naivety'.³¹ Yet a 'naivety' assessment assumes Brennan was a Voice supporter, which, as the history above shows, is not an accurate description: he was one of the earliest opponents, preferring symbolic recognition. To assume Brennan was naive thus itself seems a naive interpretation.

It must have affected Catholic support. A month before the referendum, the political scientist John Warhurst questioned why the Catholic bishops had gone soft on the Voice referendum since Labor got into power.[32] One reason was that the political right had formally opposed the Voice by this time, but another was the influence of prominent Catholics Brennan and Craven. As early as May 2022, when the religious organisations were coordinating their joint resolution in support of the Uluru Statement, the Catholics were last to sign. Apologising for the delay, a very senior Catholic explained that Brennan had advised against signing it. They ultimately signed, but, in my view, it demonstrated Brennan's efforts – both public and private – to thwart consensus-building for a constitutional Voice. And this was before Labor had proposed any constitutional drafting, so there was no legal basis for his obstruction. The joint resolution was just expressing in-principle support and calling for bipartisan action. Brennan apparently had issues even with this.

A reader's comment in response to Warhurst's article explained Brennan's impact better than I can: 'Even though he has decided to vote Yes he certainly gave discerning Catholics plenty of reason to say No.'[33] Another comment under a different piece observed how Brennan initially 'presented a case for the No campaign', enabling the right-wing press to take 'full advantage of his stance'.[34] The observations were astute. Brennan would hold himself out as a Voice supporter, but his advocacy gave voters myriad reasons to say 'No', and the Liberals excuses to withhold support – and all the while he claimed he would nonetheless vote 'Yes'. According to Brennan, he would vote 'Yes' despite the government's 'joke' of a process,[35] despite the flawed drafting that would 'clog up' the government in delay and litigation,[36] despite the ill-advised 'crash or crash through' approach,[37] and despite the 'hell of a mess'[38] it created. His message was confusing and poisonous to the referendum's chances. In my opinion, the best interpretation of this contorted behaviour is that Brennan didn't want the Indigenous leaders who had rejected his minimalistic approach to succeed with the Voice proposal he had long opposed. The great tragedy is that key conservatives, who co-conceived a constitutional Voice to both Parliament and the executive, appeared to defer to Brennan instead of defending their own work.

To me this was shocking, but I shouldn't have been surprised. Not only did the con cons and Brennan share an institutional connection through the Australian Catholic University that would have encouraged deference to the priest, but the politics had also changed. The conservatives were no longer in power. Labor was running the show. This put our conservative allies on the back foot and inflamed their tribal instincts. Brennan's arguments must have been enticing: they presented a way to attack Labor and the progressives, who needed to be publicly slammed into submission if bipartisanship was to be forged. The left had to be forced to give something big away to show the right (and the public) that the activists were conceding ground. Constitutionally sanctioned advice to the executive was a convenient thing for Indigenous people to be forced to relinquish. The tactics were misguided, however, because the prolific complaints gave the Coalition a shiny new legal justification for its opposition and probably scared sections of the public. The attacks would help sink the referendum. I believe Brennan ought to have known this, and so too our con con allies.

Additional blame must lie with the Labor government and the 'Yes' campaigns. For too long they downplayed the conservative genesis of the Voice, which made it easier for the con cons to disown their work. All of which supports the conclusion that their change of disposition was about altered politics, not law. The arguments about the executive were weapons of political warfare. Those weapons would not have been deployed if a right-wing government were proposing the same words. Finally, I too must wear responsibility: I didn't do enough to keep our radical centre alliance intact in the face of Brennan's criticism.

Ultimately, I will never understand why key conservative co-creators of a constitutional Voice joined with Brennan to help defeat their own proposal. But the media loved the Brennan–Craven duo. They dominated the narrative. They still control the post-referendum analysis.

In the end, Brennan won. Now he can say, 'I told you so.'

# 12

# A RADICAL SPLINTER

The 'Yes' case went quiet over Christmas 2022, enabling the germinating 'No' case to fill the void largely unopposed. The 'Yes' campaign wasn't ready. As Megan Davis later reflected: 'everyone went on holidays' over summer. The 'No' side spread its 'This is divisive, this will put race in the Constitution' narrative on social media. 'It was relentless,' Davis said, and opponents got the upper hand.[1] The 'No' campaign had apparently been organising since August 2022, and according to inside reports became a 'professional, lean and focused campaigning outfit'.[2] That description has not been applied to the disparate 'Yes' campaigns.

The unreadiness of the 'Yes' effort may have been partly due to a view among political advisers that voters wouldn't 'switch on' until much closer to the referendum – say, from four to six weeks out. Resources were thus saved for deployment closer to the vote, which led some to feel they had more time to get organised. This was the wrong approach. The competitive PR view – that whoever gets their message out first sets the framing and dominates the debate – now seems more correct.

When the 'No' campaign got a head start, the 'Yes' campaign was ill-equipped to combat the deluge. The muted response might also be explained by political advice that advocates should not engage in combat on the 'No' side's turf. Certain negative messages or 'frames' worked for 'No', but other positive frames worked better for 'Yes'. By refuting

'No' campaign attacks, 'Yes' advocates risked amplifying 'No' messages, which would only help opponents. I didn't always agree with this advice: the 'No' campaign's scare tactics needed to be directly refuted to win over undecided or wavering voters.

Looking back, 'Yes' advocates were unable to answer the argument, powerfully put by Price and Mundine, that a constitutional Voice would divide the country by race. They were shell-shocked by the ferocity and virality of that message, and the extent to which it delivered something for which 60 per cent of the Australian population appeared to be hungry. It was a seductive idea: *Everyone is equal. We should not be divided by race.*

Voice proponents countered that message in myriad intellectually sound ways: *This will unite the country. It is about dialogue, partnership and cooperation. It is about inclusion rather than exclusion. It is about love and friendship. Plus, the Constitution already includes racially discriminatory provisions. And what about Tasmania's equal voice in the Federation: that is not individual equality. Our Constitution doesn't protect individual equality – it does the opposite: it says race-based division is allowed.* All these arguments were correct, and I used them repeatedly. But they were nuanced. They had less cut-through than the basic, pithy objection – *this will divide us by race* – which got far more traction online. The 'Yes' campaign had no equally viral response to the racial division argument, which refutes Indigenous recognition no matter the model. It would kill symbolic recognition as much as a constitutional Voice.

This headline message was supplemented and supported by the legal scares and endless demands for more detail. It gave different audiences a variety of excuses to vote 'No'. Discerning voters who found the racial arguments distasteful and simplistic might instead be drawn by the 'no detail' argument. Those who understood that the Constitution is not the place for detail might prefer arguments about legal risk and endless litigation. Those less interested in legal and policy discussion might be attracted to the simple salience of *this will divide us by race*. The 'No' case in this way issued an effective multipronged attack that spoke to different parts of the Australian population and their various latent worries.

In January 2023, in addition to his fifteen questions about 'the detail', Dutton asked why there hadn't been any legal advice released on the proposed amendment, building on arguments floated by Albrechtsen. Dutton also picked up lines of attack relating to the Voice's ability to advise the executive. 'Could the High Court determine that the Voice can have a say in defence matters, or it can have a say in budgetary priorities that the treasurer is going to deliver?' he asked. 'What would it mean for a minister who has to make a quick decision if there's a consultation with the Voice?'[3] Fuelled by the debate in the opinion pages, every sitting week in Parliament the government faced a barrage of questions – legal and otherwise – from the Opposition, which it seemed ill-equipped to answer. It was a highly damaging period for the 'Yes' campaign.

❧ ❧ ❧

Contrary to the dominant narrative, the Labor government did appear to be seeking a compromise with Dutton on the constitutional amendment – at least on paper. On 1 February 2023, Albanese wrote to Dutton, inviting him to suggest changes. 'As I have said to you in our meetings,' the letter urged, 'if you have any practical suggestions or amendments on the wording I would welcome your contribution.' It was a direct offer to negotiate. As David Crowe reported, the letter 'held out the prospect of a constructive deal to recognise First Australians in the Constitution as long as those with concerns were willing to put forward their changes to the proposal'.[4] While it did not provide answers to Dutton's questions about detail, the letter was an important effort at achieving bipartisan agreement.

The invitation to compromise was not widely publicised. Though this was a failure of journalism and probably evidence of biased media coverage, it must also have been the result of poor media strategy. Given the damaging debate playing out about the amendment, why was the PM's invitation to Dutton not headline news? Why wasn't Albanese all over TV and radio issuing his invitation for a bipartisan constitutional compromise? Had media pressure been properly applied, perhaps Dutton would have been forced to respond. Instead, it appears he never bothered to reply. The PM's offer didn't force the Coalition to the table. It was too easily ignored.

Partisan division was better for the Liberals' electoral prospects. Pressure on Dutton to resist bipartisan cooperation must therefore have been immense. There was reportedly concern among 'many Liberals' that Dutton waiting too long to adopt a 'No' position might increase the possibility that Labor would compromise to appease right-wing demands.[5] A compromise was therefore perceived as a risk by the right, because it could undercut the Liberals' opportunity to run a partisan campaign. This illuminates why Dutton avoided compromise with Albanese, while pretending it was Labor refusing to budge so that it would wear the blame for a referendum defeat. It was a performative stand-off. Yet the prime minister could have been more assertive, if only to call Dutton's bluff. 'If we make this change, will the Liberals give the referendum bipartisan support?' could have been the PM's straightforward and public question. However, Dutton did not directly propose changes to Albanese's drafting, presumably to avoid being pinpointed in this way. The lack of any process to compel bipartisan negotiation allowed him to maintain the pretence.

That first week of February was a massive media week on the referendum, which might be another reason Albanese's compromise offer got little coverage. A headline story was the signing of a joint statement in support of the referendum by all state and territory leaders. The supporters included the conservative Liberal NSW premier Dominic

Perrottet, who felt the Voice should be 'above politics' and did not share Dutton's concerns about a lack of detail,[6] along with Liberal Tasmanian premier Jeremy Rockliff.[7] Perhaps the government felt it need not push its offer to negotiate with Dutton too hard, given other Liberal leaders in the federation were backing the 'Yes' campaign, and given Dutton didn't seem to want to play ball.

Another story concerned a surreptitious adjustment to the constitutional drafting. Albanese's letter to Dutton reinserted the introductory line of recognition that had been accidentally omitted from the drafting as conveyed in Albanese's Garma speech. The letter did not explain the change, which was reported the next day, having been endorsed by the Referendum Working Group's expert advisers.[8] It was subsequently attacked by Leeser, who had for years expressed concern about the insertion of symbolic language into the Constitution, but in this instance used the issue to highlight the shoddy process. The attorney-general, Mark Dreyfus, said the prime minister had only replicated in his letter to Dutton 'exactly what he said at Garma more than six months ago'.[9] Yet the material conveying the draft constitutional change had also omitted the introductory line and had to be updated. The government could have said it decided that a line of recognition should be included after receiving Indigenous and expert advice. It could even have explained that its inclusion echoed a suggestion made by Jeff Kennett in 2016.[10] Yet it was also telling that Leeser was not defending the proposal he helped create at this stage but exploiting every government misstep.

The big news week did not stop there. On 2 February, the Indigenous leaders on the Referendum Working Group met with Dutton and Leeser. Both said their questions on the details of the Voice went unanswered. Rather, they said they were given a presentation on the First Nations regional dialogues that culminated in the Uluru Statement – information which was six years old and already understood.[11] 'I didn't learn anything today that I didn't already know', Leeser stated afterwards,[12] indicating that the Coalition wanted a constitutional convention and delivery of the legislative detail.[13] However, it was reported that Indigenous barrister Tony McAvoy had been authorised by the Indigenous leadership to put an offer to Dutton at that meeting. If they agreed to adopt the details articulated in the Coalition's Langton–Calma report, would Dutton commit to back it? Dutton gave no straight answer,[14] which revealed the game being played. He was not truly open to a bipartisan deal.

~ ~ ~

Freeman and I were releasing a book showcasing the multifaith unity behind the Voice referendum. *Statements from the Soul* would be launched by Tom Bathurst, the former chief justice of New South Wales, on 20 February 2023 at the Great Synagogue in Sydney, kicking off the much-anticipated 'week of action' being planned by the 'Yes' campaign. The idea was to bring the debate back to the positive, moral case for the Voice. But Craven was about to 'go nuclear'. His intervention hit the headlines on the same day as our book launch, overshadowing any focus on the growing consensus.

Craven declared that the Voice's constitutional ability to advise the executive could 'paralyse' the government in an emergency military action.[15] Readers were supposed to imagine a government hamstrung, forced to wait for the advisory body's go-ahead before saving Australians from enemy attack. It laid the groundwork for a similar claim by Peta Credlin on Sky News in April 2023. If the gunman in the Lindt Café siege had been Indigenous, she asked, would the police have had to wait for the Voice's tick-off before intervening to save the hostages? 'What would have happened if the terrorist in that case had been an Aboriginal …? Would the voice need to have been consulted before we deployed terror police?'

As Chris Kenny observed on Sky News, Credlin's argument was 'desperate … an over-the-top and implausible scare campaign'. So was

Craven's. Under the proposed constitutional drafting, no one – let alone counter-terrorism forces – would have a duty to consult the Voice.[16] Yet Craven created the blueprint for Credlin's lowbrow claims – and he was a Voice co-creator, a supposed supporter. Such assertions from him were catastrophic. This was Craven's bullying tactic: if Voice advocates did not change the amendment in the way he wanted, he would continue these damaging assaults. If not fixed, Craven argued, the reference to 'the executive' would incapacitate government – a reality which would 'dynamite' bipartisanship and the referendum's chances.[17]

Craven had deployed the dynamite, blowing up what was meant to be the 'Yes' campaign's positive 'week of action'. 'I could not have dreamt this up,' I said to Noel. Never in a million years could I have imagined that the conservatives who co-devised a constitutional Voice to both Parliament and the executive would publicly help kill their own proposal after it won Indigenous and Labor support. Worse, we had encouraged Indigenous people to champion a constitutional Voice on the basis that it had the con cons' support, which made it more politically viable. Craven's position switch represented a deep betrayal.

I began to regret ever working with them. After all, Noel and other Indigenous leaders had conceded to Craven's overblown attacks once before. Back in 2012, he had blasted the Expert Panel's call for a racial non-discrimination guarantee as a 'one clause bill of rights' and a 'dog of a proposal'.[18] Noel had negotiated with constitutional conservatives to create an alternative approach – a constitutional Voice – despite Craven's bullying approach in the media (he had seemed more sensible in real life). Yet now Craven was doing the same thing again, this time undermining the very proposal he helped devise in the lead-up to a referendum. He didn't try to broker a private solution. Instead, he mounted a public assault, using language just as bad as – or worse than – his attacks on our so-called 'one clause bill of rights' ever were. Surely such poor behaviour cannot be rewarded, I thought. Craven had joined Brennan, Albrechtsen and Clegg in handing the Liberals excuses to say 'No'.

If we were going to hurtle towards a referendum without bipartisan support or con con backing, we might as well have stuck with a racial non-discrimination clause back in 2014, I mused. That proposal polled higher than a Voice ever did – at over 80 per cent in the Expert Panel days, circa 2011 (albeit absent any 'No' campaign). A message based in equality would have been a simpler sell: who could disagree that laws and policies should not discriminate on the basis of race? Rhetoric of equality was the basis of the current 'No' campaign, which was resonating successfully. Craven had convinced us to abandon that approach which we ditched in favour of a constitutional Voice – yet now he was assassinating that too.

My only consolation was knowing that a racial non-discrimination guarantee would likely have failed, because no previous attempt to insert new rights guarantees into the Constitution has ever succeeded. It would not have attracted bipartisan support. Australia has a strong attachment to parliamentary supremacy, which the Voice respected but a rights clause did not. That proposal would have been slammed by the right, and the special measures carve-out enabling the continuation of Indigenous-specific laws would have been pilloried as 'special treatment'.

Craven didn't stop there. He took aim at members of the Referendum Working Group who, he claimed, were refusing to compromise. He said they would rather 'see the referendum go down' than shift, describing the 'intransigence' and 'egotism' of Indigenous leaders who were prepared to blow it up if they didn't get their way. He could have been describing his own behaviour. The Working Group leaders were aghast.[19]

❧ ❧ ❧

I flew to Adelaide for the launch of the 'Yes' alliance ground campaign, but spent the few days in an upstairs backroom, drafting and redrafting a rebuttal from Noel and me to Craven and co.'s attacks. I could hear the energy in the packed hall below as I typed in the 40-degree heat.

Dean Parkin, campaign director of Yes23, addressed the crowd of volunteers and supportive organisations to mark the launch of the new Yes23 website and the start of community conversations. He urged campaigners to shift away from the intensely political debate and return the discussion to the community, 'where it belongs'. By voting 'Yes', Parkin argued, Australians would connect to the oldest living culture on earth. 'Not only do we get to make that simple yet profound statement,' he said, paraphrasing Craven's 'modest yet profound' description of the Voice from 2014, 'we get to do something practical as well', giving Indigenous peoples a 'real voice on the issues that affect our families and our communities'.[20] The event kicked off 'kitchen-table' conversations around the country.

Two days later, on 25 February, Noel and I published our piece in *The Australian,* defending the proposed amendment's inclusion of advice to the executive.[21] Yes23 advisers were not pleased – perhaps because it strayed onto 'No' turf by rebutting 'No' arguments, or perhaps because it detracted from the positive, community-focused vibe of the campaign launch. But our opponents were not ceasing their damaging attacks and setting out the history behind the Voice drafting was important. Our piece had utility. The prime minister began referring to it in his rebuttals of questions from the Liberals, reminding the Coalition that Leeser and other conservatives had helped devise the proposal they were now critiquing.[22]

On 28 February, Leeser's old organisation, U&R, platformed Craven, Brennan and Clegg at a conservative conference. I had raised concerns about its amplification of advocates who would harshly criticise the government's proposed amendment, while proposing unworkable solutions, and asked for a chance to rebut their claims. U&R declined to let me speak.

Brennan spoke. He again mischaracterised the Referendum Council's report and argued for removal of the Voice's ability to advise the executive.[23] Clegg again called Albanese's amendment 'too big and too radical'. It was 'a privileged voice on everything', she claimed, and a recipe for division and endless 'political disputation'.[24] U&R had apparently invited these contributions to help push a compromise and build bipartisan support – go figure. No direct refutations of their alternative proposals were presented in the other papers, though Tony McAvoy gave an excellent presentation defending the government's constitutional drafting.[25]

Leeser spoke, too, and condemned the government's failure to listen, persuade, find common ground with the Opposition or follow good process. His speech did not inform the conservative audience that he had helped devise the idea of a constitutional Voice in 2014, or that he had argued the importance of the advisory body's ability to engage with the executive, which Brennan was now so robustly critiquing. Rather, Leeser praised Brennan for having 'the patience of a saint' in the face of Labor's incompetence and criticised the government for unilaterally releasing 'Voice 1.0' at Garma.[26] It was only later, in his Press Club address in April,[27] that Leeser clearly outlined his role in co-devising the true Voice 1.0 back in 2014, which evolved into Albanese's amendment.

I mostly stopped collaborating with U&R after that week.

# 13

# A FINAL COMPROMISE

The concern about the Voice's ability to advise the executive was hype. No court was going to require a bureaucrat to implement the Voice's advice; at most, a court might imply requirements for an executive decision-maker to notify or proactively consult the Voice about an administrative decision, or consider the Voice's advice in making that decision. Not follow it. Just consider it.[1] But even constitutional implications of this kind were a remote possibility. Legislation would determine whether and how any duties to give notice, consult or consider would apply. The concern was therefore spurious and exaggerated.

The government was understandably spooked. On 13 March 2023, it was reported that it had privately urged Indigenous leaders to support a 'compromise deal' to alter the constitutional drafting to 'win over conservatives'.[2] Attorney-General Mark Dreyfus had presented the Working Group with a proposed change intended to prevent potential litigation arising from the Voice's advice to the executive. He wanted to adjust the third clause to read: 'The Parliament shall, subject to this Constitution, have power to make laws with respect to the composition, functions, powers and procedures of the Aboriginal and Torres Strait Islander Voice, *and the legal effect of its representations* [my emphasis].'[3] Adding the seven words at the end made more explicit the intention that Parliament would have power to control any legal effects potentially flowing from the Voice's advice to the executive.[4]

It was later reported that the solicitor-general, Stephen Donaghue, did not think the extra words were legally needed. He likewise did not recommend removing the Voice's ability to advise the executive, because he thought the current wording was sound.[5]

Noel raised concerns about the proposed change. He felt the new words could encourage future parliaments to legislate to undermine the operation of the Voice. Not only would the words make clearer Parliament's power to remove any obligation on policymakers to even consider the Voice's advice (a power it already had under current drafting), they might actively invite future parliaments to use this power to curtail the Voice's influence. Overemphasising this ability would basically say: 'Hey, politicians, you can legislate to undermine the voice if you like. Maybe you should?' It demeaned the spirit of the proposal. Given the consternation at the prospect of Indigenous people advising the executive at all, the possibility of future bad-faith dealings to prevent their advice from even being considered by policymakers seemed plausible.

I took on board Noel's concerns. I also felt that the fears being stoked about Indigenous engagement with the executive were specious. Implementing hasty changes to appease the fearmongers would be rewarding bad behaviour, and without any promises of conservative support in exchange. There was no evidence that Dreyfus's proposed change had been developed with Coalition members, let alone Dutton, and no indication that Liberal support would be forthcoming if the change were adopted. Yet again, a unilaterally devised compromise would mean a concession from Indigenous leaders with no political pay-off. I therefore opposed the change.[6]

There was also no assurance that fearmongers would be appeased. New scares could be raised. *The Australian*'s Chris Merritt argued the Dreyfus change would allow Parliament to usurp the judiciary's role, in contradiction to the separation of powers under Chapter III of the Constitution – creating plenty of scope for litigation.[7] This demonstrated that the proposed refinement was unlikely to minimise the wider fear campaign.

My other concern was timing. Wouldn't it be better to make drafting concessions during the upcoming parliamentary committee process, and even then only in exchange for bipartisanship? If a change were made before then, and without Coalition involvement, more changes would be demanded through the subsequent process. Plus, a change made via the committee might be better publicised than a change made via closed-door meetings.

The Referendum Working Group rejected Dreyfus's change. Further meetings resulted in an alternative compromise. It was agreed that the concerns about advice to the executive would be addressed via a different adjustment to sub-clause three, which would read: 'The Parliament shall, subject to this Constitution, have power to make laws with respect to *matters relating to* the Aboriginal and Torres Strait Islander Voice, *including* its composition, functions, powers and procedures [my emphasis].' This had a neat reciprocity. Under clause two, the Voice had broad discretion to advise on *matters relating to* Indigenous people, and the adjusted clause three gave Parliament broad discretion to legislate on *matters relating to* the Voice.[8] This created balance. It strengthened Parliament's power over the Voice and answered concerns about High Court uncertainty. The adjustment elegantly reconciled the Indigenous desire to have a voice in laws and policies affecting them with the desire of politicians to maintain parliamentary supremacy over all the Voice's interactions with Parliament and government. The expansion of Parliament's power over the Voice's operations created a refined synthesis of the competing concerns, thanks to the willingness of Indigenous leaders to shift yet again to accommodate conservative objections.

On 23 March 2023, the prime minister and the attorney-general held a dramatic press conference flanked by the Indigenous MPs and Indigenous members of the Referendum Working Group. The government announced the referendum question, which by now had been updated to comply with the *Machinery Act*: 'A Proposed Law: to alter the Constitution to recognise the First Peoples of Australia by establishing an Aboriginal and Torres Strait Islander Voice. Do you approve this proposed alteration?' They also announced the design principles that would guide the Voice's operation. And they announced the revised constitutional wording.

Asked whether the forthcoming committee process would contemplate more drafting changes, the prime minister said the adjusted words could be altered if people 'have the numbers'. But the Liberals didn't have the numbers. The thirteen-person committee included three Liberals and one National, given Andrew Gee was now independent, having quit the National Party in protest at its opposition to the Voice. The PM said it would 'take a lot of convincing' for him to support further changes. This remark did not seem to welcome bipartisan collaboration, but it was understandable: further changes would be pointless unless they delivered Liberal support.

The final constitutional compromise was not properly sold or explained. The reasons for the drafting change got lost in the noise. The 23 March press conference seemed more geared towards making the emotional case: for Australians to vote 'Yes', they needed to feel it in their hearts. The problem was that undecided or wavering voters also needed to be persuaded via their heads. If some had been spooked by the legal debate, their fears needed to be assuaged.

While Albanese tried to explain the latest drafting refinement, his explanations were unclear.[9] What he or the attorney-general needed to clarify was that sub-clause three had been changed to expand the power given to Parliament, to make it extra clear that Parliament would control all issues 'relating to' the Voice – including whether its advice needed to be considered, whether notice had to be given to the Voice about particular decisions, and whether it needed to be proactively consulted. Albanese or Dreyfus needed to explain how this change elegantly addressed concerns about unintended consequences flowing from the Voice advising the executive.

Constitutional experts were left to elucidate this independently. Government lawyers briefed the media that the inclusion of the words 'relating to' and 'including', while more subtle than the Dreyfus formulation, in fact gave Parliament even more power to control all aspects of the Voice's operations.[10] Twomey explained that the change empowered Parliament 'to specify the legal effect of the Voice's representations', which 'achieved the same thing as the seven words proposed by Dreyfus' – just in a more subtle way.[11] This was no substitute for the government explaining these things on live TV. The politicians should have spelled out that this was a compromise.

Despite the poor marketing, this final constitutional compromise is an important fact of the history. Indigenous leaders and the government made a final concession to critics. They shifted yet again to address conservative concerns. One paper called it a 'peace deal' that the government hoped would foster bipartisanship.[12] But a peace deal with whom? The final compromise arose through negotiations between Indigenous Working Group members and the Labor government, without the Coalition's involvement. The concession did not come with a commitment to bipartisanship, or any promise that key protagonists of the fear campaign about executive government would now cease their attacks. As it turned out, this final compromise might as well not have been made. It was ignored in the forthcoming debate and delivered no political pay-off.

※ ※ ※

Craven ensured that the final compromise was not seen as one. He declared the revised drafting a 'ruthless con job', not a compromise. 'The right of the voice to mesh the executive government in complication and litigation ... is unchanged,' he wrote. 'Frustrating legal challenges will multiply like cockroaches.' Craven dismissed Albanese's calls for bipartisanship as a 'joke' and said Dutton's opposition was now 'inevitable', because the 'overreaching' Indigenous radicals had got their way. This time he named the object of his acrimony: 'The standout is Megan Davis, the driving force behind the current fatally flawed proposal, and inevitable referendum defeat.'[13]

The 'No' case immediately capitalised. Warren Mundine told ABC radio that Craven's comments proved the Voice would be a debacle. 'You even have Professor Greg Craven, who was a strong conservative supporter of the Voice, now coming out saying it is a disaster. We are going to be in litigation for the next ten to fifteen years,' he said.[14] Meanwhile, Craven was reported in the *Daily Mail* as saying the revised amendment would enable the Voice to comment on 'everything from submarines to parking tickets', leading to 'regular judicial interventions'.[15] This contribution was so useful for the 'No' case that it was quoted in the official 'No' pamphlet, right under a quote from an op-ed by Davis and Appleby, which said Parliament would be unable to 'shut the Voice up'. Craven was apparently furious: as a Voice supporter, he claimed his words had been taken out of context.[16] Was he that naive? How did he expect Voice opponents to use his words?

The proximity of the two quotes in the 'No' pamphlet felt strangely fitting: like the end of an epic feud in which the protagonist's grudge comes full circle to bite him on the buttocks. Davis had been the source of much of Craven's consternation because he felt her contributions were unhelpful to the 'Yes' cause. Yet there the two quotes were – progressive and conservative, yin and yang – finessing the 'No' case with a sense of political equilibrium. The two quotes immortalised together should have been a mirror for Craven. Who was he now to throw stones at Megan Davis?

Albanese noted again that the Liberals had not been forthcoming with any proposed amendments to the drafting since July the previous year, notwithstanding his invitations to suggest changes. 'Not one suggestion' from Dutton or Leeser had been received over eight months, the PM said. 'Not a word.'[17] Despite the Liberals' intransigence, Voice advocates had yet again tried their best to address conservative concerns.

❧ ❧ ❧

Looking back, it is remarkable the extent to which key players have re-written history to sustain the fallacy that Labor and Indigenous leaders unilaterally caused the failure of bipartisanship that led to the referendum's defeat, instead of the Coalition, which rejected the Voice for electoral gain. Sitting on the ABC's referendum-night panel, Liberal MP and co-chair of the 2023 parliamentary committee Keith Wolahan stated that the Liberal Party opposed an Indigenous Voice on principle, because it would divide the country by race. When David Speers pointed out that such ideological opposition meant the Liberals would never have compromised to facilitate bipartisanship – no extra detail or redrafting of the amendment could have shifted their in-principle stance – Wolahan obfuscated. We could have had a constitutional convention to facilitate a compromise, he argued. But how would a constitutional convention have shifted the Coalition's politically and ideologically driven opposition? It would have only amplified division, as it did prior to the republic referendum.

Even Voice supporters such as Andrew Bragg, who knew the Voice was conceived as a compromise with conservatives, and whose 2021 book outlined some of the additional compromises made by Indigenous leaders over several years, adopted the 'Labor did not compromise' line. In July 2023, he told 2GB radio that the government had 'made no concessions, no changes, and insisted upon no changes',[18] ignoring the final compromise made in March. Joining the ABC panel after the 'No' result was called, Bragg further claimed that more compromise from Labor might have seen a greater number of Liberal politicians voting

'Yes', as occurred in the republic referendum when the deputy leader, Peter Costello, voted 'Yes'. Yet the Liberals were allowed a free vote on the republic, but not on the Voice. Shadow cabinet members were thus not free to contradict the party's 'No' stance in 2023: Leeser had to resign from the front bench to advocate 'Yes'. While others suggested a free Liberal vote might have been possible had there been more compromise from Labor, could Labor manoeuvring really dictate internal Liberal Party rules?

In retrospect, the final compromise – like the earlier concessions made by Indigenous leaders – should have been saved up for implementation via the committee process, where hopefully it would have garnered greater publicity and been properly explained. However, this would not have fixed the problem of bipartisan support. By the time the committee process began, Dutton had locked in his 'No' stance, which meant the elusive 'perfect compromise' forever being pressed upon Indigenous people could only be another pivot without pay-off. This was the continual charade. Indigenous people were expected to endlessly compromise in exchange for nothing, yet when concessions were made they were blasted, disowned or erased by the very people they were meant to appease. Coalition opposition has in fact followed every compromise Indigenous people have ever made in the Indigenous constitutional recognition debate.

Grasping at straws, Brennan claimed on Sky News that adopting his latest narrower proposal would at least ensure Leeser and Bragg would 'come on board'.[19] But they were already Voice supporters, so what did Brennan mean? Did he mean Indigenous leaders and Labor should adopt his preferred drafting because doing so might at the very least persuade Leeser and Bragg to cease the partisan sledging and instead help persuade Australians to vote 'Yes'? If that was the only political pay-off – that two on-the-record Liberal supporters of the Voice (including one Voice co-creator) might pull their socks up and advocate properly – it was surely the worst compromise in constitutional history.

# 14

# A NOBLE POLITICIAN

The standout character in this story is Julian Leeser. Let's rewind a little to consider his role.

During the first several months of 2023, Leeser critiqued his own proposal from Opposition. He tested the government's knowledge of the constitutional reform he helped devise and tripped them up repeatedly. Leeser knew the answers to the questions he asked. But as a lonely Voice supporter in a party of mostly opponents, he was in a difficult position. Still, we always hoped a true leader might rise above partisan politics to stand up for Indigenous people and a decent, modest reform. Ultimately, Leeser did.

In the end, Leeser showed courageous leadership in defence of our constitutional compromise, at immense and ongoing personal and political cost. Alongside Chris Kenny, Andrew Gee and Bridget Archer, Leeser became one of the best right-wing advocates for a constitutional Voice – and perhaps one of the best advocates full stop – in the months leading up to the referendum. Though his hard work didn't undo the damage done in earlier months, Leeser's ultimate stance deserves recognition. He stood up for what he believed in, notwithstanding negative career ramifications. Such conviction and principle are rare. Leeser is the only reason I retain some faith that collaboration across political divides might still be worthwhile, despite our polarised politics and the referendum result.

It took a while for him to get there. In March 2023, Leeser asked Linda Burney whether the Reserve Bank would 'need to consult with the Voice before making a decision on interest rates'. The question was designed to trip up the government. Burney responded that the Reserve Bank was independent. Later, she argued that 'not even the prime minister can influence the reserve bank'.[1] The minister could have answered Leeser's question more technically. Leeser had asked whether the RBA would 'need to consult with the Voice' on interest rates, which was an absurd suggestion. There was no constitutional obligation for anyone (or any organisation) to consult the Voice. Any such obligation would need to be articulated in legislation. And it was inconceivable that Parliament would require the RBA to consult the Voice on interest rates.[2]

The prime minister tried to hose down Leeser's questions but made mistakes, which the 'No' campaign exploited. 'The voice is about matters that directly affect Aboriginal and Torres Strait Islander people,'[3] he told reporters. Using those words – 'directly affect' – was a misstep. It did not accurately describe the Voice's proposed constitutional remit, so experts were forced to contradict the PM.[4] Opponents capitalised on the divergence, and the government looked like it did not grasp its own constitutional change.

Albanese could have explained that the Voice's constitutional remit was deliberately broad to limit litigation while maximising practical benefit. It prevented litigation about what the Voice could advise on, making this a political judgement. It also meant the Voice could alert the government to unintended impacts of laws and policies *in*directly affecting Indigenous communities, to help improve those policies. (An environmental law, for instance, might inadvertently stymie economic development on Indigenous land.) Such flexibility and discretion were essential for practical impact.

The PM could also have explained that the Voice would naturally confine its advice to matters of most importance to Indigenous communities. It would not squander its influence and resources advising on parking tickets or submarines. If it did, its influence would wane and Indigenous communities would boot their representatives out. As Burney later clarified, the Voice would prioritise health, housing, jobs and education,[5] which were the issues that mattered most to communities. And if the Voice did give unrequested, frivolous advice on submarines or lighthouses, what would be the effect? Its advice would be ignored.

In the following days, Albanese refined his answer to the legal remit question: 'The wording of the referendum … makes it very clear that it is about matters that affect the lives of Aboriginal and Torres Strait Islander people. That is what this is about – the ten-year gap in life expectancy. It is about doing something about that,' he said.

Albanese started quoting Leeser's previous assertions of support for a constitutional Voice back at him. 'The shadow attorney general has actually been involved in a deeper way in this process for longer than I have been,' the prime minister noted, characterising Leeser's questions as 'disingenuous'. The PM challenged Leeser to 'have the courage to stand up for the principled position he has historically taken on this issue'. Leeser responded that he had always supported the Voice but disagreed with the government's mismanagement of the referendum. He described the approach as secretive and unwelcoming of input from anyone except a select few Indigenous leaders. 'The prime minister should be building bridges not throwing stones,' Leeser chastised.[6]

Two sides are needed to build a bridge, I thought.

~ ~ ~

On 3 April 2023, Leeser delivered an address to the National Press Club. He now admitted his role as a co-creator of the Voice in 2014. He explained that he supported the idea because he believed 'better policy is made when people affected by it are consulted'. As a conservative, he believed in subsidiarity. By 'empowering people, building institutions that shift responsibility and decision-making closer to people and local communities, we are more likely to be successful in shifting the dial on Indigenous affairs', he said.[7] Leeser explained that he had signed up to the Voice because it worked through 'political influence not judicial veto', but clarified that the original words 'were never meant to be inviolable'. He saw our 2014 drafting as 'Voice Version 1.0'. Leeser's admission that Voice 1.0 had been co-devised by him in 2014, not in 2022 by Anthony Albanese, was an important adjustment to his narrative.

Leeser critiqued the Labor government. The prime minister had made the Voice a 'signature policy', he said, but had abandoned the 'deliberative process of the past decade' via which the Coalition had been 'finding common ground, building coalitions … and working across the aisle'. Labor instead pursued a 'top-down' approach, ignoring 'calls for a process to settle the constitutional amendment before presenting it to the parliament' and disregarding other proposals by Clegg and Brennan. Leeser noted that the PM's comment, that he would 'take a lot of convincing' before supporting any drafting changes, did 'not sound like … a person looking to reach consensus'. There had been no 'substantive engagement' to facilitate bipartisanship, Leeser argued. Occasional 'calls and chats before announcements' were 'politeness', not 'partnership'.

Leeser painted a picture of complete Labor incompetence and failure to work across the aisle. Reading his words again, I am forced to consider whether the Labor government is more to blame for the referendum result than my analysis thus far has allowed. Then I remember how this issue was in fact managed under a Coalition government, and I realise responsibility must be shared. It is not accurate, as Leeser claimed, that the Coalition years were characterised by bottom-up engagement and the forging of common ground. Notwithstanding that

Leeser, as a Voice co-creator, was in the Parliament with the Liberals from 2016, Turnbull in top-down fashion tried to manipulate the Referendum Council towards a symbolic constitutional outcome (which Leeser had long opposed for constitutionally conservative reasons). Turnbull chose not to engage with Noel's suggestion to pursue a revised legislate-first strategy, instead unilaterally rejecting the Voice in 2017 and misrepresenting it as a 'third chamber'. While Leeser, with Dodson, did good work on the 2018 Joint Select Committee on Constitutional Recognition, keeping the Voice alive in the face of a hostile Coalition, the subsequent prime minister, Scott Morrison, nonetheless echoed Turnbull's rejection. And what about the fact that Dutton had neither replied to Albanese's invitations to suggest drafting changes nor proposed any refinements during the last eight months?

While the Coalition was better than Labor at putting in place processes to progress but also delay resolution of this issue, it never took ownership of the proposal co-devised by one of their own. The Coalition had eight years since 2014 to own the Voice as a conservative reform, yet that still didn't happen after Leeser became the Shadow Minister. There is no evidence to suggest the Coalition would ever have put the Voice to the people. Turnbull's assessment that 'there was never any prospect of the voice amendment receiving formal Coalition endorsement'[8] seems in retrospect a fair summation. Leeser's analysis left out these observations. His exoneration of the Coalition was coloured by his partisan loyalty.

Leeser then made two suggestions to get the referendum process back on track. First, the government should commit to implementing local and regional voices, as outlined in the Calma–Langton report. He said the Liberals would 'back it in', but when Burney endorsed local and regional voices in May, the Liberals offered the government no praise. Second, he proposed big cuts to the constitutional amendment to address concerns raised about the Voice's ability to advise the executive. Critiquing the expert advice and the explanatory memorandum's assertion that Parliament would remain in charge of the Voice's operations, Leeser noted that 'you can't out-legislate the Constitution' – a line Peter Dutton also used in making the 'No' case. Leeser thus proposed removing sub-clause two of the Voice amendment in its entirety, deleting the Voice's function of advising both Parliament and the executive. Without this sub-clause, the amendment would just tell Parliament to set up a body with no specific role, and the rest would be left to legislation.

I was shocked by this suggestion to gut the constitutional change. It would take away the guarantee that Indigenous people could give advice on laws and policies affecting them, which was the whole point of the reform. I wondered if this was Leeser's ambit claim. Perhaps he hoped the extreme demand would prompt negotiation, which might result in a final model akin to what Brennan and Clegg proposed, removing the Voice's ability to advise the executive.

Noel and I refuted Leeser's proposal in our joint submission to the parliamentary committee, arguing it was not a constitutionally conservative suggestion, because the Constitution does not require Parliament to establish random bodies with no particular purpose. We feared that, if advice to the executive were removed from the constitutional amendment, advice on policy would most likely not be required under the legislation in any enduring way. The pushback against it had demonstrated that many in power would prefer not to have to deal with Indigenous communities when making policies about them. Yet repeated Productivity Commission reports on Australia's failure to Close the Gap confirmed that governments and bureaucrats routinely ignore advice from Indigenous communities, which is why programs and policies fail to address Indigenous disadvantage. Assuming true partnership would happen without a constitutional commitment was therefore naive. The referendum needed to compel real change. It was inconsistent to argue on the one hand, as Leeser and others now did, that the Voice must achieve practical results, but on the other hand that its constitutional role in giving advice on policy must be removed. This would remove its practical substance, undercutting the whole purpose of the proposal.

Advice to the executive was not something Indigenous people could lightly give up. Certainly not in exchange for nothing.

❖ ❖ ❖

The day after Leeser's Press Club speech, a poll showed a majority of Australians in a majority of states still supported guaranteeing an Indigenous Voice in the Constitution. The Newspoll survey signalled 'the likelihood that a referendum would meet the critical double majority test to succeed' if it were held that day, because 54 per cent of all Australian voters supported the proposition, with 38 per cent opposed.[9] But the next day, two days after Leeser's speech and four days after the Liberals lost the Aston by-election to Labor, Peter Dutton and the deputy leader of the Opposition, Sussan Ley, declared a 'resounding "no" to the prime minister's Canberra Voice'. Once the Liberal Party had declared its formal 'No' position, the 'Yes' vote began to seriously fall.

Dutton said the Liberal Party had decided to campaign against the Voice referendum because it would be a 'divisive Canberra Voice' composed of 'academics' – a mischaracterisation of the Coalition's own Calma–Langton report, which Leeser had encouraged Labor to endorse. Dutton also said unnamed Indigenous elders had urged him to oppose the referendum. He complained again about the lack of detail and said it was clear the prime minister would refuse to compromise on the constitutional drafting.

The prime minister responded on radio, reminding listeners that 'no Liberal or National Party leaders [had come] forward with any alternatives or any suggestions' since he released the draft words at Garma, despite repeated invitations.[10] Note the word 'leaders'. Leeser had put forward changes in his Press Club speech earlier that week, but Dutton's formal opposition had undercut Leeser's bargaining position, eliminating the possibility that those suggestions – or other drafting changes – could be adopted by the government in exchange for Liberal support. Bipartisanship had been taken off the table.

Reflecting on the timing of Dutton's decision, the Aston by-election was probably decisive. It was a devastating failure for the Liberals. Aston was a Liberal heartland seat, and no government had won a seat off the Opposition in a by-election since 1920. The media had predicted a Liberal victory, with Dutton supposed to appeal to less wealthy parts of the electorate. He didn't. The Aston result would have meant increased pressure to use the referendum to slam Albanese in Liberal electorates, particularly in those battler demographics the Liberals needed to win back. What better issue than race to re-engage the Liberal base?

That Dutton's decision to lock in a 'No' stance closely followed key efforts at compromise by Voice proponents is also worth noting. Given compromise was seen as a risk by the hard right, the drafting concession implemented by the government in late March might have put Voice opponents on high alert. They didn't want the public to see Labor concessions. They wanted a stark partisan battle. As poorly publicised as it was, this final compromise may nonetheless have inadvertently increased pressure on Dutton to declare a 'No' position, lest the partisan division so valuable to the 'No' camp be undermined. Leeser's proposal to drastically weaken the amendment, and his suggestion that the Liberals would 'back in' a Labor commitment to local and regional voices, might have also set alarm bells ringing. Perhaps that was why Dutton formalised his party's opposition so soon after that speech, to neutralise Leeser's moves and eliminate hopes of a bipartisan deal.

Dutton did not indicate that his opposition could be flipped if Albanese adopted Leeser's or others' changes. When asked if he would 'support a national voice if there was no obligation for the executive government to consult the Voice', Dutton avoided the question. 'I don't think the prime minister's got any intent on changing anything,' he deflected. What he supported, he said, was symbolic recognition. This did not leave room for a compromise with Indigenous people, who rejected a purely symbolic approach. Dutton nonetheless committed to holding a referendum on symbolic recognition if the Voice referendum failed – a promise he later walked back.[11] He also said he supported legislating local and regional voices, but not a national Voice, which was apparently contrary to what was agreed in Opposition party room discussions.[12]

Noel called Dutton's decision a 'Judas betrayal' of the country. He likened Dutton to an 'undertaker', preparing a grave for the Uluru Statement. 'Dutton sees his own political future tied up with getting this referendum to fail,' Noel surmised on radio. 'This is more about his calculations about Liberal versus Labor, rather than what's good for the country … He doesn't mind chucking Indigenous Australians and the future of the country under the bus so he can preserve his miserable political hide.'[13]

By May 2023, Dutton was arguing that a constitutional Voice would 're-racialise the nation'. Noel pointed out the 'duplicitous' nature of this argument, which contradicted what Dutton had told him in private meetings.[14] This was all about slamming Albanese and Labor. It had nothing to do with what Dutton personally believed.

Dutton did not allow a conscience vote on the Voice referendum, despite Leeser and others pushing for one. Former prime minister John Howard endorsed Dutton's decision, even though he had allowed a conscience vote in the 1999 republic referendum. First, he said the republic involved more structural change than the Voice, so it warranted a conscience vote whereas the Voice did not.[15] Then Howard claimed it was because the Voice was not a moral issue, but the republic was.[16] It was a baffling double standard – which no one could ever suggest was informed by racism – but Dutton agreed. Same-sex marriage had been a moral issue warranting a free vote, he told the press pack, but giving Indigenous people a Voice was not.

Leeser was absent from Dutton's announcement of the party's 'No' stance on 5 April. A few days later, after the Easter long weekend, he resigned from the shadow cabinet. On 11 April, Leeser explained his decision:

> Almost ten years ago, I sat down with a small group of constitutional conservatives and Indigenous leaders and worked on a proposal for constitutional recognition.
>
> The idea we developed was different, it was organic, it was consistent with our constitutional heritage, and it was a uniquely Australian idea designed for Australian conditions.
>
> The proposal was called the Voice.
>
> It was a voice for Indigenous communities to our national leaders.
>
> It was a way of achieving constitutional recognition that Aboriginal and Torres Strait Islander Australians have loved this land for centuries but it also had a practical aspect.
>
> It was about creating a new structure to improve the lives of Aboriginal and Torres Strait Islander people.
>
> And it was about finding common ground.
>
> I was so committed to this idea that I even set up an organisation called Uphold and Recognise to encourage constitutional conservatives to support the idea of a voice and to get involved in the debate.
>
> With a referendum due this year I believe the time for the Voice has come ...
>
> I believe the Voice can help move the dial on Indigenous education, health, housing, safety and economic advancement.

Leeser said that, despite many respectful conversations, 'the Shadow Cabinet and the Party Room and I have taken a different position in relation to the Voice'. His resignation was about 'trying to keep faith with the very chords of belief and belonging that are part of who I am'. He had 'tied his colours to the mast' on the Voice before he entered Parliament, he later told the *Australian Financial Review*. The journalist Michael Pelly said Leeser had emerged as 'the most principled politician in the land'.[17]

While Leeser said he would still advocate the drafting changes he had proposed over coming weeks, he committed to campaigning 'Yes' even if his suggestions were not adopted.[18] Leeser became one of five former Liberal ministers for Indigenous affairs who vocally supported a constitutional Voice. Ian Viner, Fred Chaney and Peter Baume, who all headed up the Indigenous affairs portfolio during the Fraser government, declared on 18 April that they supported Leeser and Ken Wyatt (who had recently quit the Liberals in protest at Dutton's opposition). They intended to vote 'Yes'.[19] These senior and respected Liberals understood the complexities and challenges of Indigenous affairs policy. Their united support was significant but gained little coverage in the media.

Leeser's resignation speech was one of the best I'd heard. We needed more of his kind of leadership in this country. Perhaps our collaboration was worth it after all, I thought.

The moment was double-edged. Jacinta Nampijinpa Price, the face of Advance's 'No' campaign, would soon replace Leeser as shadow minister for Indigenous Australians.

∽ ∽ ∽

A parliamentary committee had been established to scrutinise the constitutional alteration bill over six weeks. Dutton had locked in the Liberals' 'No' stance before its work began.

Leeser, Brennan, Clegg and U&R all advocated for changes to the amendment to address the legal concerns they had been raising. On

14 April, Craven told the committee the amendment he co-created in 2014 had morphed into a 'cyanide-flavoured icy pole' in subsequent iterations. When asked to explain why his original drafting was sound whereas the present drafting was apparently poisonous (despite their clear similarity, given both included advice to the executive), he gave no coherent answer. Yet Craven exhibited notable pride in his work on the Voice, even while he trashed his own idea. He boasted that it was 'designed in my study at ACU by me, Noel Pearson and Julian Leeser'. He was 'one of the four people in the room when it was dreamt up', he said.

In fact, there were six people in those 2014 negotiations, if Anne Twomey and I were permitted to be counted as people. It was notable that whenever Craven publicly recalled our early drafting discussions, there were never any women involved in his accounts. It was always the important men doing the work: him, Noel, Leeser and Freeman – always in Craven's 'study'. In fact, our meetings were held in other rooms too, and, unlike at the constitutional conventions of the 1800s, women participated. I wondered if Craven remembered our discussions in grainy black and white, with the men in top hats, sporting long beards and hairy noses. It might explain the vagueness of his recollections about the original legal drafting, as well as the absence of females in his memory. The erasure grated. While Leeser's public recounting always omitted me (unless I was advocating alongside him), Craven's recollections omitted Twomey as well – and she was no lowly adviser. She was one of Australia's most respected constitutional lawyers, and our chief constitutional drafter. Why did she need to be erased? I later realised there was another potential reason. Twomey had published the original drafting agreed with Craven and co., which included advice to the executive. Craven downplayed that connection probably to prolong the pretence that it was absent in the amendment he co-created.

The next day, Craven backflipped again. He explained that his support for the Voice had 'faltered' because he 'watched the Albanese government push it in problematic directions' – confirming that the flip-flopping was mostly about politics. Inspired by Leeser's resignation, Craven had now decided he would advocate 'Yes', even if his preferred drafting adjustment was not adopted. Craven's defence for his strange behaviour was that he was not a 'responsible or a reasonable man'.[20] He forgot that insight after the referendum. When listing the causes of the referendum's failure, he never includes his own actions.

~~~

The Indigenous advocates testifying before the committee overwhelmingly wanted to keep advice to the executive. 'The torment of our powerlessness is partly due to bureaucrats,' former Referendum Council co-chair Pat Anderson explained at the hearing in Canberra. 'Every time there's a change of government, a change of minister and even a new head of department? We all have to come back to Canberra and justify, explain who we are ... We can't get any traction.' Megan Davis explained how Tony Abbott's Indigenous Advancement Strategy had taken funding and resources from Indigenous communities 'without checking what worked and what didn't work'. The role of the executive was very prominent in the dialogues, she said. 'Part of the poor outcomes we have is that our people are just not at the table' with government. Davis later explained how a constitutional Voice would help Australia implement the UN Declaration on the Rights of Indigenous Peoples, which emphasised the importance of Indigenous consultation and participation in laws and policies impacting them. Marcia Langton similarly reiterated the importance of good-faith Indigenous engagement with the executive, drawing on her extensive engagement with Indigenous communities during the Voice Co-Design Process.

Advice to the executive stayed. Labor had the numbers, and the committee report endorsed the constitutional wording without further changes. Several factors contributed to this outcome. First, the floated changes did not have Indigenous support. Indigenous support was important to the government and for public perceptions. Second, none of the proposed adjustments were legally compelling. They did not fix a genuine legal problem, and in fact could create new and worse problems. This was partly because so many compromises and refinements had already been built into the amendment over nine years of evolution, which meant the weight of legal opinion endorsed the amendment without changes. This included the solicitor-general's advice of 19 April, which commended the constitutional wording without adjustment, concluding the reform would enhance Australia's parliamentary democracy. The solicitor-general comprehensively dismissed the suggestion that the Voice advising the executive would 'clog up' the courts, or 'cause government to grind to a halt'. Such advice bolstered the Labor government's decision to reject further changes to the constitutional alteration bill.

Third, while the proposed changes put to the committee were mostly rushed and driven by political tactics, none came with a clear promise of additional Coalition support, let alone a commitment of bipartisanship. Therefore, none of the changes would realistically enhance the political viability of the reform. Although the Liberals' dissenting report endorsed Leeser's proposal to delete sub-clause two, along with other proposals to weaken the amendment, it gave no indication that the Liberals would switch to a 'Yes' position if any of these changes were adopted. Andrew Bragg likewise endorsed adjustments but did not indicate that Liberal support would be forthcoming if his recommendations were taken up. Any such commitments would have contradicted the party's predetermined 'No' stance. So why would Labor agree to legally unnecessary drafting changes for primarily political gain, when no clear political gain was apparent? There had been no political pay-off for the last concession, and there was no evidence that a further concession would be any different.

There is one thing I regret about my testimony before that committee. When Liberal Keith Wolahan was interrogating me about whether

I could endorse any of the watered-down constitutional amendments that had been proposed, I should have asked him straight up: 'Keith, which of those proposed drafting adjustments comes with an offer of Liberal Party support for the referendum? If you can tell me which one comes with a commitment of bipartisan backing, then I can consider whether that adjustment should be made in exchange for bipartisanship.' The answer would have been 'None', not that Wolahan or the other Liberals would have admitted this. They would have done the usual politician thing: 'I'm asking the questions here, not you', or something along those lines. The committee deliberations danced around this central issue, which allowed the Liberals to continue the charade.

A final point must be made about constitutional 'risk', which was the topic of extensive discussion in committee deliberations. The discussions unfortunately framed the negligible possibility of unintended litigation as a negative 'risk' – the preferred term of Voice opponents – rather than as a highly improbable outcome. This ignored the fact that court processes are part of our democratic system. There is no constitutional clause or reform that carries zero possibility of judicial scrutiny. Yet Liberal committee members like Bragg unrealistically wanted the referendum to be 'presented without risk',[21] despite the fact that no constitutional or law reform could ever tick that box. A symbolic insertion, the reform preferred by the Coalition, certainly wouldn't: experts have long warned of the extensive judicial creativity a new preamble could prompt. Nor would removal of the 'race' clauses, the IPA's preferred change, entail no risk: if you remove Parliament's race power without proper replacement, from where would it get the authority to enact or amend laws for Indigenous affairs? Only judges could answer that question, probably with resort to international human rights instruments. In truth, the Voice was the least legally risky constitutional proposal – and the most respectful of parliamentary supremacy – that had ever been on the table in the Indigenous constitutional recognition debate. It is a failure of our democracy that this was not understood.

It was least risky for non-Indigenous Australians, that is. Because who really wore the risks of this proposed constitutional amendment, which began as a compromise with conservatives and already had so many concessions built in? As I argued before the committee in Cairns, the Voice amendment had evolved and been legally refined over nine years, but Indigenous people had been asking for a Voice for decades. 'Think about what they've been through,' I said. 'The dispossession, the policies of discrimination and the historical violence.' Yet 'all they're asking for is a constitutionally guaranteed advisory voice in their affairs', leaving all the details up to Parliament. For Indigenous people, this entailed the real risk that a future Parliament could detrimentally change the composition of the Voice and weaken the institution. Yet Indigenous people were prepared to wear that risk because they are pragmatic. 'This is already a compromise,' I argued. 'They are not asking for much in the grand scheme of things, and I think we should remember that before scrambling to whittle it down to almost nothing.'[22] Labor committee member and former barrister Peta Murphy – who has since passed away – found that argument compelling. 'When you put it that way, who's bearing the risk? It really is First Nations people,' she said.

# 15

# TIPPING POINTS

The months of May and June 2023 were tipping points in the referendum campaign. The constitutional alteration was soon to pass Parliament. We hoped this would spell an end to the damaging legal debate, and the focus would turn to a positive community campaign. Ever since the Liberals had formally opposed the referendum in April, however, the polls had been nosediving. By mid-June, the 'Yes' vote had dropped below 50 per cent. Some big decisions would need to be made.

We tried to ascertain which Liberal opponents would switch to support if Leeser's desired changes – or any proposed changes – were adopted. What new advocates would appear in the Liberal Party if Indigenous people agreed to further concessions? While there never seemed to be a proper answer to this question, it was clear Dutton would not change his position in exchange for some constitutional tinkering. Journalist Michelle Grattan was correct that only abandonment of a constitutional Voice and complete capitulation to symbolic recognition could possibly have delivered bipartisanship, and Indigenous people could never accept that.[1] The best we could expect was that one or two Liberals currently on the fence *might* become 'Yes' voters if certain changes were adopted. But even then it was unclear if they would become active 'Yes' advocates. We were never given a list of Liberals who would come on board if a particular change was implemented.

'These amendments are not about parliamentary colleagues,' Leeser later clarified, confirming that bipartisanship was not up for grabs. Rather, it was about 'securing the support of the Australian people'.[2] The 'electoral prospects for the Voice are not tracking as they should', Leeser warned, and the best way to improve them was 'to limit the arguments of the No case'.[3] Leeser argued that removing clause two would reduce the noise in the debate, which would make the referendum more likely to succeed,[4] but this was unpersuasive given Dutton's opposition would continue even if Leeser's change were adopted. (Plus, some opponents did not agree with Leeser's proposal. Clegg's submission to the committee argued that his suggestion would make matters worse, so that noise would still continue.) Any further drafting adjustments would likely be drowned out and dismissed, just as the March concession was erased by opponents and a compliant media. Indigenous leaders and the government therefore had little incentive to accept Leeser's proposal, which was yet another attempt to get Indigenous people to settle for far less for no payoff. His manoeuvring was unlikely to improve the referendum's prospects but was adding to the false narrative that Labor was refusing to compromise, which was providing cover for the Liberals. Perhaps this was the point. But the risk was that the few remaining right-wing Voice supporters might start recanting that support, spooked by the months-long controversy about the drafting. Leeser 'thinks that he's doing a helpful thing in terms of proposing a last-minute change', Noel reflected at the time, but his 'agenda here is actually damaging to the cause of recognition'.[5]

Leeser had also been lobbying some Indigenous leaders. On 18 May 2023, former social justice commissioner Mick Gooda called for further compromise to stop the referendum failing. 'I'm beginning to be terrified we're going to lose this,' he said. 'It seems the polling is only headed in one way, and that's down. We need to do something to arrest that slide somehow ... I know we've compromised all our lives, but right now, we're right at the pointy end, and if there needs to be a compromise to get over the line, let's do it.'⁶ He called for advice to the executive to be removed from the amendment. Yet Gooda admitted he had not talked to Dutton – so this was not about a deal with the Liberals – though he had been talking to Leeser for several weeks.⁷ After the referendum, Gooda repeated Brennan's 'crash or crash through' line, blaming Labor and the 'Yes' campaigns for the referendum defeat.⁸

Key Indigenous leaders disagreed with Gooda. Noel called Gooda a 'bedwetter' for failing to hold the line on the constitutional drafting, while Dean Parkin said changing the drafting would drag the debate back into legalese. Megan Davis agreed that further changes should not be pursued. Meanwhile, government members reportedly believed more concessions would not stop the partisan attacks,⁹ given Dutton's committed 'No' stance.

On 22 May, Dutton argued in Parliament that 'changing our Constitution to enshrine a Voice will take our country backwards, not forwards'. He claimed there was 'no comparable constitutional body in any other country' – an incorrect statement.¹⁰ He also said the inclusion of advice to the executive would result in a Voice that could advise on any matter and could not be 'shut up'. It would 're-racialise' the nation.

The NSW Liberals began repudiating former premier Dominic Perrottet's support for a constitutional Voice. The new Opposition leader, former barrister Mark Speakman, said he supported a Voice in principle but had concerns about the drafting: 'What we now have is a proposal for a Voice to the executive as well.'¹¹ He had swallowed Brennan and Craven's false narrative, revealing the damage these lies were doing. I urged Noel we should meet with Speakman to explain the true drafting history. We met over Zoom and walked him through the evolution of the amendment.

Speakman didn't come to a settled view until mid-August 2023, when he announced his full support for the constitutional change, saying the rewards would outweigh the risks. However, he said he would not actively campaign for the Voice. He also recommended splitting the referendum question in two to increase its political viability: one question on a symbolic statement of recognition, and one on the Voice. When Speakman emailed his statement of support, I urged him to consider being a proactive advocate. There were too many right-wing Voice supporters who didn't want to help persuade voters, I argued, but without their help the referendum would not succeed. I also argued against his proposal to split the referendum question – an idea Ken Wyatt later endorsed as well.[12] Dividing the question would confuse voters and suck support away from the Voice, plus Indigenous people and respected con cons opposed symbolic recognition. The vote might become split, so both questions might fail.

I didn't expect a reply, but had to try. We needed every Liberal advocate we could get.

❖ ❖ ❖

When it was clear his proposed changes would not succeed, Leeser switched to genuine 'Yes' advocacy. He began confidently answering his own questions about the Voice. This was an important turning point, which should have helped the 'Yes' campaign more than it did.

On 24 May, two days after Dutton's 'No' case speech, Leeser delivered a compelling conservative argument for a 'Yes' vote – his second-reading speech to the constitutional alteration bill that was passing through the houses. It debunked some of the key scares being propagated by the 'No' case. The most prolific was that the Voice would be 'a third chamber of parliament', 'a fourth layer of government' or 'a new House of Lords'. 'I prefer to call it what it is,' Leeser said. 'An advisory body of Aboriginal and Torres Strait Islander Australians, trying to better direct federal government funds to achieve better outcomes.' Some opponents were arguing that the Voice's advice would be so compelling it would have a de facto or virtual veto over government policy. Leeser rejected this too. 'The voice is advisory,' he told Parliament. 'It won't be Moses handing down tablets from the mountain. The parliament will still be the democratic centre of our national life. The parliament will still be supreme in matters of law and policy … And it remains with the Parliament and the executive to weigh that advice, to consider and reflect on it, and sometimes to reject it.'

Leeser then tackled whether the Reserve Bank would have to consult the Voice on interest-rate decisions. Belatedly answering his own question, he clarified that the Voice 'will have no interest in where the Department of Finance purchases its paperclips or its recycled paper, as some have claimed. It will not run programs or dish out grants, and it won't have interest in submarines, as some "No" advocates suggest, as if our subs are going to be painted with Indigenous designs like the fuselage of a Qantas plane. And if the Voice wants to lambaste the RBA on interest rates, I say: Join the queue.' If only he had been prepping the government on how to answer his mischievous question. Better still: if only he'd answered it himself weeks earlier. His speech was brave: it directly contradicted Dutton. Leeser went on to be a highly effective 'Yes' advocate.

Former Nationals member Andrew Gee also gave a rousing second-reading speech in favour of a 'Yes' vote. He reminded Parliament of the history that made the proposal for a constitutional Voice so profound, speaking of two Aboriginal women in his electorate who had suffered discrimination and indignities but who 'never allowed bitterness or hatred' to consume them. Then Gee took aim at the 'No' case, highlighting the hypocrisies of the Coalition. The Liberals 'say they want a constitutional convention on the Voice', he noted, 'yet they have muzzled debate in their own party ranks and it's now cost them their shadow attorney-general'. Gee was unpersuaded by those wanting to weaken the amendment, and noted my and Noel's argument that a Voice to the executive might have prevented the destruction of the sacred site at Juukan Gorge. He also noted that the constitutional conservatives who wanted to 'take away the Voice's ability to talk to the executive' had in the past 'advocated that it should do just that'. Their submissions 'veered towards political opinion rather than sound legal principle', he said. 'If you take out the clause which actually defines the Voice's functions you really will end up with constitutional uncertainty,' he argued. 'It's pretty simple,' Gee concluded. 'If you're a member of the Liberal Party or National Party and you support the Voice, then stand up and be counted ... Be like the member for Bass ... Look at the member for Berowra. The flame of true liberalism hasn't flickered out. So stand up. Stand up and support the Voice.'

Bridget Archer was also compelling. On 22 May, she read out sections of the Uluru Statement and talked about Tasmanian history that saw the Indigenous population depleted by violence, dispossession and disease. 'Abductions of women and children were rife from the very beginning,' she explained, 'paving the pathway towards forcibly removing children from their own loving homes, perpetrating unspeakable pain.' Archer noted how past 'government policies ... led to consistently poor outcomes for the world's oldest culture. We know we cannot change the past, but, this year, we have an opportunity to turn the page and to take the first meaningful steps towards true reconciliation in this country.'

On 14 June 2023, Andrew Bragg delivered his second-reading speech to the Senate. He noted he would vote and advocate 'Yes' because the Voice aligned with Liberal principles and was a sound idea. Bragg nonetheless criticised the government's approach and indicated that he would not do much campaigning. He said the best course of action would have been to establish a parliamentary committee in 2022. 'Instead what we received was a government bill,' he said, and the government was not really open to changes via the committee process. His remarks echoed comments he made on radio the same day:

> I'm worried about the product here. I think that people are turning away from it because they feel that some of the issues have not been

addressed ... I think a better process here would have helped build some centre ground [but] ... the government have not wanted to focus on building centre ground. The committee process we had was a joke. It did not provide a proper opportunity to improve the wording ... But their intransigence and their refusal to engage, I think, has damaged the whole agenda.[13]

The repeated negative commentary from an apparent Voice supporter – like the remarks of Craven, Brennan and, in earlier weeks, Leeser – would have convinced many undecided or soft 'Yes' voters to switch to 'No', contributing to the plummeting polls. Though the remarks criticised the government's approach, they also hurt the prospects of a 'Yes' vote, which was hurting Indigenous people. As I warned at different times: critics should be careful not to punish Indigenous people for the perceived failings of the Labor government.

Bragg's public slamming of Labor's referendum did not harm his political career. He was appointed as shadow assistant minister for home ownership in March 2024 and, after a preselection battle in May, took the top spot on the Liberal Party's NSW senate ticket. Meanwhile, Leeser, who eventually became a highly persuasive 'Yes' advocate, remained relegated to the back bench. It underscored the powerful incentives for Coalition players to use the referendum for partisan attack, rather than stand up for a just and modest reform.

Two days prior to Bragg's remarks, on 12 June 2023, *The Sydney Morning Herald* reported a 'tipping point' in Voice support. The 'Yes' vote was now below 50 per cent, and the 'No' vote was ahead. It was not only Coalition voters who were getting turned off; support among Labor voters had also fallen significantly. Only the support of Greens voters remained stable and high.[14]

Yes23 held 'Come Together for Yes' rallies across the country. The huge turnouts were a massive psychological boost for the 'Yes' campaign. I spoke alongside other advocates at the rally at Prince Alfred Park in Sydney on 2 July, where Rachel Perkins, as emcee, was keeping spirits high. 'What the polls don't really accommodate is this huge, growing movement of the Australian people,' she said to the thousands who had gathered on the sun-drenched oval for a family-friendly day of face-painting and performances. 'You don't see it necessarily on television, you don't see it in newspapers, but there's conversations happening round kitchen tables, in sporting clubs, in workplaces across the country. And that's just going to grow,' Perkins said.[15] I was anxious that the massive 'Yes' crowd should understand that they could not be complacent. The referendum's double-majority criteria would only be fulfilled if every 'Yes' supporter did the hard yards to persuade as many people as they could. 'Persuade, persuade, persuade,' I urged. 'Let's drag this thing over the line.' A woman on stilts roamed the crowd while two guys in kangaroo suits bounced and posed for pictures. My son got his face painted with sparkles in Aboriginal colours.

But while the 'Yes' campaign desperately tried to bring the conversation back to the community, the 'No' campaign framed the referendum as an elitist left-wing project. That weekend, Dutton blasted corporations backing a 'Yes' vote, saying they lacked the 'backbone' to withstand the woke mob. They craved popularity in the 'Twittersphere', he told Sky News.[16] Conversely, months after the referendum, he told business leaders they had a 'moral obligation' to speak up on economic policy, lest they leave a vacuum to be filled by the left.[17] Free speech, for the new right, clearly depends on what you want to say.

The community campaign was heartfelt but inadequate. As Noel once commented, 'We are doing the trench warfare, but we have no air cover. There's no advertising.' Of course, there was advertising. But the costly ads did not persuade enough voters. There was a strange focus on free-to-air TV ads, despite messaging channels being fragmented by streaming services and social media.

A Yes23 ad released in May 2023 emphasised the need to recognise Indigenous peoples in the Constitution and appeared to downplay the Voice. This aligned with advice Noel had received from Mark Textor: the referendum would win if it was about recognition but would fail if it was about the Voice. Some government members disagreed with this strategy: they felt it was vacating the field and playing into the hands of the 'No' campaign.[18] I thought the Voice could not be hidden away in the messaging. The referendum was about recognition through a Voice: the two issues could not be separated. To de-emphasise the Voice would seem sneaky and dishonest. On 22 May, Dutton argued that the prime minister was being 'tricky' trying to conflate the 'two separate issues' of the Voice and recognition in his referendum proposal. 'He wants to leverage the overwhelming public support for constitutional recognition to piggyback his poorly defined, untested and risk-ridden Canberra Voice model,' Dutton said. 'And isn't it telling that the "Yes" campaign's first video ... mentions recognition – but it fails to mention "the Voice" even once?'

The Uluru Dialogue's 'You're the Voice' ad, released in September, was also quickly neutralised by the 'No' campaign. Dutton had a witty response, which linked the song's words to the 'no detail' critique. 'The key line in the lyrics there is ... "you're the voice, try to understand it". I honestly don't think most Australians understand it,' he told Sky News.[19]

A few months earlier, on 12 June 2023, the same day disastrous polls showed the 'Yes' vote had dropped below 50 per cent, Noel publicly admitted that the 'Yes' messaging was confused. He also conceded that he had made mistakes by indulging in personal attacks and vowed to be more disciplined. Noel wanted one united message to come out of the 'Yes' campaign.[20] That was going to be difficult with different campaign entities pursuing different strategies, but Noel took the challenge seriously. With the help of a dedicated team, he became tireless and controlled with his messaging. He stuck to positive themes like love, unity and Closing the Gap. This was about giving Indigenous peoples an advisory Voice to achieve reconciliation and practical results, Noel argued, trying his best to stay optimistic no matter what trouble was brewing in the polls.

❧ ❧ ❧

Why did the Labor government proceed with the referendum, absent bipartisanship and with insufficient support in the polls? Key decision-makers must have at some point considered whether the referendum should be cancelled or postponed. A decision must have been made to carry on. One reason might have been pressure from some Indigenous leaders to keep going. This was Labor's Indigenous-led campaign. Perhaps it was determined to be politically better for the Australian people to reject the Voice, rather than the PM breaking his promise and disappointing some Indigenous leaders by cancelling the referendum. As Victorian Indigenous campaigner Marcus Stewart commented post-defeat, 'We asked for this referendum and the government facilitated the process. The loss of this referendum falls fairly and squarely on us as Aboriginal campaigners.'[21]

Some 'Yes' proponents suggested a change in strategy, however, including some Indigenous advocates. The Uluru Dialogue's Eddie Synot revealed on social media that 'many of us pushed for extension of the referendum date'. The prime minister's office was evidently not keen: the PM had a trip to the US planned later in the year, among other possible reasons. Extending the Voice debate would have been politically undesirable because it would distract from other issues and intrude on the next election.[22] Yes23 were also resistant to postponement, due to the complex investments and planning which made stopping and restarting untenable. No one sought my views, but I didn't think a short-term postponement would help decisively. The polls would fall more with increased time for divisive debate, and campaign funds would become more depleted. Big structural shifts in the campaign's approach were also unlikely, given what I knew of the landscape. Nor would a short-term delay fix the absence of bipartisanship.

In retrospect, the real problem was not that the referendum was held too early, but that it was held too late. The vote came too late in our nation's history. Australia should have resolved this fundamental question in 1901 or in 1967, when it was easier for voters to directly see the problems that needed to be fixed, and when our politics was more amenable to bipartisan cooperation. The discrimination against Indigenous people was more visible back then, their disadvantage more in your face. Indigenous suffering was not so hidden away or packaged up in glossy Closing the Gap reports. Back then our national failure was not veneered by corporate Reconciliation Action Plans, compulsory cultural sensitivity training or prolific acknowledgements of country. These efforts at cultural deference on the one hand have generated misplaced complacency that we are already fixing what needs to be fixed at the heart of our country (which we are not). On the other, they have prompted fatigue in some Australians – including those seated next to me on flights, shifting uncomfortably or muttering 'I'm so over it' when the acknowledgement is recited upon landing. How much more genuflecting did the Indigenous people want?

The longer in history we waited, the harder the challenge became. Our politics became more polarised, and sensible policy discussion more elusive. Social media, the culture wars and identity politics have made it more difficult to build consensus on recognising the rights of the Indigenous minority. The problem was not just right-wing identity politics, which denies that there should be any recognition of Indigenous difference in our society while hypocritically targeting Indigenous people with identity-based smears. Left-wing identity politics also made consensus-building harder. As 3 per cent of the population, Indigenous people desperately needed scores of non-Indigenous advocates to speak out in favour of this change, yet in the present 'pass the mic' era, the non-Indigenous right to speak on this issue was regularly questioned – except, that is, when it came to old white men such as Frank Brennan and Greg Craven, whose verbiage is somehow universally accepted as authoritative. Others were readily attacked for vocalising support, with any wrong move seized upon.

When organisers failed to secure a replacement after the Indigenous speaker pulled out of a pro-Voice multifaith event due to injury on the day, diverse non-Indigenous supporters carried on without an Indigenous spokesperson. I was subsequently admonished online by an Indigenous Voice advocate for contributing to the erasure of Indigenous women, which was 'colonial and violent', I was warned. This kind of thing was common. It was a sign of the times – of the fragmented nature of contemporary progressive politics. Colonial 'divide and conquer' dynamics sometimes seemed more insidiously effective in the tribal age of social media than they had been in the past. Voice proponents could be found trolling each other in defence of a purist Indigenous-led discourse, but to the detriment of a relaxed, inclusive and consensus-building conversation. The dynamic rendered diverse 'Yes' allies more divided and distracted than we should have been, which worked in favour of opponents.

Fifty-six years prior, the non-Indigenous Indian–South Sea Islander and Scottish advocate Faith Bandler, famous for her prominent advocacy during the 1967 referendum campaign, was not accused of 'colonial violence' or erasing Indigenous voices by taking a stand. She was far more prolific and impactful on a national scale than the non-Indigenous advocates who spoke at our small event, yet her contribution was celebrated and her non-Indigenous heritage was not a focus. Back then, there was a level of solidarity that is absent in today's progressivism due to identity-based infighting and bickering over the spotlight. This is evident not just in Indigenous affairs, but across all policy issues. It hampers the left's ability to have the inclusive conversations needed to build broad coalitions to combat shared opponents and propel real reform.

In 2023, any potential 'Yes' advocate who was non-Indigenous faced a double risk. If you spoke out in favour of 'Yes', you would be viciously attacked online by right-wing opponents of the Voice, and you might also get scolded by the left-wing guardians of the conversation constantly policing who gets to speak. In this era of identity politics gone mad, both left and right were contributing the kind of shouty self-righteousness that causes ordinary people to switch off and potential advocates to feel it might be easier to stay silent. Yet the 3 per cent could not win this referendum without widespread vocal allies.

With these factors considered, it might have been the worst time in history for Australians to vote on an Indigenous Voice referendum. Focus-group insights should have raised alarms early on. They revealed that mentioning 'fairness' or statistics on Indigenous disadvantage tended to put voters off, as did talking about the wrongs of history, because it made people feel guilty. This glimpse into the mindset of the electorate in hindsight suggests the referendum was likely a lost cause. For how do you make a case for reform to give Indigenous peoples a Voice, so that better laws and policies can be made, if you are not allowed to talk about the unjust laws and policies of the past? The Voice's practical approach was all about fairness and closing a gap that had its ultimate roots in the dispossession and disempowerment of Indigenous people. Yet campaigners were told they had to 'thread the needle' by providing just enough information to make the electorate feel good about saying 'Yes', but not enough that voters might start to feel guilty about past or present failures. By calling it divisive, amplifying fears and platforming Indigenous spokespeople who made Australians feel okay about voting 'No', anti-Voice advocates effectively destroyed any possibility of the 'Yes' teams threading that needle. Their approach exploited non-Indigenous voters' inherent uncertainty and fearfulness about their own, and Indigenous peoples', place in this country. The messy debate made too many Australians want to tune out, to go back to avoiding the discomfort that lies at the heart of our nation's foundational story.

As these forces played out and the polls kept dropping, the more dramatic prospect of cancelling the referendum – at least until bipartisanship could be achieved, which might take a long time – was apparently not raised on the 'Yes' side. When I've since asked Noel if it was a mistake not to cancel, he says in retrospect it was, but the idea was never discussed. A key reason was that the main 'Yes' campaigns were separate, so these crucial issues were never properly brought to a head within the Indigenous leadership. When I asked if political advisers ever suggested cancelling, Noel said they never did. I now wonder if they were too timid, out of respect for the Indigenous-led campaigns. Yet experienced political experts also confidently influenced important choices made by both the government and Indigenous leaders. There is a bolshie style many advisers and PR people possess; their self-assurance and expertise can be seductive. It is hard to imagine them being shy.

On the right there was Mark Textor, who had been sceptical of the Voice early on[23] but later joined the 'Yes' campaign. The cognisance of the need for bipartisanship is reflected by the fact that Yes23 worked with Textor and other right-wingers, such as Tony Nutt (former chief of staff to John Howard) and Simon Frost (former head of the Victorian Liberal Party and adviser to Josh Frydenberg). While some have questioned whether their Liberal affiliations could have biased the strategic advice provided to Yes23,[24] and Noel often sensed avoidance of any action too critical of the Liberals, Textor's firm, Crosby Textor, also would have lost Liberal friends for helping the 'Yes' side – insights that cancel each other out. The firm has since announced it will no longer work with the Liberal Party on elections.[25] On the left there was Tim Gartrell, former head of advocacy group Recognise. In the early years,

Gartrell had also seemed dubious of our push for a constitutionally guaranteed advisory body, but his view had also evidently shifted: he became Albanese's chief of staff and a key adviser to the government during the referendum. There were many other influential advisers and experts too.

I don't doubt that everyone helping the 'Yes' campaigns was doing their best to win. Nonetheless, I had concerns with elements of the strategic approach. The 'Yes' side had long expressed confidence that polling between 54 and 57 per cent was enough to win the referendum, often sharing these figures publicly to build confidence and demonstrate that the referendum was on track to succeed. My worry was that these numbers were not high enough, because support would drop when the 'No' campaign heated up. 'The pollsters know about polls,' Noel would say in response to my concerns. While my preference would have been to grow the campaign much earlier to increase baseline support, knowing it would fall as the referendum drew nearer, funding and logistical constraints meant this was easier said than done. My other concern was that 'Yes' communications – flyers and explainer documents – were not hitting the mark. Amid the frantic campaigning, however, this problem was not fixed.

Polls kept falling. A fundraising dinner on 30 August 2023 saw Noel, Rachel Perkins and other Indigenous leaders address potential donors, with the prime minister as the headline speaker. At that time the 'Yes' vote was around 44–46 per cent and dropping.[26] The political experts told the audience the vote was winnable. That advice kept coming as polls fell further, with the experts hoping the numbers would turn around, until one day a few weeks before the vote, the consensus became 'This is not winnable'.

I also did not advise Noel or anyone else that the referendum should be cancelled. Partly, I could not see how the freight train could be halted. Partly, I wanted it to be put to the people, to reach its conclusion. Whether there was bipartisanship or not, Indigenous people needed an answer to their request. If the answer was 'No', they needed to be told so they could move on to other strategies. I didn't want to see the referendum postponed – for the cause to drag on for another decade of no bipartisanship and no progress. I couldn't see the government or the 'Yes' campaigns changing strategies decisively, because the same structures would likely remain in place for the foreseeable future. In retrospect, however, this was the wrong attitude. Perhaps my tiredness clouded my judgement. I regret not telling Noel the referendum should be cancelled, because defeat has been disastrous for Indigenous people and the country.

I can now ponder whether the sceptics were right all along: maybe the Voice was unviable because the Coalition was fundamentally closed to the possibility of changing a system that is so badly failing Indigenous Australians. Noel and I, and so many Indigenous advocates, tried hard to work with the right because we knew bipartisanship was crucial. But our experience of the position-shifting of Coalition politicians perhaps contributed to a feeling of resignation, given politics trumped principle for too many on the right, and a determination to try to change things despite their intransigent opposition. For what did bipartisanship mean when so many politicians would tell you one thing in private, then announce the opposite in public? What did bipartisanship mean when some of the conservative co-creators of the Voice proposal failed to defend it in the face of attacks by their conservative colleagues, and at crucial junctures began to attack it themselves? What did bipartisanship mean when Indigenous advocates compromised repeatedly – doing everything possible to accommodate conservative concerns without caving in completely to bullying – while Coalition politicians neither budged nor negotiated? Bipartisanship is meaningless absent a basic level of good faith that makes genuine negotiation possible. There was no good faith from the vast bulk of the right in the end, and no willingness to explore a middle ground with Indigenous leaders. Compassionate and rational conservatism in Australia had dwindled to obscurity. But Indigenous people fought for change regardless.

These observations do not fully answer my question. It will take me years to figure out why we went ahead without the bipartisanship that had been the focus of our whole strategy for more than a decade. Maybe there will never be an answer other than 'hope'. Indigenous people had to try. And as Noel asked back in 2021: 'If not now, then when?'[27] He was paraphrasing the Jewish scholar Rabbi Hillel, to whom the phrase is usually attributed. Anthony Albanese used the same catchcry. Many in the 'Yes' camp probably believed this referendum was 'if not now, then never' – which may have been true. For Indigenous leaders, this was their last, best chance at constitutional recognition, even if the chance was dismal.

# 16

# BROKEN HEART

I was flying around the country advocating for a Voice in the Constitution while my dad was dying in Melbourne. He'd had six months of chemotherapy after getting a pancreatic tumour cut out. He was cancer-free. But the chemo had awakened latent tuberculosis in his system, probably contracted during his childhood in India. The misguided oncologist couldn't believe it was TB; she thought the cancer had come back, though blood tests showed no evidence of that. It was terminal, not treatable, the expert presumed. Mum urged quick TB treatment. She thought Dad could be saved. But Dad, a GP like Mum, listened to the oncologist instead of his wife's medical opinion. He delayed TB treatment, awaiting further tests on the expert's advice. Maybe he was sick of harsh medicines. Maybe he was not thinking straight. But the weeks of inaction meant the disease spread through his body and infected his brain. He died in November 2023, a few weeks after the referendum, while getting belated treatment for TB. Bad advice can be a killer.

I didn't know the full details until it was too late to intervene. I was travelling and advocating: my parents didn't want to bother me. It was only after the referendum was lost that I realised what had gone wrong. By that time, dad had weeks left. Given my efforts could have made little difference to the referendum result, I wonder now if I should have left it to others and made more of a difference with Dad. Regret will be my bedfellow as I wonder 'What if?', both for my father and my country.

୶ ୶ ୶

Noel and I advocated hard while the 'No' campaign's contagious messages infected the brains of Australians. We were doing everything we could, but that was not enough. The 'Yes' side was out-campaigned in traditional media and social media, even as Noel was reassured the situation was not so bad: there were big-name influencers sharing 'Yes' messages, and more ads were coming, campaigners were told. But the promised final wave of advertising never appeared, and the kick-arse social-media strategy didn't materialise.

All we could do was try harder, at event after event. I sometimes spoke at over ten events a week in the lead-up to the referendum. I still felt under-utilised, though I was hardly ever home. My husband picked up the slack while I was away, looking after our two-year-old, who had learned to recognise the 'Yes' logos: 'Vote "Yes"!' he would exclaim, pointing at T-shirts or signs.

Noel and other Indigenous leaders worked harder than me. Noel had his team line up as much media and as many events as possible, as the formal campaign lacked that organisational ability, I presume due to limited resources. He did shopping-centre walks with 'Yes'-voting politicians and handed out flyers at train stations. He spoke to big and small corporations, plus organisations such as the Association of Rhodes Scholars, the Australian Institute of Superannuation Trustees, the Victorian Nurses and Midwifes Conference and Rotary – to name just a few. There was a standout event run by the Australia Day Council in South Australia in May, where John Farnham's song 'You're the Voice' made a rousing debut. The hall was packed and the feeling buoyant.

Working with Yes23's multicultural consultant, Brad Chilcott, Noel and I did extensive multicultural and multifaith engagement, together and separately. Noel spoke to the Queensland African Communities Council – a festive event with dancing, food and rousing interjections during Noel's remarks. They expressed immense empathy for Indigenous people's struggles for acceptance. He turned up to Friday prayers at multiple mosques and found deep solidarity in the Muslim community. He spoke at churches and temples. We engaged extensively with the Indian community, especially in Western Sydney, and Noel did several events with Amar Singh, the Australian of the Year, who took off in a van around Australia to help convince multicultural communities to vote 'Yes'.

We spoke to Aboriginal communities. Noel did two inspiring events on Thursday Island, where the commitment to the Uluru Statement was again passionately declared by local elders, including family members of Mabo and the other plaintiffs. Journalists were invited to travel up, but they didn't make the trip and barely covered the story. He spoke at the Queensland Media Club with the Indigenous mayors of Cape York, all expressing their desperate need for a Voice. Yet volunteers on referendum day were asked on the booths: 'Why haven't we seen any of the women from Aurukun standing up for this?' In fact, those leaders advocated at multiple forums, including forums at which I spoke. Aurukun elder Phyllis Yunkaporta brought one room to tears with her impassioned plea for support following Noel's talk in leafy Ashgrove. Women lined up for hugs and photos with this powerful Indigenous advocate. These moments were publicised and posts were shared, but they got no cut-through in media or social feeds. There was a massive event in Alice Springs with a huge contingent of local Indigenous women rallying for 'Yes'. Jacinta Nampijinpa Price claimed it was a 'rent-a-crowd' and she got more media than the grassroots women. It was hundreds of local Indigenous women saying 'Yes' versus one Jacinta Nampijinpa Price saying 'No', but the press gave Price more than half the airtime.

Noel gave a brilliant lecture to a standing ovation from a packed auditorium at Federation University. He did politics in the pub events and rallies aimed at keeping 'Yes' volunteers energised. He did a multi-party beach walk in Bondi with teal MP Allegra Spender, plus some Liberal representatives, and spoke at community picnics. He went doorknocking, chatting to people in their homes. He spoke alongside Labor heavyweights, including Anthony Albanese, Tanya Plibersek, Linda Burney and Jim Chalmers, but also did events with Liberals like Julian Leeser and Bridget Archer, plus a host of enthusiastic teal independents, who were arguably the most proactive 'Yes' advocates. He even advocated alongside Greg Craven (for some reason). I organised community events for Noel, Leeser and me in Leeser's electorate of Berowra, in Sydney, with my auntie, a local teacher, emceeing. Noel was characteristically compelling while Leeser's localised arguments provided reassurance and calm perspective.

Noel's best persuasion occurred via informal chats at airport baggage carousels. His conversion rate was impressive. Fellow travellers recognised him. There was a constant flow of people either offering support, or saying they were 'No' voters who wanted to learn more, then converting to 'Yes' after a productive conversation. Children and adults lined up to get selfies. Many expressed gratitude that Noel was 'trying to change our country for the better'. Some were in tears, cognisant of the enormity of the struggle and the fractiousness of the debate.

Some inspiring connections were forged. On the Gold Coast, a family who had lost their daughter to suicide was finding it cathartic to make 'Yes' friendship bracelets, which Noel wore religiously throughout the campaign. There was an event with Afghan cameleers in Queensland who had crafted a generous response to the Uluru Statement, which Noel read out to the massive gathering. 'We, the Gold Coast Afghan community, have heard your call,' it declared. 'With tear-filled eyes, open hearts, and resolute spirits, we pledge to walk with you.' In these moments, love was truly in the air. Hope bubbled in our chests.

At his Press Club address on 5 October 2023, Noel made the case for a 'Yes' vote as an expression of love. 'I mean not love in a saccharine or sentimental way, nor romantic or patriotic love,' he explained. 'I mean in the sense the late English philosopher Roger Scruton called Oikophilia: *oikos*, the Greek for "home", and *philia* for "love" – the Love of Home.' Noel recalled the hundreds of conversations he had had at forums and train stations, in shopping malls and town halls, and under the shade of mango trees. 'It is the love of our Country that joins us all as Australians,' he said.

Noel spoke, too, of the practical challenges a Voice could help address – such as the scourge of rheumatic heart disease, which was 'largely eradicated in the rest of the world but allowed to fester in the Paradise of Cape York and the remote communities of Australia'. The disease kills two Indigenous people per week. Yet upon searching *Hansard*, Noel realised the local member for Cape York, Warren Entsch, 'ensconced in his safe seat for twenty-six years', had never once mentioned rheumatic heart disease in parliamentary debate. It demonstrated the need for an Indigenous Voice to raise such issues with government and Parliament. Entsch was incensed. CYI received an email from a constituent who had emailed the member for Leichhardt to complain about politicians' lack of attention to the disease. They were informed that Entsch had phoned the woman 'within hours' of her email. 'He spoke at length (20 mins or more) on what he had done in the issue, but mostly expressing very vehement criticism of Mr Pearson which bordered on defamation in my opinion.' The woman was 'quite shocked by his aggression towards Noel'.

I advocated alongside other inspiring Indigenous leaders – like Rachel Perkins, Dean Parkin, Jade Appo-Ritchie, Sean Gordon, Stan Grant, Marcia Langton, Thomas Mayo, Tony McAvoy, Jill Gallagher, Tania Major, Fiona Jose, Kirsty Davis, plus the hard-working Empowered Communities leaders, including the calm and compelling Tyronne Garstone in the Kimberley, Shane Phillips from Redfern, plus Vickie Parry and the young and passionate Gary Field of Central Coast, New South Wales – and so many more.

I spoke at African, Chinese, Indian, Sri Lankan, Iranian, Greek, Jewish, South-East Asian and Islamic community events around the country, and worked with filmmaker Perkins on a video showcasing the growing multicultural support for the Voice. I spoke at an Indian seniors' gathering, and unexpectedly had to dance with some of the old ladies while another performed karaoke. The chair of U&R, Sean Gordon, Labor MP Andrew Charlton and I debated the Liberal minister Alex Hawke and Warren Mundine at an India Club event in Sydney. The 'Yes' team won the room and the feedback was positive. I felt the Indian community was with us, galvanised by the inspiring 'Desis for Yes' group and others. To my dismay, however, the Hindu Council of Australia, which had publicly supported the joint resolution of peak religious organisations in May 2022, organised nothing to assist community understanding of the referendum – despite my pressing. Prior to the vote, they issued a newsletter platforming 'No' and 'Yes' arguments, with the 'No' proponents taking primacy. They had been happy to support the Voice while the cameras were rolling in May 2022, but, influenced by the Liberal Party, their support appeared short-lived. Too often, community leaders would express support, then equivocate under pressure from Liberals in their ranks. Noel and I got kicked out of a multicultural Lions Club meeting in Sydney, where Noel was meant to give a speech, presumably for partisan reasons.

I spoke at a Greek seniors' gathering, with a translator relaying my words, and my team ran an online forum for the Persian community that was translated into Farsi. I spoke at a Chinese Australian dinner, where I was booked to appear on a panel with Warren Mundine and two other Indigenous advocates. Mundine didn't turn up. With a Liberal contingent in the room, it was a robust and sometimes painful discussion continuing well into the night. It was exhausting, but the organisers did a survey to assess the support of attendees at its conclusion: the vast majority had decided to vote 'Yes', and several more

Chinese Australian organisations signed up to the Multicultural Australia for the Voice website as a result.

These efforts garnered commitments of support from over two hundred ethnic and cultural community organisations. We even launched *Statements from the Soul* at a multicultural event in Hobart with Liberal premier Jeremy Rockliff – a Voice supporter. However, I worried that our extensive multicultural engagement was not reaching enough voters. At a Greek forum, a key leader of a peak organisation complained that while multicultural organisations (his included) were supporting the Voice, information was not reaching their communities. *You as a leader are supposed to help with that*, I thought. While some leaders, such as Amar Singh and Harish Velji, were incredibly proactive in sharing information, others tended to passively complain rather than step up and assist. Together with Yes23, we signed up 'Multicultural Ambassadors for Yes' all around the country. But after they signed up, most went quiet and took no action.

Saying you support something is easy. Actually doing something to assist takes effort many were unwilling to expend, especially in the politically fractious environment. Reticence and inertia were most evident in the many Liberal 'Yes' supporters (politicians and other leaders) who chose to stay quiet rather than help persuade and educate the public. Some swam valiantly against the tide. Former Liberal MP Pat Farmer, for example, self-funded his inspiring run around Australia to raise support for the referendum, using his own vehicle, friends and family as his pit crew and some crowdfunded money to help with fuel. The Indigenous Empowered Communities regions supported Farmer along his route.

Noel and I did webinars for the Buddhist Council, the Anglican Church, the Uniting Church and the National Council of Imams, at which Albanese also spoke. I spoke at carer organisations and healthcare institutes. I educated staff at big and small corporations via lunchtime sessions. These staff sessions were valuable because they enabled me to engage with undecided voters. I also did events organised by local councillors and some Rotary Club meetings. I appeared at a church event alongside Liberal NSW politician Matt Kean, a Voice supporter and one of the most impressive advocates. The host gave me a massive jar of nuts as thanks, handing it over with tears in his eyes. I ate half in my hotel room for dinner, my stomach churning at the prospects of a failed referendum.

I spoke at 'Yes' events with federal MPs – Jim Chalmers, Tanya Plibersek, Chris Bowen, Malarndirri McCarthy, Linda Burney, Leeser and others, including many of the teals – plus one event with former National MP Andrew Gee, in Bathurst. He gave one of the most compelling conservative arguments for a constitutional Voice I had heard. At a politics in the pub event with Plibersek, I spoke to a man who was leaning 'No'. 'Ask your questions, then let's talk after,' I urged. He approached me when it was over and told me he would now vote 'Yes'. I was jubilant and wanted to hug him. I controlled myself and we high-fived. A 'Yes' organiser later texted to tell me the pub had been full of soft 'No' voters and most had switched to 'Yes'. I was happy, but those shiftable audiences were too rare.

I debated Mundine and Jacinta Nampijinpa Price at a CIS event, joining Indigenous barrister Tony McAvoy on the 'Yes' team, but Yes23 preferred that I didn't do debates in front of mostly 'No' audiences. This seemed like another effort to prevent 'Yes' advocates straying into 'No' frames that helped the opposing side. We needed to stick to our positive 'Yes' message, not get dragged onto 'off-ramps' by rebutting the 'No' campaign's scaremongering. Despite these efforts to control the messages being delivered by the multitude of 'Yes' proponents spanning the country, mistakes were made. On 28 September 2023, journalist Ray Martin attended a rally with the PM in Marrickville. Martin criticised the 'No' campaign's 'If you don't know, vote "No"' slogan: 'If you're a dinosaur or a dickhead who can't be bothered reading, then vote "No",' Martin dared Australians. The 'No' campaign used it to demonstrate the 'Yes' campaign's elitism: 'People aren't stupid, they aren't dinosaurs,' Dutton protested on 2GB radio.[1] The mistake was deriding potential 'No' voters as the Australian equivalent of Trump's 'deplorables'.[2] Martin still did a big Channel 7 debate against Jacinta Nampijinpa Price and Lidia Thorpe – the embodiment of the far left teaming up with the right to oppose the Voice. Martin joined Labor senator Malarndirri McCarthy on the 'Yes' team, framing the 'Yes' case squarely as a leftist agenda. Andrew Bolt, with his limited repertoire, attacked Martin's fair skin in his blog.

Despite harnessing right-wing expertise, the whole 'Yes' strategy was by now fatally skewed to the left. And though my engagement with right-leaning outlets was discouraged, it was nonetheless noticed in unlikely places. When I travelled to Indigenous communities, I was shocked to hear Indigenous people – especially women – say they watched those Sky and CIS debates and learned much from them. 'Go, sister!' they would say. These comments buoyed my spirits. There was solidarity across ethnic difference on the 'Yes' side after all, I reflected. I felt it more in remote Australia than in urban centres.

I joined the Kimberley Land Council's referendum 'roadshow' in Western Australia, visiting Halls Creek, Dubbo, Fitzroy Crossing and Kununurra with Dean Parkin, Tyronne Garstone, Rachel Perkins and other Indigenous speakers. It reminded me why I was putting in the effort. Urgent problems faced by these communities included unhealthy and overpriced food in local shops contributing to poverty and health crises, youth disengagement and crime, poor educational outcomes and inadequate housing. Their concerns underscored the absurdity of suggestions that the Voice would be advising on submarines, paperclips and parking tickets.

The discussions were also emotional. Participants talked of the need to right past wrongs, to create a fairer Australia and a better future for their children and grandchildren. Many carried historical wounds, yet they expressed love for their fellow Australians and hope for the future. They expressed the need for healing, and urged each other to choose friendship over fear, and unity over division. 'Please vote "Yes", an Indigenous woman said to a packed room in Derby, wiping away tears. 'I grew up on a station. I've lost everybody. It's been so hard, what we've been through. Our people deserve to be recognised in the Constitution,' she said. 'We deserve to have a Voice. So please vote "Yes". I love you all.' This was one articulation of what this referendum meant to Indigenous Australians asking for an advisory Voice in their affairs. This was the invitation Australians needed to answer, but probably failed to hear amid the partisan noise.

I appeared at the Sydney Town Hall with Noel and Thomas Mayo – a tireless and passionate advocate who had been on the road for years talking to Australians about the Uluru Statement. I was in awe of his energy and work ethic. One of the last times I saw my dad out and about was at a Melbourne Town Hall event in September 2023, when I appeared on a panel following Noel and Jill Gallagher as the headline speakers. Gallagher gave one of the most powerful speeches I had heard, talking about her family's history and their experiences under past child-removal policies. Noel spoke of his disbelief that Australia could refuse recognition of the First Peoples. He was testing out different messages on the road.

At one point, he went back to basics and started taking people through the actual amendment they would be voting on. The amendment was not usually on the Yes23 campaign flyers, but Noel got his team to create a laminated business card with the words of the constitutional change. This became his key tool and was handed out to audiences everywhere, with CYI staff carting tens of thousands of those little cards across the country. I would always show the amendment in my slides. I took to detailing the evolution of the drafting over nine years as well, to show how it had become more modest over time – and to refute the lies voters were hearing about Labor's radicalisation of the proposed change. Time and again, I was told how helpful these explanations were. 'Why are we only hearing this information now?' people would ask. I didn't know how to answer.

As well as explaining the constitutional provisions, Noel's oratory was big and inclusive. He never stopped talking about the three stories that entwine to make Australia: the Indigenous ancient heritage, our inherited British institutions and our multicultural richness. He said the Uluru Statement was an expression of Indigenous Australians' love for their fellow Australians. That love being unrequited was his 'worst nightmare'.

The scariest nightmares happen when you're awake. Not sleepwalking but striding fully conscious into calamity.

As the months of hard work wore on, I knew it was insufficient. Most who attended the events were already 'Yes' supporters – a perennial problem of campaigning. How do you get undecided or uninterested voters to attend and engage? Often you can't. I began to see the same supportive faces at multiple events. Sometimes, I flew interstate to speak at an event with only a handful of mostly 'Yes' voters, with some repeat attendees. It became dispiriting and exhausting. In desperation, I started making social-media videos to refute 'No' arguments. These travelled a bit, but without money behind them they probably had little impact.

I got bad conjunctivitis, then Covid, and did online forums from my bedroom. I can't imagine how tired the Indigenous advocates were. They were more booked up than me, and many suffered serious health problems. Noel had health issues that sometimes hampered his efforts. The inspiring Tanya Hosch advocated through the loss of a leg, caused by diabetes.[3] Patrick Dodson had to retreat from campaigning due to cancer. Linda Burney revealed she had suffered a ministroke and heart problems, requiring medicines that affected her speech.[4] This was the lived reality of Indigenous inequity. They kept advocating through that hardship, even as the polls showed impending defeat.

Noel's optimism started to wane. In a speech at Gilbert + Tobin in the days before the vote, he reflected that Australia was a 'hard country now'. Nothing seemed to persuade white Australians that the Constitution did not 'entirely belong to them'. Noel regretted that the faith he had asked Indigenous Australians to place in white Australia was proving to be misplaced. 'No amount of obsequiousness on our part, humility, love, seems to ever melt their hearts,' he marvelled, noting the modesty of the proposal that was about to be rejected. 'If you were me, and you represented a minority who were the original peoples of the land, would you have been satisfied with a Voice to the bloody parliament?' he asked.[5] This was what was gutting. Australians were rejecting a small ask from the original peoples, who had been mistreated more than any other group in the country. 'Frankly,' Noel remarked days earlier, 'the Voice is a proposal so pathetically understated that I'm amazed most Indigenous people are settling for it. After all, I helped design it as something so modest that no reasonable non-Indigenous Australian could reject it. More fool me.'[6]

Noel said that if the referendum was lost, and this modest reform was rejected, he would never again 'be an advocate for conciliation and compromise'. He would never again urge 'a middle path', because a 'path based on recognition and reconciliation' would no longer be viable. 'We'll have gotten a very clear answer this weekend that those like me, who've championed a middle path, our arguments have not been proven. They'll have been proven to be incorrect.'

Once the middle path dies, we are left only with extremes.

༺ ༺ ༺

We needed cut-through advertising and a winning social-media strategy to get the referendum over the line. The 'Yes' side had neither, despite having more money than the 'No' team. It is unclear why, but making the positive and rational case for reform in a pithy and impactful way is difficult. It is easier to shoot something down than to advocate for nuanced reform. Especially these days. As ALP national secretary

Paul Erickson conceded in December 2023, social media was central now fewer Australians consumed news from traditional sources, but the 'Yes' side was beaten on digital platforms.[7] Yet the dynamics of the online universe were always going to favour 'No', because platform algorithms incentivise negativity, lies, division and hate – campaign strategists must have known this. Without a successful social-media presence, 'Yes' advocates were unable to effectively communicate with voters. By contrast, the 'No' campaign's message – *this will divide Australia by race* – travelled well on social media.

The biggest weakness felt on the ground was that the 'Yes' team's slogan was just that: 'YES'. Volunteers had to explain the Constitution and positively relay the arguments for a Voice in the face of a more incisive 'No' message. Refuting 'No' arguments about racial division involved explaining the history of colonisation and the fact that the Constitution contained race-based clauses, including one that gave Parliament a necessary power to make special laws and policies for Indigenous people. It meant explaining that Indigenous people had been treated unfairly in laws and policies of the past, and that a Voice would help prevent repeat injustice and deliver better outcomes. Volunteers did a good job, but it was a complicated sell. Suddenly, you were bogged down in deep policy conversation. *This will divide us by race* was much easier and simpler.

The 'No' campaign was reportedly facilitated by the Australian branches of the international Atlas Network which, according to UTS researcher Jeremy Walker, is a global infrastructure of 500-plus think tanks, including the Centre for Independent Studies and the Institute of Public Affairs, with experience proliferating disinformation campaigns against climate-change policy.[8] There were reports of involvement by US religious conservatives,[9] while a July report by the Australian Strategic Policy Institute found various X (Twitter) accounts likely connected to the Chinese Communist Party sharing negative referendum content. Experts linked this to a 'covert campaign' by the Chinese government 'to undermine Australia's social cohesion and trust in government'.[10] Prior to the referendum, a 2023 Senate committee argued that Australia's laws were inadequate to combat 'malign foreign interference' in the referendum,[11] but it is unclear what (if anything) was done to address this threat.

QUT expert Timothy Graham warned of a coordinated misinformation campaign on social media, with bots and dummy accounts spreading 'No' messages.[12] Advance created multiple Facebook pages, with one fitted out to look like an unbiased news site, and another featuring left-wing critiques of the Voice as too weak and 'not enough'.[13] On the ground and via the phones, Advance's volunteers had been trained not to identify themselves as 'No' campaigners but to instead raise fears that financial compensation would be paid to Indigenous people in the event of a 'Yes' victory,[14] among other falsities.

The Australian Election Commission (AEC) was targeted with mistruths, including the conspiracy theory about ticks and crosses on the ballot paper, which conjured fears about a rigged process. Dutton amplified that Trumpian lie: 'I don't think we should have a process that's rigged,' he warned on radio, 'and that's what the prime minister has tried to orchestrate from day one.'[15] The AEC's Disinformation Register listed and refuted prominent lies about the referendum voting process. These included claims that postal votes were not safe, that the pencils used in the polling booths meant AEC officials would erase votes, that the referendum would be split into two questions, whereby your vote on one would overrule your vote on the other, and that the AEC would throw out all the 'No' votes.

Other disinformation included the claim that a successful referendum result would allow Indigenous people to confiscate homes, force through treaties and enable a UN takeover of Australia.[16] One TikTok video claimed the Voice was a 'Trojan Horse': it was actually 'a radical call for the establishment of … literally an Indigenous country within Australia'. Another user commented that a 'Yes' vote would enable the 'corporate aboriginals' to 'take our country'. Some voters were told Indigenous people would receive free home loans, free cars or university degrees if there were a 'Yes' outcome.[17] Migrants were targeted with tailored lies via WeChat and other platforms: if you vote 'Yes', your business will have to do 'zero dollar buying' (giving away stuff to Indigenous people), was one warning. Asian students will need to 'score much higher' in exams to compete with Indigenous people for university entrance, was another claim, and your kid's scholarship could be given away to a black.[18]

These were all variations on the same prejudicial message: the Voice will give Indigenous people special treatment, which will disadvantage all other Australians. Noel asked me to play Paul Kelly's 1992 song 'Special Treatment' at an Anglican online forum we addressed. I didn't realise the sound was cutting in and out, but the words are haunting:

*Grandfather walked this land in chains,*
*A land he called his own.*
*He was given another name,*
*And taken into town ...*
*He got special treatment,*
*Special treatment,*
*Very special treatment.*

*My father worked a twelve-hour day,*
*As a stockman on the station.*
*The very same work but not the same pay,*
*As his white companions.*
*He got special treatment,*
*Special treatment.*
*Very special treatment ...*

*Mama gave birth to a stranger's child,*
*A child she called her own.*
*Strangers came and took away that child,*
*To a stranger's home.*
*She got special treatment.*
*Special treatment.*
*Very special treatment ...*

*I never spoke my mother's tongue,*
*I never knew my name.*
*I never learnt the songs she sung*
*I was raised in shame.*
*I got special treatment,*
*Special treatment.*
*Very special treatment*

I wish someone had created a 'Yes' TV ad with that song as the soundtrack, and its lyrics played in full.

❦ ❦ ❦

Many commentators have argued racism was not the main reason for Australia's 'No' vote. It is nonetheless part of the story. Racism was the fuel that made the lies travel.

The referendum reopened the race-based 'wedge politics' playbook followed by John Howard in 1990s. That playbook stoked division, envy and fear on racial grounds. In 2023, Howard became its champion again, urging Australians to 'maintain the rage' by voting 'No'. Rage against the 'woke left', presumably, but the remark could also be intereprated as a provocation of anger against Indigenous people. Howard's unstatesmanlike contribution was indicative of the deterioration of compassionate, rational conservatism. There was hardly any left. No wonder the right failed to appreciate or value the conservative credentials of a constitutional Voice that had been designed with the con cons to respect the nation's rulebook. The political right was now dominated by reactionaries.

Noel responded to Howard's incitement to 'rage' by declaring the 'Yes' campaign would 'maintain the love'. He had to say that. The 'Yes' campaign could not call out the racism animating their opponents' tactics. *When they go low, we go high*, was the discipline. Yet the 2023 'No' campaign was a variation of the 1990s 'two sets of laws' lie (concerning land rights) that Howard had exploited three decades prior – only this time the messages were supercharged by engagement-driven algorithms. Yes23 had been utilising Coalition political experts, including former Howard affiliates Nutt and Textor, with long experience in these kinds of politics. Despite the advice of various Liberal hardheads, however, the 'Yes' campaign could not formulate a cut-through antidote to the prejudice unleashed. There was no easy cure, because generating fear and hate is easy. Inspiring love and generosity is hard.

I was reminded of Noel's 2022 Boyer Lectures, which painted a depressing picture of the barren soil in which 'Yes' campaigners had to sow their message of friendship and hope. 'We are a much unloved people,' Noel reflected. 'We are not popular and we are not personally known to many Australians. Few have met us, and a small minority count us as friends … Australians hold and express strong views about us, the great proportion of which is negative and unfriendly. It has ever been thus,' Noel observed, and though it was 'worse in the past', it was 'still true today'. Noel's striking prediction was that a referendum predicated on Indigenous people's popularity would fail. 'It will not take much to mobilise antipathy against Aboriginal people' or 'conjure the worst imaginings about us and the recognition we seek', he foretold. 'For those who wish to oppose our recognition, it will be like shooting fish in a barrel. An inane thing to do – but easy. A heartless thing to do – but easy.'[19]

The 'No' campaign excelled at shooting captured fish. They effectively exploited longstanding stereotypes of Indigenous people – as welfare layabouts with their hands out for cash, lazy blackfellas looking for 'special treatment' to get ahead, as Aborigines who want to take your land – and repackaged them as scares neatly tailored to the referendum. When the *Australian Financial Review* published an Advance cartoon depicting Thomas Mayo with his hand out for money (the newspaper later apologised), the prime minister responded, 'We'll continue to be positive.' Albanese could not say the ad was racist. He was already falsely accused of calling 'No' voters racist: he could not prove this true. Leeser and some other Liberals like Matt Kean could be more forthright; as right-wing advocates, perhaps they had more freedom. Leeser criticised the 'No' campaign's personal attacks on figures like Mayo, saying the referendum was about constitutional change, not particular individuals. He also countered accusations of elitism and rebutted nonsense claims that the constitutional change was big and radical: 'Based on a lifetime of work ... this is a small change to the constitution,' Leeser insisted.[20]

The digitally amplified dog whistle whipped up something primal. Some 'Yes' events were disrupted or cancelled due to racist threats. Trolls with Nazi motifs on their screens joined some online events. CYI received hundreds of racist emails and letters as the campaign heated up, offsetting the positive correspondence Noel received after media appearances. 'The majority of Aboriginal people don't work but survive on Centrelink benefits!' Lindsay Lake emailed Noel and the Indigenous Labor MPs. 'Your bullshit lying mouth' has been 'fact checked', emailed Wayne McKee after Noel's Press Club address. 'Noel you are a dickhead because all white people could not give a shit with the voice ... Just build a BWS LIQUOR STORE IN DARWIN YOU CAN ALL GET PISSED BECAUSE THATS ALL YOU PRICKS ARE GOOD FOR,' emailed Mark Johnson. Mark Petherick attacked the 'MORONIC KUNT CALLED NOEL (I'm a FUCKHEAD) PEARSON on ya BOOK'S so ya just a DIRTY FILTHY LYING LITTLE BUNCH OF FLOGS'. 'Fuck that nigger Noel,' emailed Lachlan K. 'Die in a fire faggot.' Meanwhile, Kym Whelan told Noel:

> If you have been unable to enrich and improve the lives in 'Cape York', then you do not get to be ensconced into our 'Constitution', to do even more damage, than you have already done, you 'Nasty Divisive Racist'! ... Yes, You are the Racist and your 'Psychotic Ramblings', one minute spewing hate, the next preaching love, doesn't fool any of us! When this 'Trojan Voice' goes down, your racist hypocrisy will be top of the list, as to why it failed ... You are all nothing but 'Racist Elitist Snobs' riding a mythical gravy train, which has reached the end of the line and we say 'NO' to you all!

Others preferred to use caps lock, like the author of this anonymous letter:

> WHY DON'T YOU AS WELL AS ALL THE OTHER FERRAL ABO COONS WAKE UP TO WHAT YES WOULD DO TO THE TRUE AUSTRALIAN PEOPLE - THE ONES THAT FEED YOU BLACK CUNTS FAR FAR TOO MUCH AS IT IS.
>     GO BACK TO THE CAVES WHERE YOU BELONG!!!!!!!!!!!!!!!!!!!!!!!!!!!!!!!!!!!!!!!!!!!!!!!!!!

An Advance TikTok video questioning Mayo's motives attracted comments disputing his Indigeneity. 'I looked at his genealogy, I am more of an Australian than he is. His dad is of Philippines Malay decent,' one user commented. 'Thomas Mayo, real name Thomas Mayor, he is not indigenous,' said another. 'I know he aint Australian and has no aboriginal blood at all. Vote no.' 'Thomas Mayo is a communist grub vote no.' 'He['s] not even Australia blood. go back to the Philippines.' Eddie Synot also received abuse. 'Mass dislike of ghastly boongs,' messaged John Drew via Facebook. Then, to clarify: 'On referendum day it sank like a stone due to the mass dislike of ghastly boongs.'

We can take some solace in the thought that not all the negative and often racist trolling was driven by real humans. As Leeser noted in a speech at Garma, the 'No' campaign was fuelled by online bots and careful 'gaming' of social media algorithms.[21] Real humans came up with that strategy, however, which speaks to the baseness of our politics.

The hate was not only aimed at Indigenous advocates, though they copped the worst. A prominent female surgeon of Asian background received a letter that attacked her for being a 'Yes' supporter. The sender was happy the referendum loss meant 'virtue-signalling, fake lefty abo loving cunts like your good self' would 'stew in your own vaginal juices'.[22] I had to trawl through the comments under my posts and videos daily, deleting, hiding or blocking the coordinated onslaught of racism and hate. I couldn't keep up, which I guess was the idea. I was told numerous times to shut up and go back to India or Pakistan or Sri Lanka. I was told I was an Indian posing as an Aboriginal person. One commenter said my people were still 'burning brides' while Aboriginal people were 'eating their toddlers'.

Around 40 per cent of electors voted 'Yes', while approximately 60 per cent voted 'No'. A comprehensive ANU study of 4000 voters provided insight into the attitudes that informed the referendum results.

It found voters still support Indigenous constitutional recognition, and they support giving Indigenous people more of a say in laws and policies that affect them. Despite the referendum outcome, they still want reconciliation. However, more than half of those surveyed agreed with the suggestion that if Indigenous people 'tried harder they could be just as well off as non-Indigenous Australians', notwithstanding that more than two-thirds also agreed that many Indigenous Australians remained disadvantaged today 'because of past race-based policies'.

The researchers discerned from this data that Australians place responsibility on Indigenous people to overcome the effects of past policies themselves.[23] Ironically, this is exactly why Indigenous people were asking for a Voice: so they could better realise their 'right to take responsibility' and offer solutions to overcome their disadvantage. They wanted to share both responsibility and blame for progress on Closing the Gap. 'By all means, blame us,' Noel argued during the campaign, 'but give us a say in the decisions that are made about us before you do.'[24] This message did not cut through to voters. The Coalition was contradicting it, saying the Voice would not help close the gap. According to the researchers, too many voters did not believe the Voice was the right approach to alleviate Indigenous disadvantage. Australians also voted 'No' because they didn't want division and were wary of extra rights being given to some Australians. This indicates that the 'No' arguments resonated.

The study suggested lack of bipartisanship was a key reason for the referendum's failure.[25] It confirmed that the vote was viewed as a left-wing cause: 'left/right identity' was a factor in voting choices, and voting results were 'tied closely to the two main party leaders'.[26] Our conservative case for the Voice did not translate into conservative electoral support.[27] Labor and minor-party voters were most likely to vote 'Yes', while Coalition voters were most likely to vote 'No'.[28] Electorates represented by a Labor member had a higher 'Yes' vote than those represented by a Coalition member.

Other trends were also evident. Women were more likely to vote 'Yes' than men, and younger Australians were much more likely to vote 'Yes' than older Australians.[29] Those who voted 'No' were more likely to speak a language other than English at home, have lower levels of education and live outside urban centres and in low-income households. 'No' voters were more likely to dislike Albanese, trust social media and view land rights as unfair.³⁰ By contrast, voters who leaned left, disliked Dutton, trusted the federal government, supported reconciliation and felt land rights had not gone far enough were more likely to vote 'Yes'. The more highly educated the voter, the more likely the 'Yes' vote. Those with higher incomes living in capital cities were also more likely to vote 'Yes'.³¹

Crucially, the study noted that very few people switched from 'No' to 'Yes' during the campaign, highlighting the ineffectiveness of the 'Yes' teams' persuasion. It was estimated that only 4.8 per cent of those who said they would vote 'No' in January 2023 ended up voting 'Yes'. By contrast, 42 per cent of those who in January 2023 intended to vote 'Yes' ended up voting 'No', with the 'Yes' vote declining by 21.4 per cent between August and October 2023.³² The 'Yes' vote fell most among Coalition voters.³³ In October 2023, the Coalition 'Yes' vote was approximately one-quarter of what it was in January 2023, confirming that Coalition opposition had a decisive impact. Despite our efforts in multicultural communities, the 'Yes' campaign struggled to connect with non-English speaking voters, who may have been swayed by targeted scare campaigns. Their vote declined significantly, especially late in the campaign.³⁴

The results underscore the success of the 'No' campaign in getting right-leaning soft 'Yes' voters to switch to 'No', and the failure of the 'Yes' campaigns to reassure those slipping away. For me, it underscores the damage done in those crucial months in 2023: Dutton formalised his party's opposition and began robustly advocating 'No'; Craven and Brennan stoked legal fears about the constitutional change, handing effective lines to the 'No' side; and the Labor government and 'Yes' campaigners failed to provide effective explanations to counteract these forces. There were many other factors too. The double-majority requirement, compulsory voting and the lack of bipartisanship made success extremely difficult. The trend in referendums is that the 'Yes' vote declines as the referendum draws near. While international experience shows that celebrity endorsements may decrease the 'Yes' vote in referendums,[35] elements of the 'Yes' campaign utilised celebrity and corporate backing, which may not have helped perceptions of elitism.

The research found that voters over the course of 2023 had become 'far less satisfied with democracy, less confident in the government, less satisfied with the direction of the country, and less satisfied with their own life'[36] – which could reflect growing cost-of-living pressures, interest-rate rises and related financial stress.[37] While dissatisfaction in our democracy grew between January and October 2023, trust in the judiciary declined more than for other institutions between the May 2022 election and the October referendum. This raises the possibility that the divisive legal debate about unintended High Court interpretations of the Voice amendment might have had a broader impact on how Australians view the judicial arm of our democracy – though who can really say? Worryingly, given the extent to which online disinformation proliferated, the one institution that gained trust during this period was social media – with 39 per cent saying that they did not trust social media at all in May 2022 declining to 32.8 per cent in October 2023.[38] Trust in social media was associated with a 'No' vote.

⁓⁕⁓ ⁓⁕⁓ ⁓⁕⁓

Maybe we were foolish to think common ground between Indigenous people and conservatives could be found. Yet things could have played out differently. I've had so many 'if only' moments while writing this book.

If only the Coalition had refined, owned and championed a Voice referendum during their time in government. If only Turnbull had not rejected the Voice in 2017 but supported and helped polish it when he was prime minister. If only the Coalition government had convened broader deliberative dialogues after the Uluru Statement, to foster community consensus and understanding, and progress the constitutional amendment. If only Abbott, Porter, Jeff Kennett, Alan Jones, Chris

Merritt and so many others had not switched from 'Yes' to 'No' when it suited their political purposes. If only Greg Craven and Frank Brennan had not attacked the constitutional drafting and been strong and persuasive 'Yes' advocates throughout the referendum campaign instead. If only Leeser had not wavered and Bragg had not gone soft. If only key constitutional conservatives had not disowned and discredited the proposal they co-created at crucial junctures. If only the constitutional compromises Indigenous people made had been saved for when politicians and the public were paying closer attention; and if only their many concessions were valued by those they were intended to assuage. If only the Labor government had explained the constitutional change more effectively and had developed processes to encourage – or force – Coalition co-ownership of the constitutional change co-devised by one of their own. If only the Liberals had supported the Voice once Labor got into power, notwithstanding it becoming a Labor-led referendum. If only the 'Yes' campaigns had had stronger advertising and social media, and had prosecuted a more coordinated and united strategy. If only the left had been more welcoming of non-Indigenous advocates and expertise, and less enamoured of identity politics. If only 'Yes' advocates had started campaigning in earnest much earlier, knowing support would drop when the 'No' campaign began. If only Mundine had not switched from 'Yes' to 'No' to please preselectors, who were nonetheless not pleased, and Price had not used this issue to catapult her career. If only Lidia Thorpe had opted for pragmatism instead of perpetual protest. If only 'Yes' had had better strategies for countering disinformation, lies and racism. If only the media did not prosecute false balance, elevating mistruths without adequate critique. If only we had better politicians: a bit smarter on the left, and much kinder on the right. If only we were better Australians, more generous with our love and less susceptible to fear.

What I do not accept is that Indigenous Australians should have settled for constitutional minimalism. It remains their choice, but why should they accept symbolism without substance, poetry without any power? After murder, usurpation of land, decades of discrimination, removal of children, non-payment of wages, and given the resultant disadvantage that carries on today, why do we demand they be satisfied with a symbolic acknowledgement without any improvement to the way this nation manages Indigenous affairs? No one can dispute the current system of top-down policy is failing. Rheumatic heart disease is rife in remote communities, diabetes ravages Indigenous people in central Australia at the highest rates in the world, Indigenous women and children are thirty-four times more likely to be hospitalised due to violence, while Indigenous women are six times more likely to die due to family violence. Most Closing the Gap targets are not on track to be met. In some areas, we are going backwards: in children's early development, rates of children in out-of-home care and rates of adult imprisonment and suicide. The rate at which Indigenous juveniles are jailed has increased, while the number of remote Indigenous youth who are employed or participating in a traineeship or study has fallen. Australia is failing the next generation of Indigenous Australians. So why should the people suffering these outcomes in a prosperous first-world democracy accept a tokenistic acknowledgement that does nothing to improve life in their communities?

My dad would put the argument differently to me – he turned rather radical in his later years. 'The Australian Constitution is illegal,' he would say, to which I would roll my eyes. 'Indigenous people are being too meek, asking for just an advisory body. It is not enough!' But he would rock up to 'Yes' campaign marches with Mum, emaciated in the T-shirt. They met their local Liberal member, Zoe McKenzie, to complain about her 'No' stance. I'm told she lectured them on why the Voice was divisive and the constitutional amendment legally unworkable, repeating key lines from Greg Craven.

I can't escape the conclusion that non-Indigenous Australians failed Indigenous people. We failed them comprehensively on 14 October

2023. We failed them as political leaders, advisers and collaborators. My twelve years of work with Indigenous leaders did their communities little good in the end. Through the Uluru Statement, Indigenous Australians were asking for our help to make things better. They were asking us to promise to do things in a better way; to abandon the failed top-down approaches of the past and present, and commit instead to listening, dialogue, partnership and mutual respect. Despite everything they had been through in our history, they were asking to be let in – to be formally recognised by a country and Constitution that has long shunned and excluded them. We said 'No' to their modest request, despite the compromise it represented, and despite the multiple additional concessions they made to elicit our support. We now have no real plan to address Indigenous disadvantage or tackle injustice. Their pragmatic consensus offered an answer. But while six million Australians voted 'Yes' to their solution – a fact Indigenous leaders note with optimism – an overwhelming majority of Australians said 'No' to this middle way.

The result raises questions for Australian democracy. For if the middle path proves too many times to be unfruitful, all we will be left with is ideological extremes. If collaboration across political divides continues to fail as it failed in 2023, then all we can look forward to is growing polarisation and division, which is bad news for sensible reform and, ultimately, democratic stability. If Australians lack the skills to build consensus to sensibly change our Constitution – as we increasingly seem to – then we are missing a crucial tool in our own democratic self-governance. Section 128 of the Constitution – the double-majority requirement – has become a lever we increasingly don't know how to manoeuvre: we have been unable to reform our Constitution since 1977. That is almost half a century of failed attempts to evolve our national rulebook. The way we conducted the Voice debate tells us much about the health of Australian democracy, and the picture is not pretty. The next phase will be learning from this failure so we can better understand how to work together, despite our disagreements and differences, to achieve worthwhile reform in the national interest. If we can't figure out how to collaborate across divides when needed, our nation's future will be at risk.

With time to reflect on the referendum's failure, Noel retains hope in the possibilities of radical centre solutions:

> In the wake of the referendum loss, we have to find a third way. I am disillusioned because I thought the Voice was a third way. But I cannot help but return to the fact that belonging to Australia is the only way forward for us. After the referendum defeat there are three possible responses. One, just capitulate and admit defeat. Two, being bitter, disillusioned and alienated. And the third way – that we keep making the case we belong to Australia, we belong to this nation. Our advocacy has got to be about belonging. We are part of the nation. We have nowhere else to go. This is our country and we have to keep making the case for unity and inclusion.[39]

I hope the reformers of tomorrow discern lessons from this book so they can succeed with better ideas where we failed. I hope they generate hope from the embers of this defeat. As I urged readers at the start of these reflections: be energised. Try harder, work smarter, learn from our missteps, persevere with new and superior strategies. Don't be scared to try to change things, even though change is hard. Don't be afraid to fail, even though failure hurts. Try your best to do something great. That's what advocates for the Voice referendum did: we tried to do something good for Indigenous people and for the country. We tried to collaborate across divides. We failed, despite our earnest efforts. I hope future generations can succeed where we did not.

# ACKNOWLEDGEMENTS

This book would not have been possible without generous philanthropic support from Mark Carnegie. I am immensely grateful for his support. Two years of engagement with multicultural and multifaith communities was also only possible with the backing of Foundation Donors Henry and Marcia Pinskier, who enabled the establishment of the Radical Centre Reform Lab at Macquarie University Law School. I am grateful to them, the Law School and Macquarie University for their warm encouragement of work towards the Voice referendum. I thank my Law School colleagues: the dean, Professor Lise Barry, for her leadership, and my collaborator, Professor Sarah Sorial, for her personal support. I acknowledge the work of the Reform Lab team – research assistants Billy McEvoy and Georgia Cam (who also valuably assisted with social media research for this book), for over two years of referendum awareness-raising – and our wonderful team of interns: Maya Buhrich, Gavin Choong, Simran Kaur, Meg La Macchia, Grace Slatyer, Jackson Bradney, Caroline Xu and Ruby Jeffrey. The Black Inc. and La Trobe University Press team has been remarkable to work with – especially chief editor Chris Feik, whose advice and insights have helped improve the book immensely. Thanks for supporting this work. I am deeply grateful to Cape York Institute for our ongoing collaboration, and I especially thank Zoe Ellerman, Kerie Hull, Tracey Kluck and Noel Pearson, whose advice and input on various drafts has been invaluable. To Noel and so many other Indigenous leaders all around the country, who worked so hard towards a constitutional Voice, I feel honoured to have worked alongside you and am thankful for the opportunity. To 'Yes' advocates across left and right who worked passionately to change the country for the better: thank you and do not give up the fight. To my husband and children, family and friends, deep gratitude are owed to you who continue to support my writing and reform endeavours.

# NOTES

**INTRODUCTION**
1. Editorial, *The Australian*, 27 December 2023.
2. Frank Brennan, 'Why I'll vote Yes to Indigenous Voice to Parliament, despite the flaws of the process', *The Australian*, 2 September 2023; Frank Brennan, 'The Voice referendum: Bringing the country with us', *Eureka Street*, 1 September 2023.
3. Greg Craven, 'Mick Gooda's speech a decisive step away from "we was robbed" rhetoric', *The Australian*, 24 February 2024.
4. Chelsea McLaughlin, '"What would you do?" Nakkiah Lui has one question for all non-Indigenous Australians', *Mamma Mia*, 3 June 2020.
5. Summer May Finlay, 'How to be a good Indigenous ally', *NITV*, 28 May 2018.
6. Amnesty International, '10 ways to be a genuine ally to Indigenous communities', 23 May 2018.
7. Amy Dale, 'From the Heart: Enshrining constitutional recognition', *LSJ Online*, 6 July 2021.
8. Shannon Molloy, 'Thomas Mayo, one of the main architects of the Voice to Parliament, issues a plea to No voters', *News.com.au*, 21 January 2023.

**CHAPTER 1: COUNTERFACTUAL**
1. Noel Pearson, 'Who We Were, Who We Are, and Who We Can Be', ABC Boyer Lectures, 4 November 2022.
2. Captain Russell, 1890 Australasian Federation Conference, Parliament House, Melbourne, Tuesday 11 February 1890.
3. Section 127 of the Constitution excluded Indigenous people from being counted as part of the population for voting purposes. Section 51(xxvi) of the Constitution excluded Indigenous people from the ambit of the race power. These exclusions were removed after the 1967 referendum.

**CHAPTER 2: A FAILED 'RADICAL CENTRE' REFERENDUM**
1. Noel Pearson, 'White guilt, victimhood and the quest for a radical centre', *Griffith Review*, no. 16 (2007): 34–72.
2. Noel Pearson, 'Conservatives leave door open to progressive change', *The Australian*, 9 March 2018.

3   Noel Pearson, 'Hunting the radical centre for Australia's future', Speech to the Press Club, 27 January 2016, Canberra.
4   Galarrwuy Yunupingu, 'Truth, tradition and tomorrow', *The Monthly*, 1 December 2008.
5   Greg Craven, 'Keep the constitutional change simple', *Australian Financial Review*, 6 February 2012.
6   Shireen Morris, *Radical Heart: Three Stories Make Us One*, Carlton: Melbourne University Publishing, 2018, p. 85.
7   Ibid., ch. 6.
8   Brennan, 'Why I'll vote Yes'; Brennan, 'The Voice referendum'.
9   Warren Mundine, 'Practical recognition from the mobs' perspective', Uphold & Recognise, 2017.
10  AAP, 'Warren Mundine enters recognition debate', *Nine News*, 19 May 2017.
11  Julian Leeser, Address to the Sydney Institute, 3 October 2023.
12  Anne Twomey, 'Putting words to the tune of Indigenous recognition, *The Conversation*, 19 May 2015.
13  'Australia PM Abbott wants indigenous referendum in 2017', *BBC News*, 12 December 2014.
14  Julian Leeser, 'Uphold and Recognise', in Damien Freeman and Shireen Morris (eds), *The Forgotten People*, Carlton: Melbourne University Press, 2016, p. 87.
15  Greg Craven, 'Noel Pearson's Indigenous recognition plan profound and practical', *The Australian*, 23 May 2015.
16  Frank Brennan, 'Contours and prospects for Indigenous recognition in the Australian Constitution', AIJA Oration in Judicial Administration at the Federal Court of Australia, Melbourne, 16 October 2015; Frank Brennan, 'Acknowledging Indigenous heritage a good beginning', *The Weekend Australian*, 16–17 May 2015.
17  See Morris, *Radical Heart*, pp. 129–34.
18  Megan Davis, 'The long road to Uluru: Walking together – truth before justice', *Griffith Review*, no. 60 (2018): 32–45.
19  Erwin Chlanda, 'Uluru Statement: A year later the debate goes on', *Alice Springs News*, 26 May 2018.
20  Ibid.
21  RMIT Fact Check, 'Anthony Albanese says surveys show between 80 and 90 per cent of Indigenous Australians support the Voice. Is that correct?', *ABC News*, 2 August 2023.
22  Jordyn Beazley, 'Indigenous communities overwhelmingly voted Yes to Australia's Voice to Parliament', *The Guardian*, 15 October 2023.
23  Thomas Mayo, 'A dream that cannot be denied: On the road to freedom day', *Griffith Review*, no. 70 (2020).
24  Referendum Council, *Final Report of the Referendum Council*, Canberra: Commonwealth of Australia, 2017, p. 38.

**CHAPTER 3: REPUDIATING THE RADICAL CENTRE**
1   Shireen Morris, 'Imagining an affirmational republic', *UNSW Law Journal*, vol.

44, no. 3 (2021): 1202, 1219.
2. Bertrand Tungandame, 'Lidia Thorpe opposes Voice to Parliament, seen as a powerless tool in a colonial and racist constitution', *SBS*, 12 October 2023.
3. Paul Kelly, 'Johnson symbolises conservative crisis', *The Australian*, 13 July 2022.
4. Shireen Morris and Damien Freeman, 'Giving Voice to Indigenous people in a constitutionally conservative way: Walter Bagehot, Edmund Burke and the Uluru Statement from the Heart', *Law and History*, forthcoming.
5. Karen Middleton, 'The making of the Uluru statement', *The Saturday Paper*, 3–9 June 2017.
6. Giovanni Torre, 'Coalition, Labor combine to sink Senator Thorpe's bill to enshrine Indigenous rights', *National Indigenous Times*, 6 December 2023.
7. Referendum Council, *Final Report*, pp. 22, 24.
8. AFP, 'UN Indigenous rights expert backs Australia "Voice" vote', *Barrons*, 5 October 2023.
9. Josh Butler, 'Lidia Thorpe brands leading no group "deceptive" for using her quotes in Voice Facebook campaign', *The Guardian*, 24 May 2023.
10. Calla Wahlquist, 'Most Australians support Indigenous Voice to Parliament plan that Turnbull rejected', *The Guardian*, 30 October 2017.
11. Simon Benson, 'Bill Shorten raising Voice a winner with voters: Newspoll', *The Australian*, 20 February 2018.
12. Lorena Allam, 'More Australians want an Indigenous Voice protected in constitution, survey suggests', *The Guardian*, 30 November 2020.
13. Taken from *Q&A* transcript of the show. See also Neil McMahon, 'Q&A recap: Old foes Alan Jones and Kevin Rudd finally find common ground', *The Sydney Morning Herald*, 31 October 2017.
14. Jeff Kennett, 'As a nation, we need to be reconciled', *Herald Sun*, 8 June 2016.
15. Greg Brown, 'Jeff Kennett adds voice to call for Indigenous recognition', *The Australian*, 20 July 2019.
16. Lisa Visentin, 'Albanese "owes it to the public" to release Voice details: Jeff Kennett', *The Sydney Morning Herald*, 12 January 2023.
17. Jeff Kennett, 'Voting No to the Voice is merely a matter of principle', *Herald Sun*, 5 September 2023.
18. Ibid.
19. Kennett, 'As a nation, we need to be reconciled'.
20. Chris Merritt, 'Koori Court the exception that proves Dicey's principle', *The Australian*, 2 June 2017.

**CHAPTER 4: THE ILLUSION OF BIPARTISANSHIP**
1. Josh Nicholas, 'How the Indigenous Voice referendum could have passed with bipartisan support – in charts', *The Guardian*, 29 November 2023.
2. Scott Bennett, 'The Politics of Constitutional Amendment', Parliament of Australia, Research Paper No. 11, 2002–03.
3. Cheryl Saunders, 'The Australian experience with constitutional review', *Australian Quarterly*, vol. 66, no. 3 (1994): 49.

4   See for example Paul Kildea, 'Getting to "Yes": Why our approach to winning referendums needs a rethink', *AusPubLaw*, 12 December 2018.
5   Anne Twomey, 'The Constitution was designed to be hard to change. It was not meant to be impossible', *The Sydney Morning Herald*, 16 October 2023.
6   John Howard, 'The right time: Constitutional recognition for Indigenous Australians', speech to the Sydney Institute, 11 October 2007.
7   Troy Bramston, 'Pearson rues former PMs' missteps', *The Australian*, 28 April 2023.
8   Shireen Morris, '"The torment of our powerlessness": Addressing Indigenous constitutional vulnerability through the Uluru Statement's call for a First Nations Voice in their affairs', *UNSW Law Journal*, vol. 41, no. 3 (2018): 629.
9   Referendum Council, *Final Report*, pp. 5, 68, 88.
10  Mark McKenna, *First Words: A Brief History of Public Debate on a New Preamble to the Australian Constitution 1991–99*, Canberra: Department of the Parliamentary Library, 2000.
11  Noel Pearson, 'A Rightful but Not Separate Place', ABC Boyer Lectures, 11 November 2022.
12  Paul Kelly, 'Howard's sway: The former PM speaks out on the Voice', *The Australian*, 19 November 2022.
13  Janet Albrechtsen, 'Former prime minister John Howard denounces Noel Pearson's Indigenous Voice to Parliament "Judas" attack on Peter Dutton', *The Australian*, 8 April 2023.
14  Victoria Lane and Natasha Robinson, 'Time to get a move on with recognition: Ken Wyatt', *The Australian*, 10 July 2015.
15  The Kirribilli Statement was presented to the prime minister and the Opposition leader at the H.C. Coombs Centre, Kirribilli, Sydney, 6 July 2015.
16  Morris, *Radical Heart*, pp. 182–85.
17  Peter van Onselen, 'Indigenous Voice to Parliament: To get to Yes, try a little respect, not hectoring', *The Australian*, 24 June 2023.
18  Frank Brennan, *No Small Change: The Road to Recognition for Indigenous Australia*, St Lucia: University of Queensland Press, 2015, p. 275.
19  David Crowe, 'Crunch week for Albanese with no turning back on Voice referendum', *The Sydney Morning Herald*, 18 June 2023.
20  N. Biddle, M. Gray, I. McAllister and M. Qvortrup, 'Detailed analysis of the 2023 Voice to Parliament Referendum and related social and political attitudes', Research article, ANU Centre for Social Research and Methods, November 2023.
21  Michelle Grattan, 'ANU research suggests referendum confined to Indigenous recognition might have passed', *The Conversation*, 27 November 2023.
22  See Shireen Morris and Noel Pearson, 'Indigenous Constitutional Recognition: Paths to Failure and Possible Paths to Success', *Australian Law Journal*, vol. 91 (2017): 350.
23  See Leeser, 'Uphold and Recognise'.
24  See, for example: Jeremy Clark and Jill Gallagher, 'Why Indigenous Australia will reject a minimalist referendum question', *The Sydney Morning Herald*,

20 March 2017; David Ross and Barbara Shaw, 'Indigenous Australians know removing race from constitution is pretend change', *The Guardian*, 10 April 2017; Cheryl Axleby and Klynton Wanganeen, 'Constitutional recognition must make Indigenous lives better. Otherwise what's the point?', *The Guardian*, 20 April 2017.

25   Paul Karp, 'Peter Dutton walks back offer of second referendum after Voice poll', *The Guardian*, 16 October 2023.
26   Cameron Gooley and Georgina Mitchell, 'Indigenous Voice referendum should be held by 2024, Liberal senator says', *The Sydney Morning Herald*, 14 April 2022.
27   Referendum Council, *Final Report*, p. 10.
28   Murray Gleeson, 'Recognition in keeping with the Constitution: A worthwhile project', Speech to Gilbert + Tobin, 18 July 2019.
29   Malcolm Turnbull and George Brandis, 'Response to Referendum Council's report on constitutional recognition', Media release, 26 October 2017.
30   Greg Brown, '"Take it or leave it" a risky approach on Voice, says Josh Frydenberg', *The Australian*, 19 August 2021.
31   Karla Grant, 'Malcolm Turnbull: All Australians are equal', *Living Black*, 16 June 2020.
32   Joint Select Committee on Constitutional Recognition relating to Aboriginal and Torres Strait Islander Peoples, *Final Report*, Canberra: Parliament of the Commonwealth of Australia, 2018, p. ix.
33   See for example Frank Brennan, 'An Indigenous Voice', Advent McKinney Lecture, 22 November 2022.
34   Referendum Council, *Final Report*, pp. 6, 34, 35, 37, 38, 104, 163.
35   Ibid., pp. 36–37.
36   Ibid., p. 30.
37   Turnbull and Brandis, 'Response to Referendum Council's report on constitutional recognition'.
38   Malcolm Turnbull, 'Australia's constitutional history told us the Voice referendum was unwinnable. Sadly, that was right', *The Guardian*, 22 October 2023.

**CHAPTER 5: GRAB THEM BY THE LAPELS**
1   Morris, *Radical Heart*, pp. 144–45.
2   Renee Viellaris, 'Malcolm Turnbull risks war with Labor and Indigenous groups after rejecting Referendum Council's "radical" blueprint"', *The Courier Mail*, 25 October 2017.
3   Noel Pearson, 'Betrayal', *The Monthly*, December 2017 – January 2018.
4   Morris, *Radical Heart*, pp. 210–13.
5   Ibid., pp. 146, 157–58, 186–87.
6   Stephen Fitzpatrick, 'Christian Porter lashes out at lawyer Shireen Morris in recognition row', *The Australian*, 8 December 2017.
7   Dennis Shanahan, 'Push for Indigenous Senate seats on Abbott's mind as bush visit begins', *The Australian*, 15 September 2014.

8   Morris, *Radical Heart*, pp. 123–24.
9   Ibid., pp. 107–10, 189–90.
10  Amy Remeikis, 'Barnaby Joyce "apologises" for calling Indigenous Voice a third chamber of Parliament', *The Guardian*, 18 July 2019.
11  Morris, *Radical Heart*, p. 133.
12  Nakari Thorpe, 'Morrison maintains "third chamber" position on Indigenous Voice', *NITV*, 26 September 2018.
13  Deborah Snow, 'Morrison pledges recognition but will take "as long as needed"', *The Sydney Morning Herald*, 26 May 2019.
14  Ken Wyatt, 'Walking in partnership to achieve change', Speech to the National Press Club, Canberra, 10 July 2019.
15  Rick Morton, 'Co-designing the Voice to Parliament', *The Saturday Paper*, 16–22 November 2019.
16  Ken Wyatt, 'Looking Forward; Looking Back', Vincent Lingiari Memorial Lecture, Charles Darwin University, Northern Territory, 15 August 2019.
17  Deborah Snow and Ella Archibald-Binge, 'Keeping hope alive: The push to revive the Statement from the Heart', *The Sydney Morning Herald*, 30 May 2020.

**CHAPTER 6: ON CONSTITUTIONAL COMPROMISES**
1   See for example Brennan, 'Why I'll vote Yes'; Brennan, 'The Voice referendum'.
2   Peter van Onselen, 'Indigenous Voice to Parliament: Referendum for change brought low by hubris', *The Australian*, 14 October 2023.
3   David Crowe, 'The PM was mugged by history. Here's how to win a referendum in future', *The Sydney Morning Herald*, 19 October 2023.
4   Pearson, 'A Rightful but Not Separate Place'.
5   Twomey, 'Putting words to the tune of Indigenous recognition'.
6   Pearson, 'A Rightful but Not Separate Place'.
7   Cape York Institute, Submission No. 2720 to National Indigenous Australians Agency, *Indigenous Voice Co-Design Process*, 30 April 2021. I also argued for such a process in Shireen Morris, 'Refining and Agreeing on a Constitutional Amendment for a First Nations Voice', *UNSW Law Society Court of Conscience*, vol. 16 (2022): 11.
8   Lorena Allam, 'Government appoints First Nations leaders to guide referendum on Indigenous Voice', *The Guardian*, 8 September 2022.
9   Wahlquist, 'Most Australians support Indigenous Voice to Parliament plan that Turnbull rejected'.
10  For more on this idea, see Sarah Sorial and Shireen Morris, 'Mini-publics and the legitimacy dilemma: How theoretical tensions are resolved in practice', *Public Law* (forthcoming).
11  Pearson, 'Who We Were'.
12  Pat Anderson et al., Submission No. 479 to Joint Select Committee on Constitutional Recognition relating to Aboriginal and Torres Strait Islander Peoples, Parliament of Australia, 3 November 2018, p. 6.
13  Ibid., p. 8.

14  Gabrielle Appleby, 'The Uluru Statement is not a vague idea of "being heard" but deliberate structural reform', *The Conversation*, 24 July 2020.
15  Andrew Bragg, *Buraadja*, Redland Bay: Kapunda Press, 2021, p. 165.
16  Anne Twomey, 'There are many ways to achieve Indigenous recognition in the Constitution – we must find one we can agree on', *The Conversation*, 8 July 2020.
17  From the Heart, 'No compromised position on Uluru Statement from Heart', *Mirage News*, 10 July 2020.
18  Paige Taylor, 'New Voice proposal by Uphold & Recognise to placate both sides', *The Australian*, 22 January 2021.
19  Michael Pelley, 'Why is Noel Pearson upset with Murray Gleeson?', *Australian Financial Review*, 13 October 2023.
20  Committee Hansard, Joint Select Committee on the Aboriginal and Torres Strait Islander Voice Referendum, Friday 14 April 2023.
21  Senator Jacinta Nampijinpa Price, 'Shadow Minister for Indigenous Australians', Speech, National Press Club, Canberra, 18 September 2023.
22  'Jacinta Price is "misleading" the public about the Voice: Chris Kenny', *Sky News Australia*, 18 September 2023.
23  Julian Leeser, 'Speech on the Aboriginal and Torres Strait Islander Voice, House of Representatives', 24 May 2023.
24  See for example Shireen Morris, 'Don't let No scare tactics get in the way of the Indigenous Voice to Parliament', *The Australian*, 30 May 2023.

**CHAPTER 7: FLIP-FLOPPERS**
1  Thorpe, 'Morrison maintains "third chamber" position on Indigenous Voice'.
2  Twomey, 'There are many ways to achieve Indigenous recognition in the Constitution'.
3  Taylor, 'New Voice proposal by Uphold & Recognise to placate both sides'.
4  Rob Harris, '"Not our policy": Scott Morrison rejects push for referendum on Voice', *The Sydney Morning Herald*, 18 March 2021.
5  Andrew Bragg, Maiden speech, 24 July 2019.
6  David Penberthy, 'First Indigenous Voice to be adopted by South Australian parliament', *The Australian*, 7 May 2021.
7  Rob Harris, 'Gladys Berejiklian backs the Voice, urges embrace of Indigenous reconciliation', *The Sydney Morning Herald*, 8 June 2021.
8  Bragg, *Buraadja*, pp. 167, 202.
9  Katharine Murphy, 'Josh Frydenberg won't endorse objective of Andrew Bragg's book on Indigenous Voice to Parliament', *The Guardian*, 18 August 2021.
10  Katharine Murphy, 'Essential poll: Majority of Australians want Indigenous recognition and Voice to Parliament', *The Guardian*, 12 July 2019.
11  Paige Taylor, 'Crossbenchers would support Indigenous Voice referendum', *The Australian*, 15 April 2022.
12  AAP, 'Fearmongering making Voice debate difficult: Pocock', *National Indigenous Times*, 15 June 2023.

*Notes*

13 David Coleman, 'ABC News afternoon briefing with Greg Jennett', 3 April 2023.
14 Tim Wilson, 'My journey on the road to recognition', remarks at Uphold & Recognise event at the University of Melbourne, 25 May 2017; see also Preface to Warren Mundine, *Practical Recognition from the Mobs' Perspective: Enabling Our Mobs to Speak for Country*, Uphold & Recognise Monograph Series, North Sydney: Uphold & Recognise, 2017.
15 Morris, *Radical Heart*, pp. 116, 172, 188–89.
16 Greg Brown, 'Don't put Voice to the vote, says Mundine', *The Australian*, 12 July 2019.
17 Tim Rowse, 'Is the Voice already being muted?', *Inside Story*, 1 February 2021.
18 Russell Broadbent, 'Just as I see it: Uluru Statement from the Heart', Statement, 20 January 2021.
19 Russell Broadbent, 'A Divine Invitation', in Shireen Morris and Damien Freeman (eds), *Statements from the Soul: The Moral Case for the Uluru Statement from the Heart*, Collingwood: La Trobe University Press, 2023.
20 Karen Middleton, 'Liberal "Yes" supporters threatened with losing preselection', *The Saturday Paper*, 9–15 September 2023.
21 Rachel Eddie, 'Long-serving Liberal MP Russell Broadbent faces preselection challenge', *The Age*, 15 June 2023.
22 Lisa Visentin, 'This Aboriginal elder is voting No. She's persuaded her Voice-backing MP to do the same', *The Sydney Morning Herald*, 10 September 2023.
23 Paul Sakkal and Kieran Rooney, 'Veteran Liberal Party MP Russell Broadbent quits party, moves to crossbench', *The Sydney Morning Herald*, 14 November 2023.
24 Paul Karp, 'Warren Mundine indicates he won't run for vacant NSW Liberal Senate seat', *The Guardian*, 22 September 2023.
25 Andrew Messenger and Eden Gillespie, 'Indigenous Queenslanders in "double mourning" as state's pathway to treaty loses bipartisan support', *The Guardian*, 19 October 2023; Benita Kolovos and Adeshola Ore, 'Treaty could make people "feel more divided", Victorian opposition leader says, as Coalition withdraws support', *The Guardian*, 22 January 2024.
26 Paul Sakkal, 'No campaign dumps campaigners over racist remarks, distances itself from Adler', *The Sydney Morning Herald*, 15 August 2023.
27 Daniel Hurst, 'Gary Johns faces calls to resign from no Voice campaign over "offensive" comments', *The Guardian*, 24 July 2023.
28 Sarah Collard et al., 'Indigenous Voice: No campaign event reinforced "racist stereotypes", watchdog says', *The Guardian*, 5 April 2023.
29 Samantha Maiden, 'Warren Mundine accuses Anthony Albanese of dividing nation on race over the Voice,' *News.com.au*, 30 August 2023.
30 Rosie Lewis, 'Yes campaign for an Indigenous Voice to Parliament says No camp hosted by extreme group', *The Australian*, 24 July 2023.
31 Natassia Chrysanthos, '"Time is now": Australia-wide campaign to call for referendum on Indigenous Voice', *The Sydney Morning Herald*, 2 May 2022.
32 Ibid.
33 Natassia Chrysanthos and Angus Thompson, '"Why would I?": Morrison rules out referendum on Indigenous Voice if re-elected', *The Sydney Morning*

*Herald*, 2 May 2022.
34  Leeser, Address to the Sydney Institute.
35  Kelly, 'Howard's sway'.
36  Malcolm Turnbull, 'I will be voting yes to establish an Indigenous Voice to Parliament', *The Guardian*, 15 August 2022. See also Malcolm Turnbull, 'Why my government didn't back the Voice, but I'm now voting yes', *The Sydney Morning Herald*, 30 August 2023.
37  Josh Butler, 'Yes campaign groups received more than five times as much in donations as no side in Voice referendum', *The Guardian*, 2 April 2024.
38  Daniel Hurst, 'Julie Bishop backs Indigenous Voice as "step in the right direction"', *The Guardian*, 26 July 2023.
39  Carla Masceranhas, 'Australia could vote to become a republic as soon as 2026, Malcolm Turnbull predicts', *News.com.au*, 20 December 2023.
40  Malcolm Turnbull, 'Voice lessons for republicans? Don't give up on constitutional reform', *The Sydney Morning Herald*, 13 January 2024.
41  Joe Hildebrand, 'Catastrophic move that changed Voice to Parliament', *News.com.au*, 15 April 2023.
42  Paul Sakkal and Hamish Hastie, 'Frydenberg rules out Kooyong run as Wyatt laments his absence', *The Sydney Morning Herald*, 21 September 2023.
43  Brown, '"Take it or leave it" a risky approach on Voice, says Josh Frydenberg'.
44  Matt Cunningham, 'Peter Dutton tours Northeast Arnhem Land for Voice to Parliament', *NT News*, 25 February 2023.

## CHAPTER 8: ALBANESE'S VOICE

1  Michelle Grattan, 'Albanese releases draft wording for Indigenous "Voice to Parliament" referendum', *The Conversation*, 29 July 2022.
2  Anthony Albanese, 'Address to the Garma Festival', 30 July 2022.
3  Janet Albrechtsen, 'Questioning Albanese's Voice isn't idiotic, racist or ideological', *The Australian*, 31 August 2022.
4  Noel Pearson and Shireen Morris, 'Conservatives eat their own words on Voice', *The Australian*, 25 February 2023.
5  Anthony Albanese, Interview by Patricia Karvelas, *Breakfast*, Radio National 1 March 2023.
6  Nick Tabakoff, 'ABC reporter starts "reparations" debate amid Voice discussion', *The Australian*, 8 August 2022.
7  Anthony Albanese, Interview by David Speers, *Insiders*, ABC Television, 31 July 2022.
8  Karina Okotel, 'Why a First Nations Voice will meet Dutton's demand for practical change', *The Sydney Morning Herald*, 1 June 2022.
9  Paul Kelly, 'Conviction not enough for PM on the Voice', *The Australian*, 3 August 2022.
10 Janet Albrechtsen, 'Libs left limp as Voice poses legal nightmare', *The Australian*, 1 August 2022.
11 Janet Albrechtsen, '"Bonfire of cash": The small motley No crew that beat Yes', *The Australian*, 15 October 2023.

12   Albrechtsen, 'Libs left limp'.
13   Albanese, 'Address to the Garma Festival'.
14   Jacinta Nampijinpa Price, Maiden speech to Parliament, 27 July 2022.
15   Ian Trust, 'Listen to our Voice, stop going behind our backs', *The Australian*, 5 December 2022.
16   Price, Maiden speech to Parliament.
17   'The Voice debate: Tackling one of the biggest issues of a generation', *Sky News*, 4 September 2022.
18   Trust, 'Listen to our Voice, stop going behind our backs'.
19   Beazley, 'Indigenous communities overwhelmingly voted yes'.
20   Paul Karp and Eden Gillespie, 'AEC responds after Jacinta Nampijinpa Price questions "conduct" in Indigenous communities that voted yes', *The Guardian*, 15 October 2023.
21   Ellie Dudley, 'The Nationals will not support an Indigenous Voice', *The Australian*, 28 November 2022.
22   James Massola et al., '"Emotional blackmail": Nationals to oppose Voice to Parliament in blow to referendum', *The Sydney Morning Herald*, 28 November 2022.
23   Chris Kenny, '"Doesn't make any sense": Nationals oppose Voice to Parliament', *Sky News*, 28 November 2022.
24   Lucy Barbour, 'David Littleproud declares he will challenge Barnaby Joyce for National party leadership', *ABC News*, 28 May 2022.
25   Paul Karp, 'Nationals MP Andrew Gee quits party citing its opposition to Indigenous Voice', *The Guardian*, 23 December 2022.
26   Lisa Visentin et al., 'Bitter war of words as Nationals split on opposition to Voice', *The Sydney Morning Herald*, 29 November 2022.
27   Lesley Turner, 'Jacinta Price doesn't speak for my people – and her stance shows why Australia needs the Indigenous Voice', *The Guardian*, 1 December 2022.
28   Paige Taylor, 'Indigenous leaders condemn Jacinta Price, Nationals over opposition to Voice to Parliament', *The Australian*, 1 December 2022.
29   See for example 'Why remote communities haven't heard of the Voice', *ABC Radio*, 4 July 2023.
30   Michael Koziol, '"This is nuts": Tingle calls out false balance at ABC over Voice coverage', *The Sydney Morning Herald*, 14 October 2023.
31   Daniel Hurst and Amy Remeikis, 'David Littleproud is a "kindergarten kid" whose Nationals will be "left behind" on Voice, Noel Pearson says', *The Guardian*, 29 November 2022.
32   Nic White, 'Jacinta Price hits back with single photo after "bully" Indigenous leader claimed she was "punching down on blackfellas in redneck celebrity vortex" as her feud with "angry men claiming to speak for Aboriginals" gets nastier', *Daily Mail*, 29 November 2022.
33   Lech Blaine, *Bad Cop: Peter Dutton's Strongman Politics*, Quarterly Essay 93, Collingwood: Black Inc., 2024, p. 90.
34   AAP, 'Albanese didn't say Voice opponents are "racist"', *AAP Factcheck*, 28 July 2023.

*Notes*

35  Paul Sakkal and Lisa Visentin, 'Yes campaign "snookered", says Noel Pearson in call for major campaign shift', *The Sydney Morning Herald*, 12 June 2023.

**CHAPTER 9: WHERE IS THE DETAIL?**

1   Katharine Murphy, 'Peter Dutton saying maybe to the Indigenous Voice but meaning no is not a cost-free exercise', *The Guardian*, 3 December 2022.
2   Josh Butler, 'Cracks emerge in Nationals over opposition to Indigenous Voice as Ken Wyatt blasts party's "laziness"', *The Guardian*, 30 November 2022.
3   Noel Pearson, 'It's Time for True Constitutional Recognition', Speech delivered at the National Museum of Australia, 17 March 2021.
4   Paul Karp, 'Indigenous Voice model revealed – but no national representation until after 2022 election', *The Guardian*, 17 December 2021.
5   Paige Taylor, 'Labor to lay out key elements of its Indigenous Voice by Christmas', *The Australian*, 25 July 2022.
6   See Damien Freeman, 'Labor is failing badly on the Voice referendum', *The Australian*, 29 November 2022.
7   Megan Davis, 'Constitutional recognition: Two decades on', *Indigenous Constitutional Law*, 1 March 2021; Megan Davis, 'A Voice of recognition', *The Australian*, 16 July 2022.
8   Dana Morse, 'Indigenous Voice report authors "disappointed" by argument the proposal lacks detail', 5 December 2022.
9   Davis, 'A Voice of recognition'.
10  Sky News, 'The Voice debate'.
11  Teela Reid, 'Turnbull is not the referendum messiah he thinks he is', *The Sydney Morning Herald*, 17 August 2022.
12  Gabrielle Appleby and Eddie Synot, 'What do we know about the Voice to Parliament design, and what do we still need to know?', *The Conversation*, 6 December 2022.
13  Paige Taylor, 'Expert warns against too much Voice detail', *The Australian*, 7 December 2022.
14  Caitlin Fitzsimmons and Jack Latimore, 'Raising Indigenous voices on a Voice to Parliament', *The Sydney Morning Herald*, 20 January 2023.
15  Marcia Langton, 'Fighting for a Voice', *The Saturday Paper*, 7 January 2023.
16  Katharine Murphy, 'What the ghosts of campaigns past – and Dirty Dancing – can teach the PM about the Voice referendum', *The Guardian*, 28 January 2023.
17  Anthony Galloway, ' "Nonsense and mischief": Pat Dodson slams critics of the Voice', *The Sydney Morning Herald*, 4 February 2023.
18  Finn McHugh and Anna Henderson, 'Liberals deliver "resounding no" to Labor's Voice plan, but back constitutional recognition', *SBS News*, 5 April 2023.
19  Josh Butler, 'Peter Dutton and the Voice: What the Liberal party has got wrong about Indigenous recognition', *The Guardian*, 7 April 2023.
20  Anthony Galloway, 'Burney commits to regional voices in concession to Liberal MPs', *The Sydney Morning Herald*, 20 May 2023.

## Notes

**CHAPTER 10: TOPSY-TURVY WORLD**

1. Greg Craven, 'Voice cannot happen without the right', *The Australian*, 28 May 2022.
2. Janet Albrechtsen, 'The Albanese amendment ensures a Voice will be a disaster', *The Australian*, 13 August 2022.
3. Greg Craven, 'Chicken Littles are wrong: Voice won't make legal sky fall', *The Australian*, 18 August 2022.
4. Louise Clegg, 'A more modest option could lift prospects for Voice', *The Australian*, 25 August 2022.
5. Shireen Morris, *A First Nations Voice in the Australian Constitution*, Oxford; New York: Hart Publishing, 2020, p. 146.
6. Albrechtsen, '"Bonfire of cash"'.
7. Frank Brennan, 'Most Australians are tolerant and inclusive, so stop the hectoring on our national day', *The Australian*, 26 January 2022.
8. Their drafting refers to laws made under 's. xxxvi'; however, I assume this is an error and that s. 51(xxvi) was the intended power. See Megan Davis and Rosalind Dixon, 'Constitutional recognition through a (justiciable) duty to consult? Towards entrenched and judicially enforceable norms of Indigenous consultation', *Public Law Review*, vol. 27, no. 4 (2016): 255, 262.
9. Frank Brennan, 'Why their Voice must be heard', *The Australian*, 20 August 2022.
10. Morris, *A First Nations Voice in the Australian Constitution*, p. 146.
11. Nicole Hegarty, 'Legal experts worry the words "executive government" could lead to Voice referendum court battles', *ABC News*, 25 March 2023.
12. Albrechtsen, '"Bonfire of cash"'.
13. Albrechtsen, 'Questioning Albanese's Voice isn't idiotic, racist or ideological'.
14. Albrechtsen, '"Bonfire of cash"'.

**CHAPTER 11: BLACK ROBE RETURNS**

1. Twomey, 'Putting words to the tune of Indigenous recognition'.
2. Albrechtsen, 'Libs left limp as Voice poses legal nightmare'.
3. Frank Brennan, 'The Path to a Referendum: From Uluru Via Garma to Canberra and on to the People', Newman Lecture, Mannix College, 17 August 2022, pp. 11–12.
4. Craven, 'Chicken Littles are wrong'.
5. Greg Craven, 'Voice far from won outside centre-left bubble', *The Australian*, 14 November 2022.
6. Greg Craven, 'We need to work out how Indigenous Voices can be heard', *The Australian*, 13 September 2014.
7. Ibid.
8. Craven, 'Voice far from won outside centre-left bubble'.
9. Greg Craven, 'Indigenous Voice to Parliament referendum rewrite is a tragedy in the making', *The Australian*, 31 March 2023.
10. Referendum Council, *Final Report*, pp. 6, 34, 35, 37, 38, 104, 163.
11. Brennan, 'An Indigenous Voice'.

Notes

12  Bragg, *Buraadja*, p. 165.
13  Frank Brennan, 'Lessons from the referendum', *Eureka Street*, 7 February 2023.
14  See for example Jenny Brinkworth, 'Wording critical to Voice referendum: Brennan', *The Southern Cross*, 31 March 2023; Frank Brennan, 'Voice to Parliament: Look for wording all stakeholders can support', *The Australian*, 25 February 2023; Brennan, 'The Path to a Referendum, p. 11–12, 18.
15  Paul Kelly, 'The Voice', Robin Speed Memorial Lecture: Rule of Law Series, 1 June 2023.
16  Frank Brennan, *An Indigenous Voice to Parliament: Considering a Constitutional Bridge*, Mulgrave: Garratt Publishing, 2023, p. 5.
17  Brennan, *An Indigenous Voice to Parliament*, p. 38.
18  See also ibid., pp. 53, 76. It was only after the referendum defeat – when it was too late to matter – that, in his 2024 book, Brennan quoted the original drafting. Even then, his description of the amendment did not admit that advice to the executive was a key element all along. Contrary to all evidence, and with no explanation, Brennan claimed the streamlined 2018 version was 'much more broad ranging' than the Twomey original: Frank Brennan, *Lessons from Our Failure to Build a Constitutional Bridge in the 2023 Referendum*, Brisbane: Connor Court, 2024, p. 93.
19  Brennan, *No Small Change*, p. 275.
20  Brennan, 'Acknowledging Indigenous heritage a good beginning'; Brennan, 'Contours and prospects for Indigenous recognition in the Australian constitution'.
21  Twomey, 'Putting words to the tune of Indigenous recognition'.
22  Brennan, *An Indigenous Voice to Parliament*, p. 55.
23  Gleeson, 'Recognition in keeping with the Constitution'.
24  Michael Gordon, 'Noel Pearson slams advocate for "modest" Indigenous recognition', *The Sydney Morning Herald*, 3 July 2015.
25  Michael Gordon, 'Academic Marcia Langton blasts Frank Brennan's recognition plan', *The Sydney Morning Herald*, 3 June 2015.
26  Brennan, *An Indigenous Voice to Parliament*, pp. 38–39.
27  Morris, *Radical Heart*, pp. 151–52.
28  Janet Albrechtsen, 'Voice proposal is a legal minefield waiting to explode', *The Australian*, 16 November 2022.
29  Kenneth Hayne, 'Fear of the Voice lost in the lack of legal argument', *The Australian*, 28 November 2022.
30  Ian Callinan, 'Examining the case for the Voice – an argument against', *The Australian*, 17 December 2022.
31  Sarah Ison, 'Yes campaigner Frank Brennan says Anthony Albanese called him "politically naïve" for publicly raising concerns over Voice', *The Australian*, 1 March 2024.
32  John Warhurst, 'In the chorus of Yes, why aren't the bishops joining in?', *Eureka Street*, 14 September 2023.
33  Comment from 'Damien' in response to Warhurst, 'In the chorus of Yes'.
34  Comment from Michael D. Breen in response to John Warhurst, 'Frank Brennan and an Indigenous Voice to Parliament', *Eureka Street*, 4 May 2023.

35 Patrick Hannaford, 'Voice advocate Father Frank Brennan explains where Albanese government went wrong in referendum debate', *Sky News*, 9 October 2023.
36 Frank Brennan, Submission to Joint Select Committee on the Aboriginal and Torres Strait Islander Voice Referendum, 13 April 2023.
37 Brennan, 'Why I'll vote Yes'.
38 Rosie Lewis, 'Frank Brennan says Indigenous Voice to Parliament referendum has "sent race relations backwards"', *The Australian*, 3 October 2023.

## CHAPTER 12: A RADICAL SPLINTER

1 Michael Pelly, 'The inside story of the Voice campaign', *Australian Financial Review*, 13 October 2023.
2 Albrechtsen, '"Bonfire of cash"'.
3 David Crowe, 'Albanese writes to Dutton to salvage a deal on the Voice', *The Sydney Morning Herald*, 2 February 2023.
4 Ibid.
5 Albrechtsen, '"Bonfire of cash"'.
6 Lisa Visentin, '"Failure of the process": Opposition questions new recognition line in Voice proposal', *The Sydney Morning Herald*, 3 February 2023.
7 Lorena Allam and Sarah Collard, 'PM, state and territory leaders formally back Indigenous Voice to Parliament with statement of intent', *The Guardian*, 3 February 2023.
8 Lisa Visentin et al., 'Indigenous Australians to be formally recognised in Voice proposal', *The Sydney Morning Herald*, 2 February 2023.
9 Visentin, '"Failure of the process"'.
10 Kennett, 'As a nation, we need to be reconciled'.
11 Visentin et al., 'Indigenous Australians to be formally recognised in Voice proposal'.
12 'Peter Dutton commits to continue to meet with Voice referendum working group', *ABC News*, 2 February 2023.
13 Josh Butler, 'Peter Dutton says meeting with Voice panel did not answer his questions', *The Guardian*, 2 February 2023.
14 Lisa Visentin et al., 'The devil in the details: Inside the Yes campaign's defeat', *The Sydney Morning Herald*, 16 October 2023.
15 Greg Craven, 'In a sea of confusion, sharks circle Indigenous Voice', *The Australian*, 19 February 2023.
16 Morris, 'Don't let No scare tactics get in the way of the Indigenous Voice to Parliament'.
17 Craven, 'In a sea of confusion, sharks circle Indigenous Voice'.
18 Patricia Karvelas, 'Historic constitution vote over Indigenous recognition facing hurdles', *The Australian*, 24 January 2012.
19 Paige Taylor, 'Indigenous Voice to Parliament referendum Yes fanatics "risk silencing Voice": Greg Craven', *The Australian*, 19 February 2023.
20 Lenore Taylor, 'Voice to Parliament yes campaign launches with pledge to take conversation to the people', *The Guardian*, 23 February 2023.

21 Pearson and Morris, 'Conservatives eat their own words on Voice'.
22 Anthony Albanese, Interview, *Sky Sunday Agenda*, 9 April 2023.
23 Frank Brennan, 'Indigenous Constitutional Recognition through a Voice', Uphold & Recognise Conference, Sydney, 28 February 2023.
24 Louise Clegg, 'A modest Voice can define and unite us', Uphold & Recognise Conference, Sydney, 28 February 2023.
25 Tony McAvoy, 'Some legal issues arising from proposed constitutional reform to recognise Aboriginal people and Torres Strait Islanders', Uphold & Recognise Conference, Sydney, 28 February 2023.
26 Julian Leeser, Speech to Uphold & Recognise Conference, Sydney, 28 February 2023
27 Julian Leeser, Address to the National Press Club, 3 April 2023.

**CHAPTER 13: A FINAL COMPROMISE**
1 Shireen Morris, 'Watering down draft demeans spirit of the Voice', *The Australian*, 17 March 2023.
2 Paul Sakkal and James Massola, 'The seven extra words that could broker a compromise deal and win the referendum', *The Sydney Morning Herald*, 13 March 2023.
3 Ibid.
4 Andrew Probyn, 'Inside the late-night meetings that came to define Anthony Albanese's Voice referendum gamble', *ABC News*, 24 March 2023.
5 Paul Sakkal and James Massola, 'Solicitor-general didn't advise watering down Voice wording, working group members say', *The Sydney Morning Herald*, 29 March 2023.
6 Morris, 'Watering down draft demeans spirit of the Voice'.
7 Chris Merritt, 'Latest Voice tinkering opens door to litigation', *The Australian*, 16 March 2023.
8 All emphasis is mine.
9 Catie McLeod et al., 'Anthony Albanese announces final wording for Voice to Parliament referendum', *News.com.au*, 23 March 2023.
10 Probyn, 'Inside the late-night meetings that came to define Anthony Albanese's Voice referendum gamble'.
11 Paul Sakkal, 'Albanese's Voice announcement explained', *The Sydney Morning Herald*, 23 March 2023.
12 James Massola and Paul Sakkal, 'Albanese strikes key peace deal on Voice', *The Sydney Morning Herald*, 22 March 2023.
13 Greg Craven, 'Voice "radicals" land fatal blow to referendum hopes', *The Australian*, 24 March 2023.
14 Josh Taylor, 'Albanese hits hustings ahead of NSW election day – as it happened', *The Guardian*, 24 March 2023.
15 Danyal Hussain, 'Law expert slams Anthony Albanese's Voice to Parliament as a "ruthless con job" that's far worse than expected', *Daily Mail*, 24 March 2023.
16 Matthew Doran, 'Constitutional lawyer Greg Craven furious after being quoted in Voice to Parliament No pamphlet', *ABC News*, 17 July 2023.

17  Michelle Slater, 'Peter Dutton given "every opportunity" to ask about Voice: Anthony Albanese', *The Leader*, 24 March 2023.
18  Andrew Bragg, Interview by Ben Fordham, 2GB radio, 21 July 2023.
19  Tyrone Clark, 'Frank Brennan calls for division over Voice amendment among special advisors to be "clarified" to secure support of key Liberals', *Sky News*, 16 April 2023; see also Frank Brennan, 'Labor may need to compromise on Voice to win key Liberals' support', *The Sydney Morning Herald*, 30 April 2023.

**CHAPTER 14: A NOBLE POLITICIAN**

1  Tom McIlroy, 'Limiting the remit of the Voice impossible: legal expert', *Australian Financial Review*, 22 June 2023.
2  Shireen Morris, 'Indigenous Voice to Parliament drafting debate fuelled by "shallow tribalism" and fear', *The Australian*, 30 March 2023.
3  Josh Butler, 'Anthony Albanese criticises "very strange" question on whether Voice will have input on energy policy', *The Guardian*, 27 March 2023.
4  Rosie Lewis, 'Anthony Albanese at odds with experts over Indigenous Voice to Parliament', *The Australian*, 30 March 2023.
5  Lisa Visentin, 'Health, education, jobs and housing: Burney to give Voice priorities on day one', *The Sydney Morning Herald*, 4 July 2023.
6  Paul Sakkal, '"Have the courage to stand up": Voice split gets personal as Albanese rebukes Leeser', *The Sydney Morning Herald*, 27 March 2023.
7  Leeser, Address to the National Press Club, 3 April 2023.
8  Turnbull, 'Australia's constitutional history told us the Voice referendum was unwinnable'.
9  Simon Benson, 'Five states raise voice to back Indigenous recognition: Newspoll', *The Australian*, 4 April 2023.
10  Anthony Albanese, Interview by Dave Marchese, *Hack*, Triple J, 5 April 2023.
11  Paul Karp, 'Peter Dutton walks back offer of second referendum after Voice poll', *The Guardian*, 16 October 2023.
12  James Campbell, 'Liberal MPs say they voted for a legislated national body in lieu of the Voice to Parliament', *The Daily Telegraph*, 8 April 2023.
13  Josh Butler, 'Peter Dutton's decision to oppose Indigenous Voice is a "Judas betrayal" of Australia, Noel Pearson says', *The Guardian*, 6 April 2023.
14  Mike Foley, '"Duplicitous and dishonest": Pearson says Dutton misled him about Voice', *The Sydney Morning Herald*, 4 June 2023.
15  Kelly, 'Howard's sway'.
16  Albrechtsen, 'Former Prime Minister John Howard denounces Noel Pearson's Indigenous Voice to Parliament "Judas" attack on Peter Dutton'.
17  Michael Pelley, 'The real reason Julian Leeser quit over the Voice', *Australian Financial Review*, 14 April 2023.
18  Ellen Ransley, 'Peter Dutton stands firm after Julian Leeser resigns from Liberal front bench over Voice decision', *News.com.au*, 11 April 2023.
19  Joe Kelly, 'Three former Liberal Indigenous affairs ministers declare they will vote "yes" in Indigenous Voice to Parliament referendum', *The Australian*, 18 April 2023.

20. Greg Craven, 'Greg Craven: Why I will join Julian Leeser in Indigenous Voice to Parliament Yes push', *The Australian*, 15 April 2023.
21. Joint Select Committee on the Aboriginal and Torres Strait Islander Voice Referendum, *Advisory Report on the Constitution Alteration (Aboriginal and Torres Strait Islander Voice) 2023*, Canberra: Parliament of Australia, 2023, p. 77.
22. Committee Hansard, Wednesday 19 April 2023, p. 42; Joint Select Committee on the Aboriginal and Torres Strait Islander Voice Referendum, *Advisory Report on the Constitution Alteration (Aboriginal and Torres Strait Islander Voice) 2023*, p. 36.

**CHAPTER 15: TIPPING POINTS**

1. Michelle Grattan, 'View from the Hill: It's just too hard and too late to delay and recalibrate Voice referendum', *The Conversation*, 24 July 2023.
2. Matthew Doran, 'Indigenous Voice to Parliament referendum bill passes lower house', *ABC News*, 31 May 2023.
3. Giovanni Torre, 'Liberal MP who quit front bench to back Voice pushes changes to boost Yes vote's chances', *National Indigenous Times*, 17 May 2023.
4. Rhiannon Down and Tricia River, 'Axe "risky" Voice clause to avoid referendum defeat, Liberal MP Julian Leeser says', *The Australian*, 3 April 2023.
5. Noah Yim, '"Bedwetter": Noel Pearson rubbishes Mick Gooda's Voice suggestion', *The Australian*, 19 May 2023.
6. James Massola and Paul Sakkal, '"I'm terrified we'll lose": Voice advocate pleads for compromise to save referendum', *The Sydney Morning Herald*, 18 May 2023.
7. Paige Taylor, 'Greens and Independent senator David Pocock give Julian Leeser hope of achieving a compromise on the Indigenous Voice parliament', *The Australian*, 25 May 2023.
8. Sarah Ison, 'Yes campaign crash: Mick Gooda's anger at Anthony Albanese's Voice strategy, and aftermath', *The Australian*, 23 February 2024.
9. Josh Butler, 'Original Voice bill wording to stay as Noel Pearson calls Mick Gooda a "bedwetter" over proposed change', *The Guardian*, 19 May 2023.
10. See Shireen Morris, 'Mechanisms for Indigenous Representation, Participation and Consultation in Constitutional Systems: International Examples to Inspire Chile', *International IDEA*, 2021.
11. 'Mark Speakman "sympathetic" to the idea of the Voice but has concerns over wording', *Sky News*, 16 May 2023.
12. Paul Sakkal, 'Voice question should have been split, Wyatt says', *The Sydney Morning Herald*, 12 December 2023.
13. Andrew Bragg, Interview by Hamish Macdonald, *Breakfast*, ABC Radio National, 14 June 2023.
14. David Crowe, '"A tipping point": Support for Voice falls below a majority', *The Sydney Morning Herald*, 12 June 2023.
15. Gemma Ferguson, 'Yes advocates rally support for Voice to Parliament at events around the country', *ABC News*, 2 July 2023.
16. AAP, 'Thousands rally around Australia in support of Voice despite polls suggesting decline in yes vote', *The Guardian*, 2 July 2023.

17  Phillip Coorey, 'You have a moral obligation to speak up, Dutton tells business', *Australian Financial Review*, 21 March 2024.
18  Anthony Galloway, 'Burney commits to regional voices in concession to Liberal MPs', *The Sydney Morning Herald*, 20 May 2023.
19  David Southwell, 'Peter Dutton's dig after John Farnham backs Indigenous Voice to Parliament: Yes camp to use song "You're the Voice"', *Daily Mail*, 3 September 2023.
20  Sakkal and Visentin, 'Yes campaign "snookered"'.
21  Visentin et al., 'The devil in the details'.
22  Grattan, 'View from the Hill'.
23  Morris, *Radical Heart*, pp. 135–36; 204. Stephen Fitzpatrick, 'Indigenous Recognise campaign ditched', *The Australian*, 10 August 2017.
24  Charlie Lewis, 'Is legendary conservative campaigner C|T Group losing its touch?', *Crikey*, 17 October 2023.
25  Mark Di Stefano, 'It's over: Crosby, Textor, Liberals part ways', *Australian Financial Review*, 1 February 2024.
26  Nick Evershed and Josh Nicholas, 'Voice referendum 2023 poll tracker: Latest results of opinion polling on support for yes and no campaign', *The Guardian*, 13 October 2023.
27  Noel Pearson, 'It's Time for True Constitutional Recognition', Speech, National Museum, 17 March 2021.

**CHAPTER 16: BROKEN HEART**
1  Paul Sakkal, 'Dutton attacks Ray Martin over Voice as Jacinta Price weighs in against ABC', *The Sydney Morning Herald*, 5 October 2023.
2  Blaine, *Bad Cop*, p. 95.
3  Paul Sakkal and James Massola, 'Prominent Voice advocate's passionate speech two weeks after leg amputation', *The Sydney Morning Herald*, 30 August 2023.
4  Jacqueline Maley, 'Linda Burney reveals medical diagnosis ahead of Voice launch', *The Sydney Morning Herald*, 29 August 2023.
5  Maxim Shanahan and Michael Pelley, 'Seems nothing can melt No-vote hearts: Pearson', *Australian Financial Review*, 13 October 2023.
6  Josh Butler, 'A No vote will "bring shame upon us" and signal reconciliation is no longer viable, Noel Pearson says', *The Guardian*, 10 October 2023.
7  Peter Hartcher, 'Voters aren't hearing us: The tough advice from Albanese's inner circle', *The Sydney Morning Herald*, 2 December 2023.
8  Jeremy Walker, 'Silencing the Voice: The fossil-fuelled Atlas Network's campaign against constitutional recognition of Indigenous Australia', *Cosmopolitan Civil Societies*, vol. 15, no. 2 (2023).
9  Josh Butler, 'Indigenous Voice: No campaign's deep links to conservative Christian politics revealed', *The Guardian*, 13 July 2023.
10  Pat McGrath et al., 'Voice to Parliament referendum "prime target" for foreign interference on Elon Musk's X, former executive warns', *ABC News*, 30 September 2023.

11  See Shireen Morris and Sarah Sorial, '"Abject failure": Why Australia's scheme to curb foreign influence doesn't work and can't be fixed', *The Conversation*, 30 April 2024.
12  Emma Brancatisano, '"Extremely politicised": How "very worrying" Voice misinformation spreads online', *SBS News*, 8 October 2023.
13  Butler, 'Indigenous Voice'.
14  Paul Sakkal, 'No campaign's "fear, doubt" strategy revealed', *The Sydney Morning Herald*, 12 September 2023.
15  Blaine, *Bad Cop*, p. 91.
16  Amy Remeikis and Josh Butler, 'Voice referendum: Factchecking the seven biggest pieces of misinformation pushed by the no side', *The Guardian*, 12 October 2023.
17  Lorena Allam, 'Australia's Voice debate is being flooded with misinformation and lies. Here are some facts', *The Guardian*, 13 September 2023.
18  Clare Armstrong, 'Referendum disinformation targeting migrant groups in Australia's suburbs', *Daily Telegraph*, 26 September 2023.
19  Pearson, 'Who We Were'.
20  Josh Butler, 'Voice referendum: Julian Leeser accuses no campaign of attacking high-profile Aboriginal people to stir anger', *The Guardian*, 17 July 2023.
21  'Liberal's Julian Leeser says no campaign being driven by bots', SBS News, 6 August 2023.
22  Sarah Simpkins, '"People need to know this goes on": Doctor sent racist hate mail at work', *AusDoc*, 1 February 2024.
23  Biddle et al., 'Detailed analysis of the 2023 Voice to Parliament Referendum and related social and political attitudes', p. 64.
24  AAP, 'With a Voice, you can blame us, Noel Pearson tells voters', *SBS News*, 15 August 2023.
25  Biddle et al., 'Detailed analysis of the 2023 Voice to Parliament Referendum and related social and political attitudes', p. 42.
26  Ibid., p. ix
27  Ibid., p. 79.
28  Ibid., p. 42.
29  Ibid., p. 21.
30  Ibid., p. iii.
31  Ibid., p. 24.
32  Ibid., p. 26.
33  Ibid., p. 43.
34  Ibid., p. 28.
35  Ibid., p. 12.
36  Ibid., p. iii.
37  Ibid., p. 59–60.
38  Ibid., p. vii.
39  Noel Pearson quoted in Paul Kelly, 'The Middle East war has exposed the sheer depth of shattered values in Australia', *The Australian*, 1 June 2024.

# INDEX

#StayTruetoUluru 72

1864 Battle of Mitchell River 18
1881 Parihaka (New Zealand conflict) 19
1967 referendum 11, 190
1999 republic referendum 36, 49–51, 55, 102, 126, 171
2014 Joint Select Committee on Constitutional Recognition of Aboriginal and Torres Strait Islander Peoples 51, 68, 70, 109, 131–3
2015 Kirribilli Statement 51–2
2017 OmniPoll 41
2018 Joint Select Committee on Constitutional Recognition (Leeser–Dodson) 52–3, 60, 61, 75, 79, 81, 89, 167
2018 NewsPoll 41
2022 Boyer Lectures 15, 49–50, 74–5, 79
2023 Joint Select Committee on the Aboriginal and Torres Strait Islander Voice 10, 86
2GB radio 161, 204

*A Rightful Place* (editor Shireen Morris) 97
*AAP Factcheck* 119
Abbott, Tony (fmr prime minister) 31, 51–2, 64–8, 77, 98, 104, 175, 218
ABC 118
ABC Gippsland 96
ABC *Nemesis* documentary 64
ABC *Q&A* 42, 58
ABC radio 160
Aboriginal and Torres Strait Islander people *see* Indigenous Australians
Advance (conservative group) 110–11, 132, 135, 173, 209, 213–14
Ah-See, Roy (Indigenous leader) 83–4
Albanese, Prime Minister Anthony 1–2, 10, 38, 46, 48, 53, 55, 57–8, 73, 75, 80, 94, 106–7, 110–12, 119, 125, 129–30, 132, 141, 157, 159–61, 164–5, 169–70, 174–5, 188, 193, 195, 199, 202, 212–13, 216
  'Albanese's Voice' 11, 68, 108–9
  campaigning for the Voice 203
  a 'hand outstretched' 113–14
  Garma speech 106, 109, 111–13, 137, 149
  letter to Peter Dutton 147–9, 161
  proposed amendment to the Voice 2022 107–8, 111–12, 130–3, 135–9, 149, 154, 165
Albrechtsen, Janet (journalist) 111, 130, 135, 137, 141, 147, 151
Alexander, John (Liberal MP) 92
Allen, Katie (Liberal MP) 92
Anderson, Pat (Indigenous leader) 5, 32, 71, 75, 81, 83, 139, 175 *see also* Referendum Council; Uluru Dialogue; Uluru Statement from the Heart

245

Anglican Church of Australia  128, 202
Appleby, Gabrielle (law professor)  82, 124–5, 153–4, 160 see also Indigenous Law Centre
Appo-Ritchie, Jade (Indigenous leader)  200
APY people  115
Archer, Bridget (Liberal MP)  68, 96, 163, 184, 199
Association of Rhodes Scholars  197
Atlas Network  208
Aurukun people  198
Australasian Federation Conference  18
Australia Day Council  197
Australian Catholic Bishops Conference  128
Australian Catholic University  129, 141, 143, 174
Australian Constitution  7, 12, 15–23, 27–30, 34–6, 43–4, 47–8, 51–2, 57, 90, 100, 102, 106, 112–13, 131, 138, 152, 155–6, 159, 168, 181, 205, 207–8, 220–1 see also Australian politics
Australian Constitutional Committee 1891  15–17, 20
Australian Constitutional Convention  20–1, 59, 77
Australian Electoral Commission (AEC)  115, 209
*Australian Financial Review*  173, 213
Australian Institute of Superannuation Trustees  197
Australian National Imams Council  128
Australian politics  3, 8, 23, 25–7, 37–8, 40, 45–6, 53, 56, 76, 169–70
Australian referendums  7, 11, 36, 41–2, 49–51, 55, 68, 79, 102, 105, 113, 126, 171, 190
Australian Sangha Association  128
Australian Strategic Policy Institute  208
Australians for Indigenous Constitutional Recognition (AICR)  6, 71 see also Mark Textor; Noel Pearson; YES23 campaign group

Bandler, Faith (Indian–South Sea Islander and Scottish advocate)  190
Barton, Edmund (first prime minister)  15–17, 19, 31
Bathurst, Tom (fmr NSW chief justice)  150
Baume, Peter (Liberal MP)  173
Bell, Angie (Liberal MP)  92
Berejiklian, Gladys (fmr NSW Liberal premier)  90–1
bipartisanship  1, 7–8, 12, 25–7, 31, 37, 46–8, 52, 55–8, 62, 64, 66, 73, 76–7, 79, 99, 101, 103–4, 108, 119–20, 127–9, 132–3, 135, 138, 143, 147–8, 151–2, 159–61, 166, 170, 176–7, 179–80, 188–9, 192–5
Bishop, Julie (fmr Liberal MP)  67, 68, 103–4
Black Lives Matter debate 2020  4
Blak Sovereign Movement  36 see also Lidia Thorpe
Bolt, Andrew (journalist)  114, 204
Bowen, Chris (Labor MP)  58
Bragg, Andrew (Liberal MP)  57, 68, 82, 84, 90–2, 96–7, 104, 121, 139, 161–2, 176–7, 184–5, 219 see also *Buraadja*
Brandis, George (fmr attorney-general)  64–5
Brennan, Bridget (Indigenous journalist)  109, 111
Brennan, Frank (constitutional lawyer)  2, 29, 31, 54, 56, 61, 73, 102, 111, 133–43, 151, 153–4, 162, 166, 168, 174, 181, 185, 190, 217, 219 see also *No Small Change*
Broadbent, Russell (Liberal MP)  93, 95–6
*Broken Heart* (Shireen Morris)  1
Buddhist Council  202
*Buraadja* (Andrew Bragg)  90–1, 104, 139, 161
Burke, Edmund (conservative philosopher)  12, 37
Burney, Linda (Minister for Indigenous Australians)  39, 115, 124, 127, 164–5, 167, 199, 203, 206

## Index

Callinan, Ian (fmr High Court judge) 141
Calma, Tom 11, 53, 124–7, 138, 150
Calma–Langton report *see* Indigenous Voice Co-Design Process (Calma–Langton) report 2021
Cape York Institute (CYU) 27, 30–1, 38–9, 51, 70, 77, 200, 205
Carnell, Kate (Liberal MP) 96
Cash, Michaelia (Liberal MP) 91
Centre for Independent Studies (CIS) 203–4, 208
Chalmers, Jim (Labor MP) 199, 203
Chaney, Fred (Liberal MP) 173
Chaney, Kate (Teal independent) 93
Channel 7 204
Charlton, Andrew (Labor MP) 201
Chilcott, Brad (YES23 multicultural consultant) 197
Chinese Communist Party (CCP) 208
Clark, Inglis 16
Clegg, Louise (conservative barrister) 130–6, 138, 151, 153–4, 166, 168, 174, 180
Closing the Gap speech 2020 89
Coalition 2, 42, 45, 47–8, 51, 55–60, 62–8, 71, 77–81, 84–5, 87, 91–2, 96–9, 101, 106, 108, 120–1, 124, 153, 157, 166, 183, 218
Coleman, David (MP) 92, 94
Comensoli, Archbishop Peter 129
Costello, Peter (Liberal MP) 161
Coulton, Mark (Nationals MP) 93–4
Country Liberal Party 115, 117
Craven, Greg (ACU professor) 27–8, 31, 39, 43, 49, 86, 112, 129–32, 135, 138–9, 141–3, 150–3, 159–60, 174–5, 181, 185, 190, 199, 217, 219, 220
Credlin, Peta (journalist) 150–1
Crosby Textor consultancy firm 71, 84, 192
Crowe, David (journalist) 54, 73, 147

*Daily Mail* 160
Daniel, Zoe (Teal independent) 95
Davies, Mia (WA Nationals leader) 117
Davis, Kirsty (Indigenous leader) 200
Davis, Megan (Indigenous leader) 5, 6, 29, 32, 71, 75, 81, 83–4, 124–5, 133–4, 139, 145, 160, 175, 181 *see also* Uluru Dialogue; Uluru Statement from the Heart
design principles for the Voice 122–3
Dhupuma Barker school (Gunyangara) 105
Dilak 20–2
Dillon, Rodney (Palawa elder) 5
Dixon, Rosalind 133–4
Dodson, Pat (Special Envoy for Reconciliation and Implementation of the Uluru Statement) 39, 52–3, 60, 122, 125–6, 206 *see also* 2018 Joint Select Committee (Leeser–Dodson)
Donaghue, Stephen (solicitor-general) 155–6
Downer, Sir John 15, 17
Dreyfus, Mark (attorney-general) 149, 155–7, 159
Dutton, Peter (Coalition leader) 2, 56, 58, 66, 68, 80, 96, 103–6, 119, 121, 125, 127, 129, 147–9, 156, 160–2, 167–73, 179–81, 186–7, 204, 209, 217

Elton, Benjamin 129
Entsch, Warren (Cape York MP) 200
Eora people 16
Erickson, Paul (ALP national secretary) 208
Executive Council of Australian Jewry 128
Expert Panel on Constitutional Recognition of Indigenous Australians (the Expert Panel) 6, 27, 32, 49, 151

Farmer, Pat (fmr Liberal MP) 202
Federation University 198
Field, Gary 200
Finlay, Summer May 4

First Nations people *see* Indigenous Australians
First Nations regional dialogues 32, 43, 52, 55, 59, 61, 67, 78, 149
Fraser government 173
Freeman, Damien 6, 28, 31, 43, 66–7, 72, 82, 94, 138–9, 141, 150, 174 *see also* Samuel Griffith Society; *Statements from the Soul*; *The Forgotten People*; Uphold & Recognise (U&R)
French, Robert (High Court chief justice) 85–6, 88, 106–8
From the Heart campaign group *see* YES23 campaign group
Frost, Simon (fmr Vic Liberal Party head) 192
Frydenberg, Josh (fmr Liberal MP) 91, 104

Gadigal people 16
Gallagher, Jill (Indigenous leader) 200, 205
Garma Festival of Traditional Cultures in Arnhem Land 106, 108, 111–13, 169, 215
Garstone, Tyronne 200, 204
Gartrell, Tim (fmr Recognise advocacy head) 192–3
Gee, Andrew (National MP) 97, 116, 158, 163, 183–4, 203
Gilbert, Danny (Gilbert + Tobin law firm) 71, 85, 88, 106–8
Gilbert + Tobin law firm 85, 206
Gillard, Julia (fmr prime minister) 51
Gillespie, David (Nationals MP) 94
Gleeson, Murray (High Court chief justice) 59, 85, 91, 106–8, 140
Gooda, Mick (fmr social justice commissioner) 180–1
Gordon, Sean (U&R Indigenous Chair) 99, 200–1
Graham, Timothy (QUT expert) 209
Grant, Stan (Indigenous leader) 200
Grattan, Michelle (journalist) 54, 179
Greens Party 25, 185

Griffith, Sir Samuel (Queensland premier and first High Court chief justice) 15–19, 21–2, 31

Hall, John (New Zealand premier) 19
Hammond, Celia (fmr Liberal MP) 92
Hanson, Pauline (One Nation MP) 105, 109
Harris, Lachlan (fmr Labor government adviser) 71
Hastie, Andrew (Liberal MP) 64
Hawke, Alex (Liberal MP) 201
Hayne, Kenneth (fmr High Court judge) 141
Hegelian dialectical argument 26
*Herald Sun* 43
High Court 15, 28, 49–50, 55, 59, 75, 81, 130–3, 135, 138, 147, 157
Hildebrand, Joe (journalist) 104
Hindu Council of Australia 128, 201
Horton, Ted (advertising expert) 100
Hosch, Tanya (AFL general manager of inclusion and social policy) 71, 206
Howard, John (fmr prime minister) 48–50, 56, 64, 93, 100, 102, 171, 211–12
Hunt, Greg (Liberal MP) 93

Indigenous Advancement Strategy 175
Indigenous Advisory Council 98
Indigenous Australians 1–4, 8–13, 16, 20–1, 27–30, 31–5, 37, 39, 43–4, 48–50, 52, 55, 57, 59, 62, 70, 71, 74, 77–8, 81, 85, 93–4, 97–8, 100, 107, 108–9, 112–15, 117, 123, 132, 151, 157, 162, 164, 171, 172, 178, 193–4, 198, 205, 206–7, 209, 209–13, 219, 221–2
Indigenous constitutional recognition 1–4, 8–10, 12, 27–9, 31, 34–5, 43, 48–51, 53, 55, 57, 64–5, 83, 89–92, 97, 99, 100–2, 104–5, 107, 109, 111–12, 116, 136, 172, 177–8, 195, 204, 207, 213, 215, 219, 221
Indigenous Empowered Communities leaders 105, 117, 127, 200, 202

## Index

Indigenous Law Centre (University of NSW) 71, 124

Indigenous leaders 1–4, 8, 28, 38, 49–52, 56–8, 65–7, 73–4, 85, 87, 89, 108, 112, 126, 129, 136, 139, 143, 149, 151–2, 155, 180–1, 188, 192–3, 195, 197, 221 *see also* 2015 Kirribilli Statement

Indigenous Referendum Working Group 6, 38–9, 77–8, 122, 124, 149, 152, 155, 157, 159 *see also* design principles for the Voice

Indigenous Voice advocates 1, 3, 5, 7, 10, 15, 22–7, 29, 32, 39, 42, 48–50, 53, 56–7, 59, 61–7, 70–1, 105, 126

Indigenous Voice Co-Design Process 6, 40, 53, 69, 89, 122, 124, 126–7, 138, 175 *see also* Ken Wyatt; Marcia Langton; Tom Calma

Indigenous Voice Co-Design Process (Calma–Langton) report 2021 98, 121–7, 150, 167, 169

Institute of Public Affairs (IPA) 102, 114, 177, 208

Johns, Gary 99

Johnson, Lyndon B. (fmr US president) 63, 113

Jones, Alan (right-wing radio personality) 42, 218

Jose, Fiona (Indigenous leader) 200

Joyce, Barnaby (Nationals MP) 46, 67–8, 93, 116

Kaldas, Father Antonios (Coptic Orthodox Church) 129

Kean, Matt (Liberal NSW MP) 203, 213

Keating, Paul (fmr prime minister) 113 *see also* Native Title Act

Kelly, Paul (journalist) 37, 110, 140, 210

Kelly, Paul ('Special Treatment' song) 210–11

Kennett, Jeff (fmr Vic premier) 42–4, 149, 218

Kenny, Chris (Sky News) 42, 86, 116, 150, 163

Kingston, Charles (South Australian premier) 15–16, 19–20

Kramer, Dame Leonie 49

Labor government 1–2, 6, 8, 25, 38, 40–5, 47–8, 51, 53–4, 56–8, 65, 77, 79–80, 94, 97–9, 105, 112–13, 121, 125–30, 143, 147–8, 151, 166–7, 169, 175–6, 188, 219

Lambie, Jacqui 67

Laming, Andrew (Liberal MP) 92

Langton, Marcia 11, 15, 29, 53, 124–7, 138, 140, 150, 175, 200

Leeser, Julian (Liberal MP) 6, 28–31, 38, 42–3, 52–3, 55, 57, 60, 65, 67, 69, 72, 87, 92, 96–7, 102, 106, 108–9, 111–12, 121–2, 125, 141, 149, 153–4, 161–6, 167, 168, 169, 174, 176, 179, 180, 182, 183, 185, 199, 203, 213, 219 *see also* 2018 Joint Select Committee (Leeser–Dodson); Samuel Griffith Society; Uphold & Recognise (U&R)

Ley, Sussan (Opposition deputy leader) 169

Liberal government 48, 52, 99, 121

Liberal Party 25, 38, 41–2, 47–8, 57–8, 66, 77, 89–90, 101, 104, 108, 111, 121, 127, 148, 158, 160, 177, 184, 201

Liebler, Mark 52

Littleproud, David (Nationals leader) 56, 97, 115–6, 119

Lui, Nakkiah (Indigenous actor and playwright) 4 *see also* Black Lives Matter debate (2020)

Macquarie University Law School *see also* Radical Centre Reform Lab

Major, Tania (Indigenous leader) 200

Makarrata 20

Makarrata Commission 32, 99

Mansell, Michael 67

Maori 18–19, 19, 22

Marshall, Steven (fmr SA Liberal premier) 90–1

## Index

Martin, Ray (journalist) 203–4
Macquarie University Law School 70
Mayo, Thomas (Voice campaigner) 8, 32–3, 71, 99, 200, 205, 213–14
McAllister, Ian (ANU expert) 47
McAvoy, Tony (Indigenous barrister) 150, 154, 203
McCarthy, Malarndirri (Labor MP) 203–4
McCormack, Michael (National MP) 93, 116
McKenzie, Bridget (National Party) 68
McKenzie, Zoe (Liberal MP) 220
Melbourne Town Hall 43, 205
Melbourne University 97
Merritt, Chris (fmr legal affairs editor) 44, 156, 218–19
Middleton, Karen (journalist) 38
Morris, Shireen (constitutional lawyer) 1, 3–4, 6–7, 27, 42–3, 53, 63, 65, 67, 70, 75, 82–3, 94–5, 97, 109, 128, 136, 140–1, 143, 146, 150–1, 156, 168, 174, 177, 188–9, 194 *see also* A Rightful Place; Broken Heart; Cape York Institute (CYU); Prince Alfred Park rally; Radical Centre Reform Lab; *Radical Heart*; *Statements from the Soul*; *The Forgotten People*
Morrison, Scott (fmr prime minister) 53, 68–9, 71, 82–4, 89, 90–1, 99–101, 103–5, 167 *see also* Closing the Gap speech 2020
Morrison government 84–5, 121–2
Morton, Rick (journalist) 69
Multicultural Australia for the Voice 202
multicultural communities 4, 129, 201–2, 206, 217
Multicutural Ambassadors for Yes 202
Mundine, Karen (Reconciliation Australia) 71
Mundine, Warren (Indigenous businessman) 29, 34, 94, 97–9, 118, 146, 160, 201, 203
Murphy, Katharine (journalist) 126

Murphy, Peta (fmr barrister) 178

National Council of Churches in Australia 128
National Council of Imams 202
National Museum 122
National Party 25, 48, 68, 93, 97, 108, 115–17, 121, 158, 184
National Press Club 69, 86, 154, 165, 169, 199
National Sikh Council of Australia 128
Native Police 18
*Native Title Act* 113
New Zealand 17–19, 22, 67, 90
NewsCorp *see* Sky News
Newspoll survey 169
Ngarrindjeri Ruwe 117
Nixon, Richard (fmr US president) 25
*No Small Change* (Frank Brennan) 140
Noongar in Western Australia 20
Nutt, Tony (fmr Howard adviser) 71, 192, 212
NPY lands 117

Okotel, Karina (fmr Liberal Party vice-president; Voice supporter) 110
One Nation 25
O'Sullivan, Matt (Liberal MP) 92

Parkin, Dean (Indigenous advocate) 71, 100–1, 114, 124, 153, 181, 200, 204 *see also* YES23 campaign group
Parry, Vickie 200
Pearson, Noel (Indigenous leader) 1, 3, 5–7, 15, 25–7, 32, 39, 42, 48, 63–7, 70–2, 75–6, 81, 83–4, 88, 91, 93, 97, 99–100, 105, 108–9, 113, 118–19, 124, 126, 136, 139, 151, 153, 156, 168, 171, 174, 181, 187–8, 192–5, 197, 207, 212 *see also* Australians for Indigenous Constitutional Recognition (AICR); Cape York Institute (CYU); Indigenous Voice Co-Design Process; radical centre; Uluru Statement from the Heart

## Index

Pelly, Micahel (journalist) 173
Perkins, Rachel (Indigenous filmmaker) 71, 129, 186, 193, 200–1, 204
Perrottet, Dominic (fmr NSW premier) 148–9, 181
Phelps, Kerryn (Teal independent) 68
Phillips, Shane 200
Pinskier, Henry (philanthropist) 70
Pinskier, Marcia (philanthropist) 70
Plibersek, Tanya (Labor MP) 199, 203
Porter, Christian (fmr attorney-general) 66–9, 218
Price, Bess (NT politician) 113
Price, Jacinta Nampijinpa (Country Liberal Party MP) 34, 86, 97–8, 113–15, 117–19, 121, 146, 173, 198, 203–4, 219
Prince Alfred Park rally 186

Quarterly Essay 2014 140
Queensland African Communities Council 198
Queensland Media Club 198

Rabbi Hillel (Jewish scholar) 195
racism 4, 9, 13, 99, 119, 170, 211–16, 219
radical centre 8, 26–7, 37–8, 40, 45–6, 80, 143, 222
Radical Centre Reform Lab (Macquarie University Law School) 3, 70, 128, 129
radical centrism 26 *see also* Hegelian dialectical argument
*Radical Heart* (Shireen Morris) 1, 28, 70
Radio National 69, 118
Raffel, Archbishop Kanishka 129
Reconciliation Action Plans 189
Referendum co-design groups (2021) 6
Referendum Council 6, 10, 34–5, 43, 52, 61–2, 64, 76, 167, 175
Referendum Council 2017 report 59–62, 139, 154
Referendum Engagement Group 39
*Referendum Machinery* Act 108

Referendum Working Group *see* Indigenous Referendum Working Group (2023)
Reid, Teela (Wiradjuri and Wailwan lawyer) 5, 124
Reserve Bank of Australia (RBA) 164, 183
Reynolds, Linda (Liberal MP) 93–4
Rockliff, Jeremy (Liberal Tasmanian MP) 149, 202
Rotary Club 197, 203
Rudd, Kevin (fmr prime minister) 42, 48
Russell, Captain (New Zealand colonial secretary) 18
Ruston, Ann (Liberal SA senator) 92, 94

same-sex marriage referendum 41, 68, 79, 105, 171
Samuel Griffith Society 28, 68 *see also* Damien Freeman; Greg Craven; Julian Leeser
SBS 118
Scruton, Roger (philosopher) 198–200
Scullion, Nigel (Indigenous affairs minister) 64–5
Shanahan, Dennis (journalist) 67
Sharma, Dave (Liberal MP) 92
Sheeran, Ed (pop star) 4
Shireen Morris (constitutional lawyer) 66
Shorten, Bill (fmr Opposition leader) 52, 65
Singh, Amar (Australian of the Year) 198, 202
Sky News 42, 86, 114, 116, 118, 124, 150, 162, 186–7, 204
social media 7, 9, 12, 41, 47, 118–19, 145, 188–90, 197, 207–10, 213–15, 217–18
Speakman, Mark (fmr barrister) 181–2
Speers, David (journalist) 110, 161
Spender, Allegra (Teal MP) 199
*Statements from the Soul* (co-eds Shireen Morris and Damien Freeman) 95–6, 150, 202

Steggall, Zali (Teal independent) 68
Stevens, James (Liberal MP) 92
Stewart, Marcus (Indigenous campaigner) 188
Sydney Institute 29
Sydney Town Hall 205
Synot, Eddie 124, 188, 214–15 *see also* Indigenous Law Centre; Uluru Dialogue

Taylor, Angus (Liberal MP) 130
Textor, Mark (Crosby Textor consultancy firm) 71, 91, 99–101, 187, 192, 212
*The Australian* 1, 44, 53, 67, 73, 110, 153, 156
*The Conversation* 30
*The Courier-Mail* 65
*The Forgotten People* (co-eds Shireen Morris and Damien Freeman) 43, 66, 94
*The Guardian* 102
*The Project* 4
*The Saturday Paper* 38
*The Sydney Morning Herald* 54, 73, 100, 147, 185
Thorpe, Lidia (federal senator) 33–4, 36, 40–1, 98, 118, 204, 219 *see also* Blak Sovereign Movement
Tingle, Laura (ABC journalist) 118
Trust, Ian (East Kimberley elder) 114
Turnbull, Malcolm (fmr prime minister) 1, 34, 41, 46, 48, 52, 56, 60–70, 77, 80, 82, 94, 96, 101–4, 167
Turnbull government 61–2
Turner, Lesley (Central Land Council CEO) 117
Twomey, Anne (constitutional law expert) 28, 30, 39, 43, 47, 63, 74, 76, 82–3, 86–7, 131, 140, 159, 174 *see also* Samuel Griffith Society; *The Conversation*

Uluru Dialogue 6, 71–2, 84, 124, 187–8 *see also* #StayTruetoUluru; Indigenous Law Centre; Megan Davis; Pat Anderson
Uluru Statement from the Heart 1, 4, 7–8, 30, 32–7, 39–40, 45, 48, 52, 55, 58, 62, 65–8, 70, 72, 77–8, 82, 84, 93, 95–7, 102, 112–14, 117, 122, 128–9, 141–2, 149, 171, 184, 198, 205–6, 218, 220
UN Declaration on the Rights of Indigenous Peoples 40–1, 175
Uniting Church in Australia Assembly 128, 202
University of NSW (UNSW) 71
Uphold & Recognise (U&R) 6, 31, 72, 83–4, 89, 94, 97, 128, 130, 136, 154, 172, 174, 201 *see also* Damien Freeman; Julian Leeser

Van Onselen, Peter (journalist) 53, 73
Velji, Harish 202
Victorian Nurses and Midwifes Conference 197
Viner, Ian (Liberal MP) 173
Voice advocates 3, 5, 10, 22–4, 27, 29, 32–3, 52–3, 56–7, 59, 61, 77, 90, 100, 110–11, 114, 119, 163, 183–4, 190–1, 194, 206, 215, 222
Voice to Parliament proposal 6, 7, 9, 23–4, 29–31, 34, 36–7, 42–6, 53, 58, 60–1, 68, 75, 78, 90–4, 97, 99–107, 110–11, 114, 139, 167, 169–70, 172, 177, 194, 201, 221–2
  2014 draft proposal 1, 3, 29–33, 38–9, 42–3, 45, 52, 61, 67, 76, 79, 82–3, 87, 109, 112, 124, 131–3, 137–9, 151, 154, 165–6, 174
  2015 draft published by Anne Twomey 59, 134, 137–8, 140
  amendments proposed 43, 75, 78, 81–7, 88, 106–9, 111–12, 128, 130–5, 136–8, 139, 148–9, 154–8, 162, 166–8
  Constitution Alteration Bill 59, 173, 176–8, 182

## Index

early conservative supporters 42–4,
50, 63–4, 66, 68, 90–1, 93–8,
101–4, 116, 151, 163, 173, 219
endorsed by Indigenous Australian
majority 32–4, 37, 39, 59, 93–4,
100, 118
Indigenous constitutional advisory
body to Parliament 1, 9, 11, 21,
29–32, 42–5, 52, 55, 61–4, 66–70,
74–5, 81, 86–7, 90, 92–3, 97, 106,
108, 110–11, 114–15, 122, 124,
131–2, 134–5, 137–41, 143, 147,
150, 153–9, 164–5, 167–9, 174–6,
178, 181–3, 188, 205
in pursuit of bipartisanship 1, 7–8,
12, 25–7, 31, 37, 46–8, 52, 55–8,
62, 64, 66, 73, 76–7, 79, 99,
101, 103–4, 108, 119–20, 127–9,
132–3, 135, 138, 143, 147–8, 151–2,
159–61, 166, 170, 176–7, 179–80,
188–9, 192–5
racial non-discrimination clause
recommendation 9, 27–30, 32,
34–5, 45, 51, 70, 74–5, 131–2, 151,
152, 177
symbolic Indigenous constitutional
recognition 8, 27–32, 34, 48–57,
65–6, 78, 89, 140–1, 146, 167, 171,
174, 177, 179, 182, 220
the 'third chamber'
misrepresentation 75, 89–90,
92, 101–2, 110, 167, 182
viewed as progressive reform 25, 35,
37–41, 38–40, 45–6, 58
Voice to Parliament referendum 2–3,
5–6, 9–11, 13, 22–4, 27, 29, 31, 34–5,
38–9, 43–4, 48, 56–9, 61, 65–6,
68, 71, 77–80, 94, 97, 101, 104, 106,
109–10, 114, 122, 128–9, 148, 158, 168,
191, 208–9, 218, 222
the 'crash or crash through'
approach 2, 29, 54, 56, 73, 142,
181
defeated October 2023 1–3, 8–13, 16,
34, 53, 55, 62, 94, 103, 163, 221–2

donation by Malcolm Turnbull 103
early poll data 41–2, 45, 54, 84, 169,
179–80, 185, 187–89, 192–3
lack of cross-cultural dialogue 79
the 'No' campaign 10, 12, 34, 36,
39–41, 57, 100, 111, 119, 127, 133,
135, 141–2, 145–7, 152, 160, 164,
169–73, 186–7, 193, 197, 203,
207–9, 212–13, 215
the 'no compromise' referendum
1, 73
the peak religious organisations
resolution 128–9
political partisanship divide 7, 10,
39–40, 45–8, 78, 120, 148, 162,
169–70, 185, 216
postponing the referendum 188–9,
192–4
post-referendum analysis 144
post-referendum ANU survey 54,
215
the racial division argument 44,
105, 111, 146–7, 161, 171, 181, 208,
211
social media 7, 9, 12, 41, 47, 118–19,
145, 188–90, 197, 207–10, 213–15,
217–18
and tribalism 7–8, 41, 47, 128, 130,
143, 190
the 'Yes' campaign 4, 10, 12, 34, 54,
57–8, 70, 94, 101, 103–4, 118–19,
127, 143, 145–7, 149–53, 158, 173,
181–2, 186–8, 190, 192–5, 197–9,
204, 207, 212, 217–20

Walker, Jeremy (UTS researcher) 208
Warhurst, John (political scientist) 142
Webster, Anne (Nationals MP) 94
White Australia policy 3
Wilson, Tim (human rights
commissioner and Liberal MP) 29,
92, 94–5, 97
Wolohan, Keith (Liberal MP) 161, 176–7
Wyatt, Ken 11, 51, 53, 68–70, 69, 92, 104,
121, 125–6, 173, 182 *see also* 2014 Joint

Wyatt, Ken (*cont.*)
    Select Committee; Indigenous Voice
    Co-Design Process

YES23 campaign group  6, 70–1, 99–100,
    153, 186–8, 192, 197, 202–3, 205, 212
Yolngu people  20–1, 105, 117
Yorta Yorta people  20, 115
Yunkaporta, Phyllis (Aurukun elder)
    198

Milton Keynes UK
Ingram Content Group UK Ltd.
UKHW041920280824
447551UK00003B/142